THE
FEARFUL
MASTER

*"Government is not reason;
it is not eloquence;
it is force! Like fire,
it is a dangerous servant
and a fearful master."*

George Washington

G. EDWARD GRIFFIN

THE
FEARFUL
MASTER

A SECOND LOOK AT THE UNITED NATIONS

WESTERN ISLANDS

PUBLISHERS

BOSTON   LOS ANGELES

Direct quotations or reproductions taken from the following sources have been reprinted in this book with written permission of the respective publishers:

Rebels, Mercenaries and Dividends by Smith Hempstone (Frederic A. Praeger, Inc., New York, © 1962)

To Katanga and Back by Conor Cruise O'Brien (Simon and Schuster, Inc., New York, © 1962 by Conor Cruise O'Brien)

Who Killed the Congo? by Philippa Schuyler (The Devin-Adair Company, New York, © 1962)

In the Cause of Peace by Trygve Lie (The Macmillan Company, New York, © 1954 by Trygve Lie)

You and the United Nations, illustrated by Lois Fisher (Children's Press, Inc., Chicago, © 1958)

From the Danube to the Yalu by General Mark Clark (Harper & Row, Inc., New York, © 1954)

Library of Congress Catalog Card Number: 64-22761

Printed in the United States of America

INTRODUCTION

The Fearful Master, concisely written and well documented, sets forth the double standard which guides the UN through its devious and treacherous path toward world domination.

The author, Mr. G. Edward Griffin, has performed an outstanding service in giving the people of the free world a picture of what *has* happened, *is* happening, and *will* happen in the very near future—if we continue our course of strategic surrender to international forces.

The book opens with the story of Katanga and reveals the broken promises which the UN made to Moise Tshombe in order to deceive him, and to turn over to the central government the only province of the Congo where law and order had prevailed and where freedom was the watchword of its leaders. The murder, pillaging and rape practiced by the UN forces in Katanga can happen to any country that surrenders to UN control.

Author Griffin outlines in considerable detail the Communist infiltration into the personnel at every echelon of the UN, and he exposes the treachery and subversion that flourishes there.

The author meticulously outlines the grand design for surrender, and likens it to a jigsaw puzzle. The chief designer is well aware of the ultimate picture, but an individual working on an indiscernible piece of that puzzle does not know exactly what he is doing or where it will fit into the picture. When all of the pieces are put together, however, the finished grand design will be that of a one-world government maintained by forces against which resistance by any nation will be futile.

The Fearful Master is a book which is long overdue, but I prayerfully hope that it is not yet too late to awaken the American public. This book should be read by all Americans and demands their thoughtful and immediate attention.

James B. Utt
Member of Congress

To my beloved wife and those four precious little ones entrusted to my care; that this book may, in some small way, help to preserve them from the horror of nuclear war or the terror of Communist peace.

FOREWORD

On April 24, 1955, the Communist *Daily Worker* wrote:

> The United Nations has become an imposing institution with a fantastic pyramid of agencies and commissions, and an agenda each autumn of 75 questions. . . . There it stands—in its striking home of stone and steel and glass on the shores of the East River to which thousands of people come each week, in pilgrimages of peace and hope.

This is one of those instances where the truth is sufficiently horrible that the Communist propagandists do not have to lie. In the two decades since the United Nations was created, it has expanded into a giant international bureaucracy with tentacles reaching into every sphere of human activity from matrimony to garbage collecting. Americans by the millions have indeed made the emotional pilgrimage and genuflected before the UN "shrine of peace." But, having looked at the United Nations, most of us have not seen. We have seen the building, and the flag, and pictures of meetings where delegates listen to each other over earphones; but we have not seen the *real* United Nations—its purpose, its philosophy, its ultimate goals. To recognize these things, we will have to look much deeper than the glittering phrases about peace and brotherhood or the ringing manifestos on human rights and let the facts speak for themselves.

Wherever possible, quotations used in this book are from original sources. These sources have been thoroughly footnoted in hopes that the skeptic will check them out. Some may feel that there are too many quotes and footnotes. But this book was not meant to be one of those easy-to-read jobs that can be glanced through with one eye on the TV set. It is a documentary and should be approached as such.

Most of the documentation is taken from those people or

sources *friendly* to the United Nations. For instance, the opening sequence is a direct quote from Smith Hempstone, African correspondent for the Chicago *News*. Hempstone's views, in his own words, are as follows:

> I do not belong to the American Committee for Aid to Katanga Freedom Fighters, I am not a member of the John Birch Society, am not in the pay of the Katanga Government or *Union Miniere*, and really could not care less about the fluoridation of water. I am a registered Republican, although I did not vote Republican in the 1960 presidential election. I do believe that the United Nations has a role to play in the world today—and I believe that the U.S. should remain in the international organization.

Likewise, the forty-six civilian doctors of Elisabethville, who provided some of the most horrifying eyewitness accounts of United Nations atrocities, have declared: ". . . we believe in UNO [the United Nations]. . . . We proclaim that such an organization is necessary for maintaining peace in the world and fair betterment of the underdeveloped nations."

While on the subject of Katanga, it should be made clear that the section of this book dealing with the Congo is not meant to be a glorification of Katanga and Tshombe; it is meant to spotlight the United Nations action in Katanga. We are not being asked to pay homage to Katanga nor are we being asked to transfer our political sovereignty, our economy, and our military security to Katanga; we *are* being asked to do these things for the United Nations. It is for this reason that we need to take a close and searching look at this mammoth organization. And, just as one picture is worth a thousand words, one case history is worth a thousand theoretical arguments.

This is by no means an exhaustive treatment of the subject. If the reader wants a detailed explanation of the structure of the United Nations, how the organization functions mechanically, or what relation one subdivision has with another, he can find countless volumes in a public library. All of this is academic in the minds of most people, anyway. The citizens of Katanga who were dying under United Nations bombs were not concerned over whether the air attacks had been authorized by the Security Council, the General Assembly or the Military Staff Committee, or whether it took a two-thirds vote or only a majority vote.

Nor has the tremendous financial burden that membership in the United Nations places on the shoulders of American taxpayers been discussed. After all, mere money is relatively unimportant. If the UN really *were* what most people think it is, it would be well worth the investment. The real cost of our membership will not, in the end, be measured in terms of dollars and cents; it will be counted out in terms of lost freedoms, despair and human suffering.

This is not an attempt to present an "objective" view of the United Nations. If the reader wants to acquaint himself with the other side he need only turn on his radio or TV, or glance through the pages of his favorite newspaper or magazine. The other side *has* been presented almost without challenge by every conceivable means—books, movies, plays, speeches, editorials, pamphlets, posters, and poetry. It has been promoted by politicians, athletes, movie stars, teachers, beauty queens, and businessmen. By comparison, the case *against* the United Nations has been relegated almost entirely to the media of mimeographed news letters and hastily compiled fact sheets put out by housewives and neighborhood study groups. Radio and TV time is usually denied on the basis that such a point of view is "controversial." It is as though history had slipped back 450 years. When Galileo attempted to demonstrate the theory that the earth was not the center of the universe, he was imprisoned and condemned as follows:

> We say, pronounce, sentence and declare that you, the said Galileo, by reason of the matters adduced in this trial, and by you confessed as above, have rendered yourself, in the judgment of this holy office, vehemently suspected of heresy, namely of having believed and held the doctrine—which is false and contrary to the sacred and divine scriptures—that the sun is the center of the world and does not move from east to west, and that the earth moves and is not the center of the world. . . . Consequently, you have incurred all the censures and penalties imposed and promulgated in the sacred canons and other constitutions, general and particular, against such delinquents.

Now, as then, history will be the judge.

G. Edward Griffin

CONTENTS

PART I

KATANGA
A Case History

CHAPTER

ONE

THE FIRST SPADE

It was December 12, 1961. Christmas was coming to Katanga.

Smith Hempstone, African correspondent for the Chicago *News,* reported from Elisabethville:

> The United Nations jets next turned their attention to the center of the city. Screaming in at treetop level while excited soldiers and white civilians popped away at them with anything from 22 pistols to submachine guns, they blasted the post office and radio station, severing Katanga's communications with the outside world. . . . One came to the conclusion that the United Nations' action was intended to make it more difficult for correspondents to let the world know what was going on in Katanga, since the only way press dispatches could be filed was to drive them 150 miles to Northern Rhodesia over a road studded with tribal roadblocks and subject to United Nations air attacks. . . . By December 12, 1961 . . . mortar shells hailed down on the center of the city as the softening up process began. . . . Among the "military objectives" hit: a beauty shop, the apartment of the French consul, Sabena Airways office, the Roman Catholic Cathedral, the Elisabethville museum.
>
> A car pulled up in front of the Grand Hotel Leopold II where all of us were staying. "Look at the work of the American criminals," sobbed the Belgian driver. "Take a picture and send it to Kennedy!" In the back seat, his eyes glazed with shock,

3

sat a wounded African man cradling in his arms the body of his ten year old son. The child's face and belly had been smashed to jelly by mortar fragments.[1]

The forty-six civilian doctors of Elisabethville unanimously issued a joint report on the United Nations actions against Katanga which included the following account of the December 12, 1961, bombing of the Shinkolobwe hospital:

> The Shinkolobwe hospital is visibly marked with an enormous red cross on the roof of the administrative pavilion. . . .
>
> At about 8 a.m. . . . two aeroplanes flew over the hospital twice at very low altitude; at about 9:30 a.m. the aeroplanes started machine-gunning . . . the market square, and then the school and the hospital in which there were about 300 patients and their families. . . .
>
> The administrative building, the left wing of the four pavilions and the household buildings . . . were bombed and show hundreds of points of impact made by the machine-gun bullets.
>
> In the maternity, roof, ceilings, walls, beds, tables and chairs are riddled with bullets; a bomb exploded in another pavilion which was luckily unoccupied; the roof, the ceiling, half of the walls and the furniture have been blasted and shattered. . . . The blood from the wounded makes the buildings look like a battlefield. . . .
>
> In the maternity, four Katangan women who had just been delivered and one newborn child are wounded, a visiting child of four years old is killed; two men and one child are killed. . . .
>
> Out of the 300 patients, 240 fled into the bush, refusing to be evacuated to any other hospital, for they say . . . "the UNO prefers to aim at the hospitals and we would henceforth no longer feel safe there."[2]

[1] Smith Hempstone, *Rebels, Mercenaries and Dividends* (New York, Frederic A. Praeger, Inc., 1962), pp. 190-193. Smith Hempstone, as already noted, is the African correspondent for the Chicago *News*. He has been a working journalist ever since his graduation from the University of the South (Sewanee), except for his military service in Korea. He has worked in Africa since 1956, and in 1960 was awarded the Sigma Delta Chi award for foreign correspondence. Mr. Hempstone's personal views relating to the United Nations have already been discussed in the Foreword of this book.

[2] *46 Angry Men* (Belmont, Mass., American Opinion, 1962), pp. 60-63; originally published by T. Vleurinck, 96 Avenue de Broqueville, Bruxelles 15, 1962. The majority of the forty-six civilian doctors are Belgian, but they also include Swiss, Hungarian, Brazilian, and Spanish. They practice medi-

Professor Ernest van den Haag[3] made a personal visit to the Congo to witness firsthand the events and conditions there. In commenting on the United Nations statement that the only civilians wounded in Katanga were combatants in the resistance, he said:

> It is hard to speak, as I did, with a mother whose husband was killed at home in her presence with bayonets by UN soldiers.[4] She was in the hospital to help take care of her six year old child, severely wounded by United Nations bayonets. A child's bayonet wounds are hardly due to having been suspected of being mercenary or combatant.[5]

The doctors of Elisabethville reported the "triple and particularly heinous assassination of three elderly people" on December 16, 1961, as follows:

---

cine in the Congo, not for profit, but for the benefit of the underdeveloped populations. The political questions did not concern them. Being doctors, they had no position to take regarding matters which they felt were solely the responsibility of the Katangese government and UN authorities. What *was* their concern, however, was the health and well-being of the population in their care. The prevention of wounds was of equal concern to them as the prevention of sickness. Consequently, they were well within their role of physicians when they issued their protest and declared: "It is not as active partisans of an independent Katanga that the civilian doctors of Elisabethville have thought it their duty to warn the world conscience, but strictly as citizens of the world, besides being bound by the Hippocratic oath which compels them to fight against death wherever it may come from."

[3] After teaching at City College and the University of Minnesota, Professor Ernest van den Haag became (and still is) a member of the faculty of New York University and the New School for Social Research. He lectures widely and is the author of *Education as an Industry* and of *The Fabric of Society* (with Ralph Ross), the latter a widely used textbook in the social sciences. He has published many articles in American and foreign learned journals. Professor van den Haag is a fellow of the American Sociological Association and of the Royal Economic Society.

[4] In the original source material, the nationality of the particular soldiers involved was given. It would seem unfair, however, to implicate a whole nationality when the soldiers were completely subject to UN directives. The United Nations has never apologized for the action of these men or implied that it was not responsible for their acts. In fact, it has widely praised their performance. It will be our practice, therefore, to substitute the name *United Nations* for all future references to troops of specific nationalities serving under UN command.

[5] Ernest van den Haag, *The War in Katanga* (New York, American Committee for Aid to Katanga Freedom Fighters, 1962), p. 11.

The . . . "boy" of Mr. Derriks, Mr. André Kapenga, a witness, relates that nothing special occurred until 1:45 p.m. At this moment, the old cook, Mr. Jean Fimbo, has just brought coffee into the drawing room, and Mr. Guillaume Derriks (60-year-old Belgian) and his elderly mother (aged 87) who lives with him, are about to drink it.

At that moment, an armored car of the UNO takes up position on the path . . . and is machine-gunning the other side of the valley. . . . When the firing has ceased, [United Nations] mercenaries enter the garden . . . and machine-gun the two cars parked in the garage.

The "boy," André Kapenga, is panic-stricken; he locks himself in the food-store next to the kitchen. The [soldiers] climb the stairs leading from the garage to the kitchen and with a burst of machine-gun fire shoot Mr. Jean Fimbo, who has sought refuge under the sink . . . enter the drawing-room where Mr. Derriks who cries out in English: "Not me," is shot down by a bullet . . . and is finished off by a burst which blows off half of his face and skull.

A few seconds later, a third burst hits Mrs. Derriks in the right breast . . . and in the neck. . . .

At about 5 p.m. the "boy" Kapenga hears the soldiers once more entering the villa, where they run about looting to a slight extent before leaving. Soon after, Mr. Kapenga ventures out of his hiding place and horrified at the sight of the three bodies, runs away and hides himself in a loft.[6]

Assistant Secretary of State for African Affairs G. Mennen Williams, speaking in Detroit, accused the Katangese government of fabricating what he called "horrendous tales of indiscriminate mayhem by United Nations troops" during their December attack on Katanga. Millions of Americans read Williams' assurances in their newspapers and were relieved. Practically no one has read Smith Hempstone's reply:

Unquestionably, the Katanga Information Service had played up United Nations atrocities, real and imagined, for all they were worth. Williams might have been in a better position to judge, however, had he spent some time in Elisabethville's Leo Deux while UN mortar shells rained down during those last days before Christmas. Every newsman there had seen civilians

[6] *46 Angry Men,* pp. 27-29.

shelled with his own eyes. Each of us had seen Red Cross vehicles destroyed by United Nations fire. Or were all of us lying? Georges Alavet, the Swedish Red Cross representative, lay in his shallow grave in testimony that we were not. Sanché de Gramont of the New York *Herald Tribune* might well have sent Williams a few pieces of the shrapnel picked from his body after United Nations troops shot up the civilian car in which he was leaving Elisabethville.[7]

Much has happened since December 12, 1961. Like any point along the infinite corridor of time, it is neither the beginning nor the end. But it is a reference point, a handhold on an otherwise glass-smooth sphere too large to grasp in its entirety. The story of Katanga, its tragic struggle for freedom against the United Nations and the part that this story plays in the overall view of the United Nations itself, is so vast, so huge and overpowering that it seems impossible to find a place to begin. But, like most seemingly overwhelming tasks, it is not as important where one begins as it is that one *does* begin. To move a mountain, one must dig. December 12, 1961, is the first spade.

[7] Hempstone, pp. 221-222. For Williams' statement see "Those Angelic UN Soldiers," Chicago *Tribune* (December 28, 1961).

> *If the Congo does go Communist, it will not be
> because of Soviet strength or because the Congolese
> people want Communism; it will be because of UN
> policy in the Congo and because of the perverse
> following that induces us to support this policy
> with our prestige and our money.*
>
> Senator Thomas Dodd, November 1962

CHAPTER

TWO

PROLOGUE TO TRAGEDY

To fully understand this Christmas tragedy in Katanga, one must
be familiar with at least a few events and personalities that were
the principal parts of the prologue. It is not necessary to go into
the rich and interesting history of Africa itself over the past two
or three centuries, although such an exercise would undoubtedly
be intellectually rewarding. Nor is it necessary to catalog the
vast and varied mineral wealth of Africa and particularly of Katanga. Let it suffice to say here that such wealth is considerable.
It is undoubtedly one of the factors which has caused behind-the-
scenes manipulators from both East and West to bring their full
influence to bear on the international "front men" who have seemingly shaped the events in Katanga.[1]

In fact, we need only go back a few years in time and con-
centrate our attention on a rather small number of actors in this
tragic play. We can safely ignore the cast of millions and the supporting roles of hundreds of walk-ons and bit players who have
paraded across the stage. Most of these either have been written
into the play to dazzle the critics or else they were never really
part of the play at all—just a collection of stagehands and stand-
ins who were accidentally caught in the shifting spotlight.

[1] For background see Congressman Donald C. Bruce, "Is Katanga on
the Auction Block?" *Congressional Record* (September 12, 1962).

8

Let us set the stage. The date is now June 30, 1960. For many months radio stations in Red China, Communist Czechoslovakia and Romania have been beaming inflammatory propaganda broadcasts into Africa, attempting to agitate the populations into active support for the traditional Soviet program of anti-colonialism.[2] As defined by the Communists, this slogan means to break away all colonial holdings from non-Communist countries like Belgium, Portugal, France, and England. The Communists, of course, are not acting out of humanitarian instincts when they do this. Their purpose is twofold. First, they know that breaking away these colonial holdings will unavoidably weaken the non-Communist countries that have them and depend on them for much of their economic viability and, to some extent, for their military national security. The second reason is that a newly-emergent government with its inexperienced leadership is relatively easy to infiltrate and subvert to the cause of international Communism. So, in one fell swoop the Communists' program of anti-colonialism not only weakens their enemies but also provides them with golden opportunities to capture still more of the earth's terrain and population. Needless to say, the Communists are not interested in discussing the granting of independence to their own colonial holdings, the captive nations behind the iron curtain.[3]

Be that as it may, by mid-1960 the worldwide Communist drive of "anti-colonialism" had reached an all-time high. The Communist press in America was repeatedly instructing its read-

[2] Pieter Lessing, *Africa's Red Harvest* (New York, The John Day Company, Inc., 1962), p. 13. Pieter Lessing was born and educated in South Africa. He comes from an old Afrikaans family (descendants of early Dutch settlers in South Africa). He was a war correspondent during the Second World War, and has since served as a foreign correspondent for various British and American news services, including the BBC and the *Christian Science Monitor*. He has lived in many countries and has spent a considerable amount of time behind the iron curtain. He has also traveled extensively in Africa.

[3] In 1920 Stalin wrote: "We are *for* the secession of India, Arabia, Egypt, Morocco, and the other colonies from the *Entente,* because secession in this case would mean the liberation of those oppressed countries from imperialism, and a weakening of the position of imperialism, and a strengthening of the position of the revolution. We are *against* the secession of the border regions, a weakening of the revolutionary might of Russia, and a strengthening of the position of imperialism." Stalin, *A Collection of Articles on the National Question* (October 1920), author's preface. Republished in *Selected Works* (1953), vol. 4, pp. 385-386.

ers to whip up mass popular support for the cause. All those who questioned the wisdom of this trend were branded "imperialists" and their comments were buried in an avalanche of emotionalism. "Exploitation," "cruel and inhuman treatment of the natives," and "humanitarian consideration" were phrases shouted at anyone who doubted the wisdom of granting immediate independence to colonial areas. The great advances that had been made, the miraculous transplanting of civilization into regions totally primitive and savage, the progress that had been made in the cultural and educational levels of natives even in the bush country—these and many other considerations were rarely mentioned. Apparently they were not thought to be as good a vehicle for selling newspapers or gaining acclaim at the lecturn as the more sensational stories of exploitation and profiteering.

In keeping with the prevailing mood, Communist and Afro-Asian delegates at the United Nations had initiated a series of resolutions calling for the immediate independence of the Belgian Congo. The United States also went on record in favor of this position and exerted no small amount of pressure on the Belgian government to comply. Finally, after a few sporadic anti-colonial demonstrations in the Congo, Belgium yielded to international pressure.[4] On June 30, 1960, the Congo was granted independence.

The first character of importance to appear on-stage is one Patrice Lumumba. What kind of a man was he? What were his motives? His objectives? These questions can be answered succinctly: He was a deranged and degenerate dope addict; he was a willing agent of the Communists; he worked tirelessly to bring chaos, anarchy and bloodshed to the Congo as the necessary first stage toward his ultimate goal of complete and unlimited dictatorship with himself nominally at the top and with Communist power to back him up.

This may come as quite a shock to many who remember the

[4] In all fairness, it should be noted that there were and are many sincere Africans who had no ulterior motives in wanting independence. They believed what the Communist radio and press told them—that they would lead better and fuller lives after independence. Some of them, too, had very real grievances against the Belgians. But the fact remains that very little support for independence came from the Congo itself. Practically all of it came from outside interests.

glowing praises sung for this man a few years ago in the highest echelons of our government and in our communications media. But for the skeptic who still can't quite bring himself to believe that government officials and news editors ever could be mistaken, let the record speak for itself.

It was well known that for at least two years the Soviets had been supplying Lumumba with arms, ammunition, military vehicles and other necessary supplies to insure an appropriate "spontaneous" uprising of the people against their "colonial-imperialist masters." In addition to the hardware, they provided $400,000 a month with which to buy followers and provide them with the little extras that insure loyalty, such as cars, extravagant parties, and women. Lumumba's Communist backing was widely acknowledged and had been described in detail in both the House of Representatives and the Senate.[5]

Writing in the Brooklyn *Tablet* on April 15, 1961, Bishop Fulton J. Sheen said:

> Lumumba set up a Communist organization among his fellow tribesmen, the Batetelas, making them believe that he was the incarnation of his ancestors. During the elections, Lumumba's troops destroyed most of the ballot boxes of the other candidates. . . . The plans for the Communist revolution in the Congo were prepared in Prague, and in the first three months, Lumumba carried out the first three points of the plan: to organize mutiny in the army; put the blame on the Belgians; organize a terrorist regime.[6]

Although few Americans knew it at the time (or know it even now) evidence of Communist support for Lumumba was so plentiful and undeniable that Secretary-General Dag Hammarskjold felt obliged to reassure the non-Communist world that Soviet aid to Lumumba was actually in support of United Nations policy, and therefore presumably quite all right.[7] Even Conor Cruise O'Brien, chief United Nations representative in Katanga,

[5] Senator Thomas Dodd, *Congressional Record* (August 3, 1962). Also, Congressman Donald C. Bruce, *Congressional Record* (September 12, 1962).

[6] Statement by Bishop Fulton J. Sheen in the *Tablet* (Brooklyn, April 15, 1961). Entered in the *Congressional Record* by Congressman Donald C. Bruce (September 12, 1962).

[7] Hempstone, p. 123.

admitted that the Soviets had given Lumumba 100 trucks, 29 transport planes and 200 technicians.[8] These figures, of course, were an underestimation. For one thing, they did not include the more than two hundred Russian and Czechoslovakian "diplomats" who were by then swarming all over the Congo.[9] And finally, as revealed later by Colonel Joseph Mobutu, who had been serving under Lumumba, Red China had promised Lumumba $2,800,000 in aid.[10]

Lumumba had written: ". . . if necessary, I shall not hesitate to call in the DEVIL[11] to save the country. . . . I am convinced that with the unreserved support of the Soviets, I shall win the day in spite of everything!" [12]

Joseph Yav, a former Lumumba associate and economics minister of his government until July 17, 1960, made the following statement to Philippa Schuyler, an American reporter in the Congo at the time of independence:

> Yes, Lumumba *is* a Communist! I know it. I have proof. This does not mean Lumumba understands the ideological theories of Communism or its intellectual background. He's never read *Das Kapital*. He went Red not for mental convictions but because he was bought. On his visit to Russia and East Germany, he was given money, presents, girls and lavish hospitality. He never looked behind the glitter to see the real foundation of these slave states.[13]

This, of course, is the general pattern of recruitment into the Communist party in those parts of the world where there is not a sufficient group of so-called "intellectuals" from which to draw. The Communists much prefer the intellectual type since

[8] Conor Cruise O'Brien, *To Katanga and Back* (New York, Simon & Schuster, Inc., 1962), p. 93.

[9] Lessing, p. 142.

[10] "Bare Red Plot by Lumumba," Chicago *Tribune* (November 2, 1960).

[11] There is much evidence to indicate that "devil" is actually a code name used by African Communists when referring to the Soviet Union.

[12] *Serious and Irrevocable Decisions Reached by the Government of the Republic of the Congo*, UN document (A/4711/ADD 2 (March 20, 1961), pp. 41-42.

[13] Philippa Schuyler, *Who Killed the Congo?* (New York, The Devin-Adair Company, 1962), p. 154. Philippa Schuyler has been a news correspondent for UPI, the New York *Mirror*, Spadea Syndicate, and the Manchester, New Hampshire, *Union Leader*.

they are more easily ensnared and it is less expensive to keep them hooked on the party line. But in Africa they have to use money and flattery to accomplish what intellectual deception and flattery will accomplish for them in the more "advanced" countries. This point was graphically brought home by Gabriel Kitenge, national president of the Congolese Union party, when he told the same reporter:

> The Communists have bribed scores of Congo political leaders—with trips, girls, gifts, cars and flattery.
> The Congolese never rose above lower-middle-class living under the Belgians. So they are hungry for luxuries. They will do anything for luxuries. Ideologies and principles are vague and far off to them; it's the eloquent message of material things that they listen to. . . .
> I have tried to tell American consular officials here of the grave danger that the Congo will go Red after independence, but they don't listen to me.
> I beg of you, tell your newspaper readers in America of the grave Communist menace that threatens here. Beg them to pressure their congressmen in Washington to do something about it!
> Don't let the West abandon us! [14]

If further evidence is needed of the bond between Lumumba and his Communist masters, one need only note that Khrushchev changed the name of the Peoples Friendship University near Moscow to the Patrice Lumumba Friendship University in honor of this "great African leader." [15]

The Arabs were the first to introduce hashish cultivation to the Congo. It has since become one of the chief vices throughout the entire region. Lumumba was well acquainted with the custom. Stewart Alsop of the *Saturday Evening Post* summed it up when he said: "The notion that Lumumba was worshipped by Congolese masses was a myth. Lumumba was an accomplished demagogue, when he found the time between bouts of gin-drinking and hashish-smoking. . . . He was also roundly hated for many reasons, most of them good." [16]

Lumumba's character and Communist loyalties will be re-

[14] *Ibid.*, pp. 167-168.
[15] Lessing, pp. 110-111.
[16] As quoted by Schuyler, pp. 152-153.

vealed even further as the Congo tragedy unfolds. But this is a fairly accurate description of the man for whom Washington rolled out the red carpet.

Moise Tshombe was the second protagonist on our stage to receive world attention, though not the same type Lumumba received. To start off with, Tshombe was an anti-Communist— a handicap he never quite overcame in the American press. He was almost universally depicted as "shrewd," "a Belgian puppet," "opportunistic," and the usual journalistic innuendoes carefully designed to turn public opinion against a person about whom nothing specifically bad can be found. The truth of the matter is that Tshombe is the son of a successful African merchant, has earned a college degree, is a devout Christian, and had the overwhelming support and respect of the people who elected him to the presidency of Katanga. Not only is he a staunch anti-Communist, he is an ardent advocate of the concepts of limited government and the free enterprise system. He is a student of history and a great admirer of the success of the American experiment. He fully understands the wisdom of the traditional American political system of checks and balances with a further division of power between the Federal Government and the states. Explaining his views, he said: "We would like something rather on the American model. We are willing to have a federal president and to give the central government control of the army, the customs and that sort of thing." [17]

Even after the United Nations had initiated a bloody war against Katanga to force it to abandon this position, Tshombe held firm. Returning to Katanga after the December United Nations attack, he said, "Katanga must be unified with its brothers in the Congo but remain sufficiently free so that its fate will not be sealed on the day the shadow of Communism spreads over this country." [18]

With this background in mind, it is not hard to see why Tshombe was anathema to the Communists. Khrushchev ranted, "Tshombe is a turncoat, a traitor to the interests of the Congolese people." [19] It is interesting to note that Tshombe was also anath-

[17] As quoted by Hempstone, p. 95.
[18] As quoted by Hempstone, p. 221. Also, as quoted by Schuyler, p. 293.
[19] As quoted by Hempstone, p. 68.

ema to U.S. officials. While wining and dining almost every Communist dictator on the face of the earth from Khrushchev to Tito to Castro to Lumumba, our State Department flatly refused to grant a visa for Tshombe to enter the United States.[20]

* * *

Plans for complete chaos in the Congo had been well laid. Many uneducated Africans were told that just as soon as independence came they would automatically own all the property of the white settlers—and the settlers too! One of the campaign promises made by Lumumba was that the Congolese could have all of the European women they wanted after independence.[21]

It did not take very long. A few days after independence, the Congolese army mutinied against its Belgian officers. Lumumba reacted immediately by discharging the officers and expelling them from the country. He promoted every one of the mutinous soldiers at least one rank and moved up several to the level of general. All men received a substantial pay raise. The lowest paid soldier was getting about twice that of an American GI of equivalent rank. Devoid of professional military command and whipped up by Lumumba and his followers, the Congolese army went on a spree of plunder, murder and rape. European residents fled in terror by the thousands leaving behind their homes, their possessions, their businesses, and everything they had worked for. Currency was frozen and most of them left with only a hastily packed suitcase.

Few Americans understood what was going on. Their news sources did not help them much. All attention was focused on the pictures of crying women being helped off planes and the sensational accounts of widespread rape. We were not given any insight into why this chaos had happened or who had triggered it. It was made to appear as something that just happened. Editors by the droves speculated, "Well what can you expect? After all those years of exploiting the natives, the Belgians are just reaping the harvest that they themselves have sown."

[20] *Visa Procedures of Department of State,* report of the Senate Internal Security Subcommittee (also referred to in footnotes and text as the SISS) (August 6, 1962).
[21] Schuyler, p. 218.

Newswoman Philippa Schuyler shed a little light on how it "just happened" when she reported:

> They had been maliciously egged on to start the disorder. In the wee hours of July 9, someone rushed into the barracks shouting, "Come and fight! The whites are about to attack you! You're about to be killed!"
>
> No one was attacking the soldiers. It was a deliberate lie, with frightful consequences." [22]

The Reverend Mark Poole of the Luluabourg Presbyterian Mission and other missionaries in the Congo confirmed that the outbreaks of violence were undoubtedly Communist inspired and that they were too widespread and well coordinated to have just happened by chance.[23]

As soon as word of the chaos reached Brussels, Belgium ordered its troops back to the Congo to protect the lives and property of its citizens there. In a fit of rage Lumumba officially declared war on Belgium and called on the United Nations for military help against Belgian intervention. The United Nations complied, as we shall see. At the outset, however, Belgium called on its NATO friend, the United States, for help so that it could not be accused of trying to perpetuate its influence in its former possession. Washington refused, saying it would rather act through the United Nations. Khrushchev lashed out against the Belgians, calling them "criminal aggressors." The very same day, July 14, 1960, the United States delegation at the United Nations sided with the Soviets in a resolution stoutly condemning Belgium, demanding immediate withdrawal of her troops, and authorizing the United Nations to send troops of its own to assist Lumumba.[24] Within four days, the first four thousand United Nations troops were flown into the Congo by U.S. Air Force planes. Many additional thousands were on the way. By July 23 most of the Belgian troops had withdrawn. The territory was now in the hands of Lumumba's mutinous army and the United Nations "peace-keeping" forces.

The plunder and rape continued and spread. Smith Hempstone reported:

[22] Philippa Schuyler, *Who Killed the Congo?* (New York, The Devin-Adair Company, 1962), p. 238.

[23] *Ibid.*, p. 219.

[24] UN document S/4387.

Not only was the United Nations singularly ineffective in reestablishing order in these regions but it did little to assist in the evacuation of terrified white women and children from these provinces. The United Nations had planes available to evacuate to Stanleyville Gizengists [supporters of the Communist Antoine Gizenga] who felt themselves in danger in areas under the control of the Leopoldville government. But it showed little interest in evacuating whites from Stanleyville. . . . If a Lumumbist was maltreated, a general outcry could be expected from the Communist bloc, the Afro-Asian nations, and from liberal circles in Britain and America. If a white woman was killed or molested . . . it made little difference.[25]

Newswoman Schuyler reported:

. . . a uniformed rabble was ruling Stanleyville—there was continual extortion, brawling, beating and arbitrary arrests. Portuguese and Greeks had to pay as much as $60 to drunken soldiers to avoid arrest. Passengers arriving at Stanleyville's airport were met with a bayonet in the stomach, while Congolese loafers would scream, "We are the masters!" Congolese seized European cars right and left while UN Colonel Yohanna Chites said he could not intervene.[26]

The following account appeared in the New York *Daily News* under the heading "Congo Rebels Attack UN Train, Slay Kids":

Hundreds of rebel Baluba tribesmen yesterday massacred at least 20 Africans in three attacks on a UN guarded train taking school children home for a New Year's vacation. . . . Scores of others were injured and many passengers kidnapped by rebels after the attacks in Southern Katanga. . . . The train left Elisabethville . . . with some 300 passengers, including 100 children, and a strong guard of UN troops. But, when it reached Kamina . . . in western Katanga, only 40 people were aboard. . . . At Luena, three passengers were killed, many were kidnapped and the station was pillaged. Several African women passengers . . . were raped. At Bukama, waves of tribesmen attacked the train again with spears, clubs, rifles, bows and arrows and machetes, killing 17 passengers and kidnapping many more. . . . A spokes-

[25] Hempstone, p. 134.
[26] Philippa Schuyler, *Who Killed the Congo?* (New York, The Devin-Adair Company, 1962), p. 238.

man said that the 17 persons who died at Bukama "were killed under the eyes of the UN."

Roger Nonkel, the assistant high commissioner of Sankuru in Kasai province, stated:

> The UN are unable to restore order, and what is more, they are not even trying.
>
> In August, I asked help for Lusambo from Colonel Lasmar [chief of UN troops in Kasai]. . . . I told him that with fifty UN soldiers I could prevent war between the Batetela [Lumumba's tribe] . . . and the Baluba.
>
> He answered me coldly: "Let them kill themselves." [27]

The Communist plan for taking over the Congo was progressing as planned. Step one: Capture control of the leadership at the top. Step two: Bring about utter and complete chaos to justify the harsh police-state measures which must be used to establish firm dictatorial rule. Step three: Put the blame on non-Communists. Step four: Maneuver as many non-Communists as possible into actually doing the dirty work for them. Now came the visible beginnings of step number five, the police-state measures themselves.

On August 2, 1960, the Congolese central government decreed that any Belgian business which had been abandoned during the mayhem would be confiscated by the state unless reclaimed within eight days.

The Congo's largest and most influential newspaper *Le Courier d'Afrique* was seized by the government, forced to shut down, and its editor was thrown in jail for printing critical remarks about Lumumba. The editor was finally expelled to Belgium and the paper resumed operation with a more "acceptable" editorial policy.[28]

Lumumba moved swiftly to consolidate his totalitarian control. On September 15 he issued the following lengthy and highly revealing directive to the heads of the various provinces throughout the Congo:

> SUBJECT: *Measures To Be Applied During the First Stages of the Dictatorship.*

[27] *Ibid.*, pp. 189-190.
[28] *Ibid.*, p. 231.

Sir,

I have the honour and the pleasure to inform you that with a view to the rapid restoration of order in the country, the House of Representatives and the Senate [of the central government], meeting in special session on 13 September of this year, decided to grant the government full powers.

Full powers should be understood to mean that the government is free to act as it thinks fit in all respects, for the purpose of suppressing abuses, disorders and any action which is contrary to the will of the government over which I have presided legally since the attainment of independence by the Congo. . . .

The most effective and direct means of succeeding rapidly in our task may be summarized as follows:

1. Establish an absolute dictatorship and apply it in all its forms.
2. Terrorism, essential to subdue the population.
3. Proceed systematically, using the army, to arrest all members of the opposition. I will be personally responsible for those at Leopoldville including the Head of State and his close supporters. A few weeks ago, in view of the present situation in Katanga and Sud-Kasai, I sent the National Army to arrest Tshombe and Kalonji and even to kill them if possible. . . .
4. Imprison the ministers, deputies and senators, who sometimes abuse their parliamentary immunity. In such a case I should be glad if you would not spare them but arrest them all without pity and treat them with ten times more severity than ordinary individuals.
5. Revive the system of flogging and give the rebels 10 lashes, morning and evening, for a maximum of 7 consecutive days. N.B. Double the number in the case of ministers, senators, and deputies, reducing the number gradually according to the condition of each individual.
6. Inflict profound humiliations on the people thus arrested, in addition to the obligatory treatment described above. For example, strip them in public, if possible in the presence of their wives and children. Make them carry heavy loads and force them to walk about in that state. In case of such a walk, however, drawers may be worn.
7. In view of the seriousness of the situation of the country, which is in danger of sinking into anarchy, it would be well to imprison repeated offenders in underground cells or prisons for at least six months, never allowing them out to breathe fresh air.

N.B. If some of them succumb as a result of certain atrocities, which is possible and desirable, the truth should not be divulged but it should be announced, for instance, that Mr. X has escaped and cannot be found.

8. Those who do not succumb in prison should not be released for at least a year. In this case they shall be exiled to a country to be determined by me in agreement with certain foreign countries which have already signified their agreement in principle.

Some of the provincial presidents will say that the measures described are severe. In reply I would point out to them that certain politicians have attained power by means of dictatorship. Moreover, the measures of execution that I have indicated above constitute only the first stage of the basic regime that we hope will succeed in the Congo. The second stage will be to destroy anyone who criticizes us. . . .

In conclusion, I would point out that this letter should be communicated only to those authorities under your orders in whom you have entire confidence.

(signed) P. LUMUMBA
Prime Minister[29]

A few months later, Lumumba issued a follow-up memorandum which said: "Get to work immediately and have courage. Long live the Soviet Union! Long live Khrushchev!" [30]

When Lumumba came to the United States he was royally received on behalf of the American people by President Eisenhower who even had him stay in the official presidential guest house. He conferred with Henry Cabot Lodge, Dag Hammarskjold and Christian Herter, then our secretary of state.[31] And a few weeks later, Eisenhower announced that he had sent the first five million of an expected 100 million dollars to Lumumba to help the Congo meet its most pressing needs.[32]

[29] *Situation in the Republic of the Congo,* report of the UN Conciliation Commission for the Congo, UN document A/4711/ADD 2 (March 20, 1961), pp. 42-46.

[30] "Bare Red Plot by Lumumba," Chicago *Tribune* (November 2, 1960).

[31] New York *Times* (July 27, 1960), p. 1. Also, Schuyler, p. 222. Also, *Newsweek* (August 22, 1960), p. 40.

[32] "Lumumba Gets Pledge of U.S. Aid," Los Angeles *Examiner* (July 28, 1960), sec. 1, p. 16. Also, "Added U.S. Funds Voted for Congo," Los Angeles *Examiner* (August 17, 1960), sec. 1, p. 7. Also, *Department of State Bulletin* (October 3, 1960), pp. 510, 530; and (October 10, 1960), p. 588.

Letter to Patrice Lumumba

Whenever in doubt, consult me, brother. We have been in the game for some time and now we know how to handle the imperialists and colonialists. The only colonialist or imperalist that I trust is a dead one.

Kwame Nkrumah, president of Ghana, 1960

Letter to Kwame Nkrumah

Thank you very much for your letter of July 27th expressing your thanks for the assistance which my Government has been able to provide. . . . I agree with you that the United Nations' action in the Congo is a most heartening demonstration of the effectiveness with which the world community can cooperate.

President Eisenhower, 1960

CHAPTER

THREE

SECEDING FROM CHAOS

"I am seceding from chaos!"

With these words, Moise Tshombe declared that his province of Katanga wanted no further part of the Communist-dominated central government. He requested Belgium to return her troops to the province, to subdue the mutinous Congolese army, and to restore civil order. This they did with little difficulty. Tshombe appointed a Belgian major to reorganize the army and reestablish military discipline. With experienced European officers predominantly in charge, a whole new army was recruited. Of the original 2,800 mutinous soldiers, only 300 were allowed to remain.[1]

Within a few days, life had returned to normal throughout

[1] Hempstone, pp. 107-110.

most of Katanga. Businesses resumed operation and civilians once again walked the streets with no fear of wanton violence. As one eyewitness observer described it: "Elisabethville, a bastion of anti-Communism in a sea of Congo leftist terror, was calm and functioning smoothly in late August." [2] As early as July 21, 1960, Patrick O'Donovan reported in the New York *Herald Tribune*: "There is good order in Elisabethville. The streets are patrolled by black and white soldiers together. . . . There is almost no local opposition to Tshombe's plans."

One of the very first acts of the newly independent nation was to discharge all of the Red professors at Elisabethville University who had been attempting to indoctrinate and recruit students on behalf of international Communism. Posters began to appear on the streets: "Katanga, Africa's shield against Communism." And Godefroi Munongo, the interior minister, reflected the views of the government when he stated: "I want my country, Katanga, to be a bastion of anti-Communism in Africa. I detest Communism and will not alter my opposition to it. Katanga will stay independent, no matter what. We shall not give in." [3]

To the leaders of Katanga, independence did not mean that they were unwilling to cooperate with other provinces, to enter into a specifically limited political union with them, or even to share the rather substantial tax revenues obtained from the extensive mining operations within their territory. As mentioned earlier, Tshombe wanted a federal union and local autonomy somewhat similar to that in America.

Commenting on his vision for the future, Tshombe explained:

> Katanga is nearly as large as France. Our people have a different history, traditions, and outlook from those of the Congo. *Every people has the right to its own self-determination.* There is no reason why we should be exploited by the Congo. Because we were in the past is no reason why we should be in the future.[4] [Italics added.]

This attitude was even written into the newly established constitution. Article I read: "The State of Katanga adheres to the

[2] Philippa Schuyler, *Who Killed the Congo?* (New York, The Devin-Adair Company, 1962), p. 17.
[3] *Ibid.*, p. 172.
[4] As quoted by Schuyler, p. 163.

principle of the association with the other regions of the former Belgian Congo, *provided they themselves are politically organized with respect to law and order."* [5] As we have already seen, however, the central government had other plans—and so did the United Nations.

As to what those intentions were, one cannot readily find them in the high-sounding phrases and self-righteous platitudes of official United Nations proclamations. They are there, but one has to be experienced in the highly complex art of reading bureaucratese. While most human beings communicate with each other to *convey* ideas, politicians are prone to use language as a means of *concealing* ideas. An example of this planned deception is the blatant contradiction between the United Nations public pronouncements regarding Katanga and its actual performance.

On July 14, 1960 (the same day that the Security Council passed the first resolution condemning Belgium and authorizing the use of United Nations troops in the Congo), and again on July 20, Dag Hammarskjold stated the UN's position:

1. The United Nations force could not intervene in the internal affairs of the Congo.
2. It would not be used to settle the Congo's constitutional issue.
3. It would not be used to end Katanga's secession.[6]

In July, Ralph Bunche (as special United Nations representative for Hammarskjold) told Tshombe that the United Nations force "has received strict instructions not to intervene in the internal politics of the country." [7] On August 9 the Security Council passed another resolution which "reaffirms that the UN Congo force will not be a party to, or in any way intervene in, or be used to influence the outcome of, any internal conflict, constitutional or otherwise." [8] In speaking specifically about Katanga's secession, Dag Hammarskjold said:

> This is an internal political problem to which the UN as an organization obviously cannot be a party. Nor would the entry

[5] As quoted by Congressman Donald C. Bruce, *Congressional Record* (September 12, 1962).
[6] Hempstone, p. 111. Also, O'Brien, p. 88.
[7] Hempstone, p. 242.
[8] UN document S/4426.

of the UN force in Katanga mean any taking of sides in the conflict to which I have just referred. Nor should it be permitted to shift the weight between personalities or groups or schools of thought in a way which would prejudice the solution of the internal political problem.[9]

Nothing could have been plainer than that. Yet immediately United Nations troops began to move into position for entry into Katanga. Tshombe was leery of the whole operation and protested to Hammarskjold that since everything was calm and peaceful in his province, there was no need for United Nations "peacekeeping" forces.

On August 12 Hammarskjold personally conveyed his assurances to Tshombe that the United Nations would "not be used on behalf of the central government to force the provisional government of Mr. Tshombe to a specific line of action." [10] With these solemn pledges and under Hammarskjold's insistence, Tshombe had no alternative short of armed resistance but to allow UN troops access to Katanga.

They came by the thousands.

*　　*　　*

As mentioned earlier, Katanga was at peace. There were other places throughout the Congo that were in far greater need of UN forces than Katanga. Kasai province was in the throes of civil war and the countryside was literally red with blood, but the UN sent troops to Katanga. Stanleyville was a nightmare of lawlessness and violence, but the UN sent troops to Katanga. Away from the metropolitan areas the practice of cannibalism was being revived and missionaries were being slaughtered by the score, but the UN sent troops to Katanga. By September 1961 between twelve thousand and fourteen thousand troops, by far the greater portion of the entire United Nations force, had been concentrated inside peaceful Katanga.[11] Why were they there? Only a fool could believe that their purpose was

[9] As quoted by Hempstone, p. 242.
[10] Senator Thomas Dodd, *Congressional Record* (August 3, 1962).
[11] Senator Thomas Dodd, *Congressional Record* (September 8 and 16, 1961). Also, *Department of State Bulletin* (December 12, 1960), p. 908.

anything other than to end Katanga's secession and to bring it back under the central government.

Tshombe was no fool. In spite of the grim implications of the arrival of UN military might, he somehow managed to keep his composure and even his sense of humor. The first United Nations troops to arrive at Elisabethville's airport on August 12 were supposedly Dag Hammarskjold's personal bodyguard. When they landed Tshombe greeted them and the accompanying dignitaries by handing them each tourist brochures entitled "Elisabethville Welcomes You." [12] Then, before anyone could object, the honor guard led by Belgian officers presented the Katangese colors while a band played the newly written Katangese national anthem. What a picture that must have been—United Nations soldiers, officers and dignitaries standing rigidly at attention before a fluttering flag symbolizing the very sovereignty which they had been sent to destroy.

At this point in the drama it becomes necessary to introduce a third character—Conor Cruise O'Brien. Mr. O'Brien was formerly an Irish delegate to the General Assembly of the UN before being requested by Dag Hammarskjold to join his executive staff in the Secretariat as special advisor on African affairs. From here he was assigned to the Congo where he personally directed the United Nations political operation in Katanga. When it was discovered that he had imported his Irish girl friend to Katanga, and when she found herself unexpectedly in the news as part of an international incident, O'Brien was recalled to New York and allowed to resign. There were other good reasons for getting rid of O'Brien, too. For one thing, he was too outspoken and it soon became obvious that he had to be removed. He was not the first underling in the UN to be thrown to the wolves in order to save the reputation of a higher official.

Fortunately, however, O'Brien decided to write a book about the Katanga affair. It is a treasure of little glimpses into the innermost workings of the mind of an "international servant." He was and is a fierce advocate of the United Nations. He clings to all of the intellectual fallacies about the United Nations which will be the subject of a later chapter. Even though he had per-

[12] Hempstone, pp. 113-114.

sonally participated in and helped to execute one of the most perfidious schemes ever directed against freedom-loving human beings, he apparently did not realize what he had done, or so he says.

The important point, however, is that O'Brien speaks with authority. He was there. Obviously, a great deal of what he has to say must be taken with a large grain of salt. But what he reveals about both himself and the organization to which he is so strongly committed is, if anything, overly charitable. If O'Brien's words are incriminating in spite of his pro-United Nations bias, then they are certainly worthy of our serious consideration.

For example, consider O'Brien's description of a meeting of the "Congo club," which is the nickname for his group of top United Nations planners and advisors on the Congo. Among others, Dag Hammarskjold and Ralph Bunche (representing the U.S.) were present.

> The Afro-Asian thesis—that the secession of Katanga would have to be ended, and that the United Nations would have to help actively in ending it—was tacitly accepted round the table, and not less by the Americans than by the others. What mattered most to all of them was that the United Nations should emerge successfully from its Congo ordeal, and it was clearly seen that a condition of success was the speedy removal of the props of Mr. Tshombe's régime, thereby making possible the restoration of the unity of the Congo. The continued existence of the independent state of Katanga was recognized as a threat to the existence of the United Nations and therefore even those who, from the standpoint of their personal political opinions, might have been favourably enough disposed to what Mr. Tshombe represented, were convinced of the necessity of strong measures. . . . This was an example of the victory of an international loyalty over personal predilections. If neutral men are simply men who put the interests of the United Nations first, then Hammarskjold and all around him at that table were neutral men.[13]

Ignoring for the moment the enlightening definition of UN neutrality, one should really go back and reread this incredible statement several times to fully comprehend the extent of the calm premeditation behind the policy of deliberate decep-

[13] O'Brien, p. 58.

tion initiated by these high officials. For months they had been issuing public statements and personal assurances that the United Nations not only had no intentions of interfering in the internal matter of Katanga's secession, but that it had no legal right to do so under the terms of its own Charter. Yet, at the very outset O'Brien, Hammarskjold, Bunche and a host of other top United Nations planners sat around a conference table and quietly worked out plans for removing "the props of Mr. Tshombe's regime."

Elsewhere in his book O'Brien provided more illumination on the United Nations' total lack of integrity and respect for honesty in its pretended aims when he wrote that Mr. M. Khiary (head of UN civil operations in the Congo)

> . . . had little patience with legalistic detail, with para-
> graph this of resolution that, or what the Secretary-General had
> said in August 1960. He had no patience at all with the theory,
> often asserted in the early days by Hammarskjold, and never ex-
> plicitly abandoned, that the United Nations must refrain from
> interfering in the internal affairs of the Congo. "What are we here
> for then?" he would ask. *"Il faut faire de la politique!"* And on the
> word *politique* his brown eyes, usually so disconcertingly blank,
> would flash.
>
> He and Mr. Gardiner [another UN official] did "make
> politics," throwing all semblance of non-intervention to the
> winds. . . .[14]

*   *   *

While the United Nations was pouring troops into Katanga, things were going from bad to horrible elsewhere in the Congo. On August 4, when Lumumba returned in a Russian plane from his grand tour of Belgium, the United States and England, he found unexpected opposition awaiting. Many of his former associates had decided they no longer wanted to be identified with either him or his politics. On August 10 Lumumba was seized and stoned by an angry mob in Leopoldville and barely escaped with his life. On August 25 more anti-Lumumba demonstrations and riots broke out all over the city.[15]

[14] *Ibid.*, p. 189.
[15] Allen P. Merriam, *Congo: Background of Conflict* (Evanston, Ill., Northwestern University Press, 1961), p. 240.

Meanwhile, a small group of former British army officers from Rhodesia had entered Kasai province and formed a volunteer corps of leaders to train Baluba tribesmen for battle against Lumumba's men. They explained that they were sick of the West doing nothing to effectively fight the Congo's Reds.[16]

On September 5 Kasavubu, president of the central government and a rather weak-kneed politician (but *not* a Communist), dismissed Prime Minister Lumumba. Lumumba refused to acknowledge the action and promptly dismissed Kasavubu. At this point the lower house and the senate both convened illegally without a quorum. The house invalidated both dismissals. The senate declared its confidence in Lumumba. Complete confusion and anarchy reigned supreme.

Finally, on September 14 a young army colonel by the name of Joseph Mobutu, using what military power he could muster, picked up the pieces and seized control of the government. Kasavubu threw his support behind him and they appointed a committee of college graduates to run things temporarily. A semblance of order once again returned. The "student council," as they were nicknamed, acting under the leadership of Mobutu and Kasavubu, did a far more effective job of restoring order than the official government under Lumumba had done.

Here was obviously a bad turn of events for the Communists. They had not planned on this. Mobutu promptly ordered all the Russian and Czechoslovakian "diplomats" and "technicians" to pack their bags and leave the country. Seeing power slip from him, Lumumba sought United Nations protection and quietly moved into the Guinean embassy.

It is both interesting and significant that Lumumba chose this particular embassy for asylum. Mobutu had appealed to the United Nations to withdraw the Guinean and Ghanian contingents from its peace-keeping forces in the Congo because he had found letters in Lumumba's briefcase which clearly linked these troops with the Communists.[17]

It appeared to be common knowledge throughout the Congo that many of the United Nations soldiers were openly pro-Com-

[16] Schuyler, p. 234.
[17] Senator Thomas Dodd, *Congressional Record* (August 3, 1962). Also, Schuyler, pp. 233-234.

munist. They were apparently selected for that reason. As Philippa Schuyler reported:

> . . . there have been many complaints from anti-Communists in the Congo that UN soldiers from certain left-leaning nations have been spreading leftist or Communist propaganda or otherwise actively aiding the Red cause. . . . Some African UN officers I interviewed surprised me by revealing they spoke Russian, had visited Russia, and were openly sympathetic to the Red cause. "The UN opens the doors to Communism" was a comment I heard all over the Congo.[18]

Just as a quick aside, it is interesting to note that Kwame Nkrumah, the prime minister of Ghana, has written that he long ago decided the philosophy of Marx and Lenin was capable of solving his country's problems. He has consistently supported the Soviet Union and Cuba in the United Nations. In 1960 Red China announced that it would extend $25,000,000 in aid to Ghana over a three-year period. And in 1962 the Kremlin awarded Nkrumah the Lenin Peace Prize. In speaking of the award, his own newspaper described him as the Lenin of Africa.[19] One of the letters found in Lumumba's briefcase had been written by Nkrumah personally and said: "Whenever in doubt, consult me, brother. We have been in the game for some time and now we know how to handle the imperialists and colonialists. The only colonialist or imperialist that I trust is a dead one."[20]

Mobutu had good reason to be concerned over the presence of troops from Guinea and Ghana and he was certainly justified, in view of their activities, in requesting the UN to withdraw them. His appeal was duly considered. The next day, the United Nations specifically assigned soldiers from Guinea and Ghana to provide twenty-four-hour protection for Lumumba. The same protection was extended, wherever possible, to Lumumba's followers as well. Conor O'Brien cautiously explained it this way: "During this time, Hammarskjold and Dayal, his representative in Leopoldville . . . resisted . . . Mobutu's demand that Lumumba, who

---

[18] Philippa Schuyler, *Who Killed the Congo?* (New York, The Devin-Adair Company, 1962), p. 260.

[19] Senate Internal Security Subcommittee as quoted in the *Tidings* (Los Angeles, August 16, 1963), p. 2.

[20] "Bare Red Plot by Lumumba," Chicago *Tribune* (November, 2, 1960).

had sought UN protection on September 15th, should be handed over." [21]

On September 18 Lumumba left the Guinean embassy in a United Nations car and was taken to his well-guarded residence. He shouted from a balcony to the mob below, "I am not a prisoner! I am still master!" He accused Mobutu of being a fascist and promised that he would soon bring back the Communist embassies. That same day, a Lumumbist attempted to assassinate Mobutu who miraculously was not hurt. When Vital Pakasa, the man who organized the attempted assassination, was found and arrested he explained that the Soviets had offered him ten thousand dollars for Mobutu's death. [22]

A few weeks later, still under strong United Nations protection, Lumumba was escorted to a gala two-hundred-guest dinner party given by the general from Guinea. [23]

By this time, most of Lumumba's close supporters were fleeing to neighboring Stanleyville where another Communist dictator by the name of Antoine Gizenga ruled the roost. Finally, Lumumba decided to make a break for it to rejoin his comrades in Stanleyville. He slipped away from his UN guard and was promptly intercepted and arrested by Colonel Mobutu's forces and deported to Katanga. A few days later, he escaped from his captors. According to the story, he was seized by villagers and beaten to death.

There is also the story that Lumumba was already dead before they put him on the plane and shipped him to Katanga. (Quite possible.) There is the assertion that Lumumba's old enemy Albert Kalonji in Kasai province had agreed to dispose of Lumumba but changed his mind at the last minute. When the plane arrived, it found the runway covered with oil drums to prevent a landing. Running low on fuel, the plane proceeded to Katanga where no one expected it. (Not too plausible.) There is the UN "theory" that Tshombe personally plunged the death knife into Lumumba as he was dragged off the plane. (Unlikely, to say the least.) Regardless of which story appeals most to the

[21] O'Brien, p. 96.
[22] Philippa Schuyler, *Who Killed the Congo?* (New York, The Devin-Adair Company, 1962), pp. 233-235.
[23] *Ibid.*, p. 235.

imagination, certain facts should be kept in mind. The most important one is that practically everyone in the whole Congo hated Lumumba. When Colonel Mobutu and Kasavubu finally had him in their hands, they faced the rather sticky decision of what to do with him. They knew that the UN was doing everything possible to return Lumumba to power. They also knew Lumumba well enough to realize that if this should ever happen they would both be arrested and executed. Obviously, the safest course of action for them was to kill Lumumba or to have someone else do it. Another fact to keep in mind is that when the UN sent a special team of investigators to the Congo to look into the circumstances surrounding Lumumba's death, it was denied entry, not by Katanga, but by the central government.[24]

Be that as it may, Lumumba's death triggered off worldwide reaction. The loss to the Communists of one of their stooges was more than offset by the propaganda gain for Communist objectives. The event was skillfully used to destroy what little pro-Katanga sentiment there was in America and elsewhere. Newspaper editors eulogized Lumumba and pointed the finger at Tshombe. A howling mob stormed the Belgian embassy in Moscow. In Singapore, the American embassy was picketed. Wild street demonstrations broke out in London, New Delhi and Belgrade. In Cairo the Belgian embassy was ransacked and gutted. Belgians had to flee their homes in Egypt. There was even a phony funeral in New York while Black Muslims picketed the United Nations building.

The murder of Lumumba was a savage act. It was followed by an equally savage one. In Stanleyville nine anti-Lumumbists who had been held and mistreated for months were also murdered. The United Nations conducted no investigations. There were no outcries of indignation or protest from UN spokesmen. There were no spontaneous demonstrations around the world. There were no bleeding heart editorials in our daily newspapers.

Here is a silent tribute to the powerful hold that Communist-inspired propaganda has over the minds and attitudes of those in the non-Communist world. It is astounding that so many millions of people could be sincerely shocked and saddened over the death of a man like Patrice Lumumba while at the same time

[24] Hempstone, pp. 126, 130.

feeling little concern over the brutal murders of hundreds of anti-Communist leaders in the Congo, Eastern Europe and Red China. Here was a man who was literally unknown to the world until he led his people into chaos. And then, in spite of his clear record as an ex-convict, a dope addict, a murderer and a Communist, he was catapulted into the hearts of millions who were skillfully conditioned to think of him as a great martyred leader.

We know only too well that UN forces would bring Lumumba's agents with them.

Godefroi Munongo, August 4, 1960

THE MODERATES

For many years the United States has been financing and supporting the expansion of international Communism around the world through measures which have been presented to the American people as ways of fighting Communism. Foreign aid is probably the most obvious example. President after president has told us that we have to send billions to various Communist and pro-Communist countries in order to win them away from Soviet domination. We have shipped them military equipment, trained their officers in our military schools, sent them machine tools, built whole factories and power dams for them, and sold them subsidized wheat. Our political leaders have shrewdly borrowed the required money from our children and grandchildren who will be saddled with these debts for many generations to come. The record is truly fantastic. But the most incredible part of all is that this whole operation, which has been so necessary for Communist success, has been sold to Americans as a way of opposing Communism. A glance at a few issues of the *People's World* or the *Worker* or other Communist periodicals will cause even the skeptical to realize that our foreign aid is very near and dear to the hearts of Communists everywhere. The only criticism one finds of our foreign aid program in the Communist press is that it isn't as large and doesn't grow as fast as the Communists want. One of the prime reasons they advocate foreign aid even to countries that are not yet totally Communist but are merely in the socialist (or

33

transitional) phase, is that it helps to destroy private enterprise and strengthen socialism within these countries. The money must never be allowed to be used to develop private industry. It must be used only for government projects. For instance, back in 1955 when the Communist party of India formally announced its support of Nehru, the Communist *Daily Worker* carried a description of the event. Toward the end of the article it quoted Ajoy Ghosh, general secretary of the Communist party in India, as saying: "We want foreign aid coming at a governmental level and not with a specific purpose." He further said Indians should be "free to use the aid for anything we want." [1]

That, however, is another story. It is mentioned here merely to point up a recognizable pattern that has developed over the past few years regarding certain United States State Department policies. This pattern is involved with convincing the voters that a particular policy of the State Department or the United Nations is in the best interests of the United States when, in reality, it is just the opposite. There is no better illustration of this than the circumstances surrounding United Nations and Washington support of the so-called "moderate" central government that emerged after Lumumba's death. To tell that part of the story, however, it is necessary to take a closer look at Antoine Gizenga.

Gizenga was a minor personality in Congolese politics until he was invited to Prague, Czechoslovakia, for Communist cadre training.[2] When he returned, he became one of Lumumba's strongest supporters and worked closely with him to implement plans for the Communist take-over of the whole Congo. When Lumumba was arrested and then killed, Gizenga set himself up as Lumumba's successor. He established a Communist regime in the neighboring province of Orientale and gathered all of Lumumba's followers around him. The Soviet and Czechoslovakian diplomats and consular officials who were kicked out of Leopoldville by Colonel Mobutu popped up in the Gizenga stronghold of Stanleyville where they quickly received official accreditation. The Soviets lost no time in announcing to the world that they now

---

[1] "Indian Communists Back Nehru Position," *Daily Worker* (June 30, 1955), p. 2.

[2] Senator Thomas Dodd, *Congressional Record* (September 22, 1961).

recognized Gizenga's regime as the "only legitimate government of the Congo." [3]

With this background in mind it may still come as a shock to some to recall that at this point the United Nations swung its full support and influence behind Gizenga and did everything it could to hamper Colonel Mobutu and President Kasavubu. This is doubly hard to justify because Mobutu and Kasavubu represented the central government, which had called in the United Nations in the first place. Gizenga's little Communist satellite of Orientale province was just as much secessionist as Katanga province had been. But the United Nations made no effort to end Gizenga's secession. It passed no angry resolutions in the Security Council. It initiated no massive troop movements. In fact, as has been pointed out, it used what few troops it did have in Orientale province to protect Gizenga and his followers. Stewart Alsop, writing in the *Saturday Evening Post,* described it this way:

> The United Nations policy has been, in essence, to immobilize the forces controlled by the Kasavubu-Mobutu regime. . . . Dayal [United Nations representative in the Congo] has ruled that Mobutu's army should be permitted to make only minor troop movements. . . . With the Kasavubu-Mobutu forces thus effectively hamstrung, and with help from Egyptians and iron curtain money and technicians, Gizenga's rump pro-Communist regime quickly consolidated its position. . . . Gizenga's forces then began moving on neighboring Kivu and Katanga provinces. The troop movements were by no means minor by Congolese standards, but the United Nations did nothing. . . . Mobutu was cer-

[3] Schuyler, p. 240. On July 17, 1961, a small patrol of Katangese soldiers removing a UN roadblock were fired on by UN troops. Two Katangans were killed and the rest fled into the bush. In anger, Interior Minister Munongo called a press conference and, pointing his remarks at the lack of support for Katanga from the United States, threatened to call on Soviet Russia for assistance. No one took it seriously, however, least of all the Soviets. Radio Moscow replied by calling Munongo and Tshombe "lackies and murderers with blood-stained hands." Even Conor O'Brien admitted that in the West, Munongo's statement was a windfall for politicians who were under fire from the so-called right wing for betraying anti-Communist Katanga. Nevertheless, in Elisabethville and throughout Katanga, posters showing an African with a spear and a map of Katanga, and the words "Katanga, shield of Africa against Communism" remained in place. Munongo had lost his temper but aside from that, life went on as before.

tainly a sad and harried man when I saw him. If the United Nations under Dayal had not actively obstructed every move he made, he said, he could have dealt in fairly short order with the Stanleyville dissidents.[4]

While all this was going on, Moise Tshombe was making efforts of his own to reunite the Congo along the federal lines previously discussed. On February 28 he met with a representative of the central government and one from Kasai province. There was immediate agreement on basic principles and the conference ended with all three signing a mutual defense pact to prevent the establishment of what they referred to as a United Nations "regime of tyranny."[5] On March 8 Tshombe convened a second conference, this time expanded to include virtually every Congolese leader of importance except the Communist Gizenga. Complete agreement was reached in record time. At the conclusion of the third day, the conferees issued a communiqué revealing that they all endorsed Tshombe's basic plan calling for a "community of Congolese states." There was to be a central government at Leopoldville in a neutral zone similar to the District of Columbia. Kasavubu was to remain president, serving on a council of states made up of the presidents of the member states. Foreign policy, general internal policy, currency and military affairs would come under jurisdiction of this council of states. There were to be no customs or immigration barriers between the states. It was obviously fashioned very closely after the American pattern of government. In a final telegram to Dag Hammarskjold, the Congolese leaders warned that the dispatch of more UN troops to the Congo would "aggravate tension" between the United Nations and the Congolese population. Tshombe said at the conclusion of the conference, "We have resolved our problems ourselves and now we want both West and East to leave us alone." The Soviet news agency Tass responded by denouncing the meeting as "a conference of puppets and traitors."[6]

Here was a giant step toward unity and the restoration of order in the Congo. The United Nations, however, was not

[4] Senator Thomas Dodd, *Congressional Record* (September 8, 1961). Also, O'Brien, pp. 96, 99.

[5] Hempstone, p. 134.

[6] *Ibid.*, pp. 134-139. Also, O'Brien, p. 98.

pleased. For one thing, it was upset over the form of the new union, maintaining that it was much too decentralized. For another, its man Gizenga was not at the conference. Consequently, the UN ignored the whole thing, as though pretending the conference never took place.

United Nations troops and armaments continued to roll into the Congo—most of them to Katanga—just as rapidly as U.S. Air Force Globemasters could bring them. Congolese leaders began to see the handwriting on the wall. Few of them had the strength of conviction that Tshombe possessed, and the weaker ones began to wonder if perhaps it might not be safer to go along with whatever the United Nations wanted. Finally, on April 17, 1961, the United Nations, in spite of its promise not to intervene in the internal affairs of the Congo, pressured Kasavubu into signing an agreement which directly repudiated the principles agreed upon by the Congolese leaders. But Tshombe did not find this out until six days later when he arrived at a third conference of Congolese leaders. The atmosphere had changed completely. Kasavubu and some of the others no longer spoke of a confederation of states. Their demands were now identical with those of the United Nations. Feeling completely betrayed, Tshombe walked out of the conference and prepared to return to Katanga. As he arrived at the airport, however, he was arrested without any pretense of legality and thrown into prison. A few days later, Tshombe was formally charged on four counts of high treason, two of which were punishable by death.[7]

Tshombe was kept in prison for two months. At no time was he allowed to see his attorney. He apparently was not subjected to physical torture, but he was, nevertheless, kept in solitary confinement. He was given no exercise, nothing to read, and no one with whom to talk. A few months previously the United Nations had provided extravagant military protection for Patrice Lumumba and had loudly protested when he was arrested by Colonel Mobutu's men. Now that Tshombe was in jail, however, things were different. There were no protests or offers of protection. In fact, the world's self-proclaimed champions of justice and human rights remained strangely silent.

The enemies of Katanga expected Tshombe's arrest to set

[7] Hempstone, pp. 143-147. Also, O'Brien, pp. 99, 127.

off a power struggle among his supporters back home. They reasoned hopefully that a new shuffle would possibly bring to the top someone more pliable and more willing to go along with United Nations policies. They were wrong on two counts. First of all, the strong man in the number two spot and the most likely to take Tshombe's place was Godefroi Munongo who was, if any-thing, more like Tshombe than Tshombe himself. Also, Tshombe had earned such complete respect and loyalty from his followers that the expected power struggle never happened. His cabinet and parliament closed ranks in his absence and proclaimed their solidarity. Posters began appearing on the streets of Elisabethville with huge pictures of Tshombe and the words "He suffers for us. Let us be worthy of him."

It was fortunate for Tshombe that Lumumba was no longer top wheel in the central government. Otherwise, he would never have been seen again. But Kasavubu, even though he was now dancing to the UN tune, was not a vicious person. He was merely a weak politician who wanted to be on the winning side.

Tshombe, however, still maintained the loyalty of his follow-ers, and with the personal intervention of Colonel Mobutu he was finally released on June 22. Joyous mayhem broke out in Katanga when the news was received. A few days later, he was back at work with more determination than ever. There was an ominous note of anticipated tragedy in Tshombe's voice as he addressed the national assembly: "We shall see to it that the Katangese Nation shall endure. Let the enemies of Katanga know that they have to deal with a people." [8]

❊   ❊   ❊

Turning our attention back to the United Nations "moderates" in the central government, a new figure appears. He is Cyrille Adoula, former associate and supporter of Patrice Lumumba. He claims that he is not a Communist, but on December 28, 1957, he wrote:

> Being a socialist I am for the transformation of the present society. And for this I conceive the collectivisation of the means of production. In order to attain this goal, I see only one means: *the struggle of the classes, the permanent class struggle.*[9]

[8] O'Brien, p. 115.
[9] *Presence Africaine* (December 28, 1957). As quoted by Michel

Since the Communists advocate exactly the same thing, and since they also frequently refer to themselves as socialists instead of Communists, the distinction is not particularly reassuring. But what a man does is far more important than whether or not he may have been formally issued a membership card. If he does the work of the Communists, even unknowingly, he is just as dangerous as the most devoted and disciplined party member.

On August 2, 1961, the Congolese parliament approved Cyrille Adoula as the new premier. One of his first official acts was to invite all the Russian and Czech diplomats to return their Communist embassies to Leopoldville—which they did. Next, it was announced that Antoine Gizenga, leader of the Communist faction in Stanleyville, had been appointed to the number two spot of vice-premier. It is not clear just how much Adoula had to do with this appointment since Mr. Sture Linner (United Nations representative in Leopoldville) has publicly claimed personal credit for persuading Gizenga to accept the position.[10] Nevertheless, on August 16 Adoula visited Gizenga in Stanleyville to work out plans for their new government. A few days later they both spoke publicly and embraced each other for news photographers. Gizenga announced that he was dissolving his provisional government in favor of the new coalition and added, "The government will have to follow the Lumumba line . . ."[11] Soon afterward, Moscow radio announced that the Adoula regime would put into operation "all decisions previously made by Lumumba's government."[12]

The position of minister of the interior—which includes complete control of the police—was filled by another Prague-trained Communist, Christophe Gbenye. Gbenye had previously served under Gizenga and was the man who was directly responsible for instigating the murder, rape and terrorization of European residents in Orientale province.[13]

Counting heavily on the UN to bring Katanga's secession to

Sturdza, *World Government and International Assassination* (Belmont, Mass., American Opinion, 1963), p. 11.

[10] Senator Thomas Dodd, *Congressional Record* (August 3, 1962).

[11] Schuyler, p. 268.

[12] Lessing, p. 143.

[13] Senator Thomas Dodd, *Congressional Record* (September 8, 1961).

an end, the central government appointed Egide Bochely-Davidson as the chief administrator of Katanga province. Bochely-Davidson was not only a Communist, but a member of the Soviet secret police.[14] As the Newark *Star-Ledger* explained on September 24, 1961:

> The Reds may have . . . made a deal by which a Communist would succeed Tshombe as boss of Katanga. The central government of the Congo republic recently named Egide Bochely-Davidson—a Moscow-trained agent—as chief administrator of Katanga province. He was supposed to take over the provincial government with the support of United Nations troops. . . . If Bochely-Davidson can consolidate his position in Katanga, the Reds will be one step closer to victory in the Congo—with the aid of American dollars, United Nations soldiers, and the late Dag Hammarskjold.

The Moscow *Times* gloated:

> On August 2nd, a new government was formed in the Congo composed of 27 ministers and 17 state secretaries. Cyrille Adoula was appointed prime-minister. According to the Stanleyville newspaper, *Uhuru,* the members of political parties of the national bloc which was headed by Patrice Lumumba have 23 seats in the government, or an absolute majority. The composition of this new cabinet proves that adventurous efforts to liquidate the government of Lumumba completely failed. The decision of the parliament commits the new government to carry out all decisions made earlier by the Lumumba government. . . .[15]

[14] *Ibid.,* (September 16, 1961).

[15] Article entered in the *Congressional Record* by Senator Thomas Dodd (September 13, 1961). The Communist record of Gizenga, Adoula's vice-premier, was so well known that it embarrassed western supporters of the Adoula regime. As his pro-Communist bias became more and more difficult to conceal, it was decided to "arrest" Gizenga as proof of the central government's anti-Communism. Supporters of UN policy in the non-Communist world received much mileage from this maneuver. What most people were not allowed to learn, however, was that Gizenga was quietly set free soon afterward. According to Philippa Schuyler, his "prison" was a comfortable villa by the sea. Even Adlai Stevenson refrained from saying that Gizenga was in jail. In an article distributed by the UN association in Los Angeles, he is quoted as saying that Gizenga had been under "house arrest." See "Stevenson Answers Critics on Congo," Los Angeles *Times* (February 10, 1963).

When addressing the General Assembly of the United Nations, Adoula was careful to let everyone know exactly where he stood. He referred to the late Lumumba as his "national hero" and to Gizenga as his "good friend." [16]

This was the government that high officials in the UN and in Washington were piously describing as "moderate." The same State Department that refused to allow Tshombe to visit the United States and even went as far as to cancel the visa of the head of the Katanga Information Service in this country, rolled out the red carpet for Adoula. The following statement by G. Mennen Williams, State Department spokesman for African affairs, is typical of the kind of black-is-white pronouncements that have become all too common from State Department officials:

> A moderate parliamentary central government under Prime Minister Cyrille Adoula has been formed, and it is operating effectively and supported broadly everywhere except in Katanga. The pretensions of the opposition Orientale province government have been ended and Gizenga has been effectively neutralized. The Communists have been barred from continuing their direct support of left-wing elements in the Congo. . . . If present means do not succeed, the Adoula government may be replaced by a radical one, or, as an alternative, the Adoula government may be obliged to seek help from others than those now helping them. This would mean, in all likelihood, help from more radical sources. The net result would be to discredit the UN and the U.S. and open the possibility of chaos in the Congo—chaos which would invite Communist intervention in the heart of Africa. This alternative the world cannot contemplate with equanimity.[17]

At about the same time, Mr. George Ball, undersecretary of state, solemnly told a Los Angeles audience that Katanga's inde-

---

[16] "Adoula Receives Royal Welcome," the *Tablet* (Brooklyn, February 17, 1962). As this book is going to press, the elections in the Congo are nearing. Since the basic sentiments of the masses of Congolese people (as distinguished from many of their leaders) are anti-Soviet, the Adoula regime has recently put on a rather convincing show of anti-Communism in its public pronouncements. It has even expelled the Communist embassies from Leopoldville. Whether or not this appearance of anti-Communism will be dropped after the elections or whether it represents a true stiffening of Adoula's political backbone, will remain to be seen.

[17] *Department of State Bulletin* (November 26, 1962), pp. 804-806.

pendence "can only place in jeopardy the success of our efforts in the Congo as a whole, threaten the entire Congo with chaos and civil war, and lead to the establishment of a Communist base in the heart of Central Africa. The armed secession in Katanga plays into the hands of the Communists. This is a fact that all Americans should ponder." [18]

President Kennedy held a special luncheon in Adoula's honor at the White House. Rising to present a toast, Kennedy said:

> Gentlemen, I am sure you all join me in welcoming to this country the guest of honor and the members of his government. . . . The difficulties of our revolutionary experience, and the experiences of every other people coming into independence since the end of World War II, pale in comparison to the problems which the Congo has faced and which press upon the prime minister and his supporters. What makes him especially welcome is the courage and the fortitude, the persistence and the judgment with which he has met these challenges—which would have overwhelmed a lesser people, a lesser country, a lesser man, a lesser government. Prime Minister, we welcome you here for many reasons. The success of the Congo is tied up, really, we believe, with the success of the UN. If you fail and the Congo should fail, it would be a serious blow for the UN, upon which this country has placed so many hopes for the last 17 years. . . . [19]

[18] Department of State press release #893 (December 19, 1961).

[19] *Department of State Bulletin* (February 26, 1962), p. 335. Shortly after the assassination of President Kennedy in 1963, President Johnson addressed the General Assembly of the United Nations and confirmed that the change in chief executives had in no way altered the official United States attitude toward the UN. President Johnson said, "More than ever we support the United Nations. . . ." The only noticeable difference was that the New England twang had been replaced by a Texas drawl. See "Text of Johnson's Speech to UN," Los Angeles *Times* (December 18, 1963), sec. 4, p. 2.

His speech was softer than butter,
yet war was in his heart;
his words were softer than oil,
yet they were drawn swords.

Psalm 55:21

FIVE | IN THE LAST RESORT

While the world mourned the death of Lumumba, the United Nations expressed its own anger and concern by passing a resolution on February 21, 1961, which said:

> The Security Council . . . having learned with deep regret the announcement of the killing of the Congolese leader, Mr. Patrice Lumumba . . . urges that measures be taken for the immediate withdrawal and evacuation from the Congo of all Belgian and other foreign military and para-military personnel and political advisors not under United Nations command. . . .

This was obviously aimed at Katanga since that was the only province in the whole Congo with appreciable numbers of European military officers.

There are several interesting and revealing aspects to that resolution. First, there was the honorable mention of Lumumba, whose demise was the occasion of "deep regret" for the Security Council. Secondly, there was the outright intrusion of the UN into internal affairs of Katanga on the bold-faced assertion that it had a right to tell Katanga what it could or could not do. Nothing in the United Nations Charter gives the UN authority to dictate to a country who may or may not be employed by that country in its own army. This is clearly an internal affair of the Congo. Yet paradoxically the same resolution reaffirmed that "the United Nations force in the Congo will not be a party to or in

43

any way intervene in or be used to influence the outcome of any internal conflict, constitutional or otherwise." It went even further and acknowledged that "the solution of the problem of the Congo lies in the hands of the Congolese people themselves without any interference from outside . . ."

In the light of subsequent United Nations intervention in the Congo, one can only be astounded at the extent of hypocrisy displayed by UN officials. But hidden away in the language of bureaucratese is an indication of the UN's true, and not-so-honorable, intentions toward the Congo. In the very same resolution, the UN authorized itself to employ *"the use of force, if necessary, in the last resort."* There it was—the first glimpse—the clear and unmistakable outline of the mailed fist beneath the velvet glove.

Promising not to interfere in Katanga and at the very same time authorizing the use of force to interfere is the kind of double-talk that politicians through the ages have used to make their grab for unlimited power appear to be legal and proper. These pronouncements do not happen accidentally, nor are they the result of ignorance and incompetence. They are the mark of corrupt political skill, the product of unlimited cynicism tempered by years of experience. The men who have mastered this skill are proud of their accomplishment and are quick to admire it in others. Conor O'Brien was such a man. Expressing his unqualified approval of the United Nations resolution, he wrote:

> The contradictions and equivocations in that mandate allowed them a good deal of leeway, and this, as I have mentioned, Hammarskjold was adept at using. Sometimes, as I heard some feat of interpretation, some especially refined harmonization of S/4426 paragraph 4 with A/Res. 1474 paragraph 2, and noted how neatly it fitted the political needs of the moment, I was reminded of an excellent formula invented by a Central American chairman of the first committee, when he found it desirable to stretch the rules a little for the benefit of Mr. Cabot Lodge: "Under the rule," he said, "it would seem that the delegate is not permitted to speak at this stage. I shall, however, interpret the rule in the spirit of the principles of philosophical jurisprudence. I give the floor to the representative of the United States."
> The men round the table on the 38th floor [the "Congo club"] were often inspired by the spirit of philosophical juris-

prudence, and indeed the Congo operation, if it were to be carried on at all, demanded such a spirit.[1]

At four o'clock in the morning on August 28 while Elisabethville slept in peace, the United Nations, exercising its philosophical jurisprudence, launched a surprise attack on the city. In the early hours of morning darkness it took over all communications centers, put a blockade around the foreign minister's residence, surrounded the barracks of the Katangese army, and arrested over four hundred European officers and noncoms. Simultaneously, it began arresting and expelling from the country hundreds of other European residents who were suspected of being technicians or advisors. There was practically no resistance, since, as it was learned later, the Belgian officers who were on loan to Tshombe's army were under orders from their government not to fire on United Nations troops.[2] In one fell swoop, Katanga's army was decapitated of its professional leadership. Soldiers and civilians alike were taken from their families at bayonet point, rounded up in detention centers, and expelled from the country, often with nothing but the clothes on their backs. There were no charges brought against them, no hearings, no habeas corpus, no right of appeal, no opportunity to put their personal affairs in order. It was a police-state operation.[3]

Time magazine described it this way:

> The 11,600 black Katangese troops remained passive, possibly because UN soldiers staged furious public bayonet drills and small arms exercises in a pointed show of power. Remarked one senior . . . UN officer: "We have these soldiers scared witless." [4]

The forty-six civilian doctors of Elisabethville shed further light on the action when they reported:

> Hundreds of houses were searched by the men of the UNO without result, dozens of European civilians arrested and threatened with the foulest brutalities if they did not admit having helped, sheltered or simply known "mercenaries" or volunteers.

[1] O'Brien, p. 61.
[2] *Ibid.*, p. 221.
[3] *46 Angry Men*, pp. 44-45.
[4] Article entered in the *Congressional Record* by Senator Thomas Dodd (September 8, 1961).

Houses searched without any result? Alas, not always. Failing to find mercenaries, which was perhaps dangerous, one fell back upon a nice little compensating looting, which is not so dangerous when one is . . . armed; and if the house which was being visited was empty, a . . . little ransacking was included.[5]

Operation Rumpunch (the UN code name for the August attack) was a success. Only a handful of European officers remained in the Kantangese army. The mercenaries, as the UN called them, had been expelled.

❈   ❈   ❈

As we have seen, the UN—in the beginning, at least—justified its action against Katanga on the claim that it had to remove Tshombe's mercenaries. Aside from the fact that the composition of the Katangese army is not the concern of the UN, United Nations troops themselves were mercenaries of the first order. Irish, Swedish, Italian, Ethiopian and Gurkha troops were fighting as hired agents of the UN. If the mercenary issue was a real one, why did not the United Nations insist that the Ghanian Communist Kwame Nkrumah get rid of the British officers in his army? What would one call the American officers serving in Laos? The truth of the matter is that the whole mercenary issue was nothing but an excuse for the United Nations to initiate military action against Katanga with the ultimate objective of bringing it under the control of the Communist-dominated central government. By removing the professional leadership from Katanga's army, the UN not only reduced the chances of effective military opposition to its own future plans, but also greatly enhanced the return of civil disorder and chaos to Katanga province—the very thing that it professed to be there to prevent.

At any rate, Tshombe did not throw in the towel as the UN apparently expected. Katanga did not fall apart. Tshombe had been expecting something like this and had initiated a crash program to train African officers and noncoms for effective leadership. The program was far from complete, but sufficient progress had been made to enable Katanga to stand firm in its determination to remain independent. Tshombe appointed a Colonel Muké as commander of the army, and Katanga now had not only an

[5] *46 Angry Men*, p. 47.

African president and an African government but an African commander as well. It soon became obvious that if Katanga were to topple, even stronger measures would have to be taken.

On the morning of September 11, Conor O'Brien met with Moise Tshombe and once again gave his personal assurances that the United Nations had no intentions of intervening in the internal affairs of Katanga or of using force in the settlement of any issue.[6] That very same day, however, he met in secret with other UN officials and helped lay detailed plans for another surprise military attack on Elisabethville. The following is O'Brien's own description of those plans:

> As regards Tshombe, we were to arrest him only in the last resort. His residence was to be cut off, the entries and exits to it sealed, and then I was to parley with him, making it clear that his only hope lay in cooperating with the United Nations, and in peacefully liquidating the secession of Katanga. Meanwhile, UN forces were to secure the post office and the radio studios and transmitters, and to raid the offices of sûreté and ministry of information and remove the files. Europeans and senior African personnel working in these departments were to be apprehended if possible. The flag of the Republic of the Congo should be run up at the earliest appropriate moment on public buildings and on UN buildings; we had a supply of these flags which Michel Tombelaine had recently brought back from Leopoldville. The central government would send down a commissaire d'etat to take over authority, in cooperation with Tshombe if possible, in cooperation with the United Nations in any case. . . .
>
> We all knew, of course, that the mercenaries still at large would be likely to undertake some action, but we did not take this very seriously because of their small numbers. . . .
>
> As regards the timing, Khiary said that the operation should be carried out either *before* three o'clock on the afternoon of Wednesday, September 13th—the time that Hammarskjold was due to arrive in Leopoldville—or after Hammarskjold's departure, estimated for three days later. Hammarskjold had given authority for these operations, but it would be embarrassing for him if fighting were actually going on in Katanga while he was in Leopoldville. . . .
>
> Khiary asked how long, if fighting did break out, it would

[6] Senator Thomas Dodd, *Congressional Record* (September 16, 1961). Also, Sturdza, p. 39.

take to bring the situation under control. Raja [UN military commander] said that the points where there was a danger of resistance were the post office and the radio studio. Even if this were determined resistance, it could be ended in, at most, two hours. In this, Raja's prediction was perfectly correct.

In the light of my insistence on urgency, and Raja's assurance of the duration of possible resistance, Khiary agreed that the operations should be carried out early on the morning of September 13th.[7]

Operation Morthor, as it was called, went off according to schedule. Once again moving under cover of early morning darkness the United Nations "peace-keepers" stormed the communication and transportation nerve centers of Elisabethville. Within hours the UN-controlled radio station announced, "The secession is over! Arrest the whites! The secession is over! Arrest the whites!"[8]

Egide Bochely-Davidson, the Communist who had been appointed by the central government to administer Katanga province, was flown by UN plane to Elisabethville's airport to take control just as soon as the fighting stopped in the center of the city. (Dag Hammarskjold had said previously: "United Nations facilities cannot be used, for example, to transport civilian or military representatives, under the authority of the central government, to Katanga against the decision of the Katanga provincial government."[9])

At this point, however, Operation Morthor began to fall apart. Katangese troops launched a counterattack on all fronts as full scale fighting spread to practically every sector of the city. Control of the radio station moved back and forth between forces as one of the obviously important military objectives. Bochely-Davidson impatiently paced up and down at the airport as the distant sound of machine-gun chatter and mortar explosions grew louder by the minute. This time Katanga was fighting back.

American newspapers carried the following account:

[7] O'Brien, pp. 249-251.
[8] *Ibid.*, p. 282. When this was called to their attention at a later date, UN officials in Katanga apologized and said that they had made a mistake and meant to say "white officers."
[9] UN document S/4417/ADD 6 (August 12, 1960), pp. 3-4. Also, UN document A/4711/ADD 2 (March 20, 1961), pp. 62, 68, 73. Also, van den Haag, p. 22.

The battle for Elisabethville exploded into full war today, with casualties estimated in excess of 1,000. The UN declared martial law and . . . Michel Tombelaine of France, deputy UN civilian commander, announced over the UN controlled radio that any civilians found in illegal possession of arms will be summarily executed.[10]

Michel Tombelaine was identified as a member of the French Communist party by a subcommittee of the United States Senate on August 6, 1962.[11]

In an effort to capture and control the post office, the United Nations set up strategic military positions under the protection of a large hospital which they had conveniently established across the street. To their credit, the United Nations doctors there finally resigned en masse, stating "the building was being turned into a support fortress." [12]

The forty-six civilian doctors of Elisabethville reported:

The hospital of the Italian Red Cross, which is situated behind the post office and opposite the Banque du Congo, was militarised by the UNO. The personnel of this hospital wore the uniforms of the UNO. Already before September 13, 1961 [when the attack began], this hospital was in a state of armed defence: sandbags, shelters for riflemen and machine-gunners. . . .

. . . on the morning of September 13th, the alleged defences were really used as combat stations from which, at the beginning of the attack on the post office by the mercenaries of the UNO, a well-sustained fire helped the massacre of the defenders of this public building.[13]

UPI correspondent Ray Moloney drove a hundred miles to Bancroft in Northern Rhodesia to file the following eyewitness account:

I watched the counterattack from inside the UN Red Cross hospital which had machine guns set up along the terrace. United Nations troops were firing from the hospital in the shadow of a

[10] Newspaper article entered in the *Congressional Record* by Senator Thomas Dodd (September 16, 1961).

[11] *Visa Procedures of Department of State,* report to the Senate Committee on the Judiciary (August 6, 1962), p. 28.

[12] Newspaper article entered in the *Congressional Record* by Senator Thomas Dodd (September 16, 1961).

[13] *46 Angry Men,* pp. 68-69.

giant Red Cross flag. . . . I also saw UN troops fire on a Katangese ambulance as it tried to reach the twitching bodies of unarmed Katangese police who were ripped to pieces by UN machine-gun bullets after the cease fire sounded.[14]

Frustrated in its anticipation of an easy victory, the United Nations began to turn Operation Morthor into Operation Terror. Blue-helmeted soldiers displaying the UN emblem of peace fired wantonly at civilians, ambulances, automobiles—anything that moved. A Roman Catholic priest was murdered on his way to collect the Holy Sacrament from St. Paul's Convent; the charred remains of his body were later found in the burned shell of his automobile which had been hit by a bazooka shot from a United Nations armored car. An ambulance man, dressed in white and wearing a Red Cross armband was machine-gunned while stepping out of his ambulance to help the wounded; his leg had to be amputated to save his life. A housewife was murdered while riding with her husband down a peaceful street to buy groceries. These and literally hundreds of similar cases have been carefully documented. There are always unfortunate killings of innocent civilians as the accidental by-product of any war. But the consistent pattern of such atrocities in Katanga clearly reveals that they could only have been the result of deliberate design.

Beginning on September 18 and continuing several times daily, UN convoys traveling along the Boulevard Rhine Elisabeth and Avenue Stanley fired machine guns at virtually every home they passed. The one dwelling that received the most punishment of all was the home of a Dr. and Mrs. Szeles, Hungarian refugees who fled from similar treatment at the hands of the Communists in 1948. His home was clearly identified by an enormous Red Cross flag. Several ambulances were usually parked in front. For days on end UN troops machine-gunned this house twice a day— as convoys were deployed in the morning and when they returned in the late afternoon. On one occasion hand grenades were thrown in the windows. Mrs. Szeles, who had sought shelter in the corridor, was badly wounded by the explosions. Dr. Szeles counted 355 bullet holes in the walls of his home. All the windows were broken, the furniture smashed to pieces, the whole house reduced to shambles. Fleeing from Communist terror in Hungary at the age of fifty, Dr. Szeles came to Katanga to start a new life. Ten years later, at the age of sixty, he is once again deprived of his home—thanks to the organization that was supposedly created "to save succeeding generations from the scourge of war." [15]

At the height of the UN attack on Elisabethville, Mr. Georges Olivet, the Swiss international Red Cross representative there, cabled an appeal to his Geneva office to persuade the United Nations to stop firing on Red Cross vehicles. A few days later he disappeared while on a mercy mission to UN headquarters. It was not until eleven days afterward that his wrecked ambulance was found. It had been hit with bazooka rockets and machine-gunned by United Nations troops. In an attempt to conceal the crime, the UN soldiers had hurriedly buried Mr. Olivet and his two companions in a shallow grave next to the road. The United Nations issued two contradictory explanations of what happened. The first one charged that European mercenaries of the Katangese army had kidnapped Olivet. Later, when the evidence was disclosed, it admitted that the vehicle had been struck by UN fire but claimed that it was an accident caused by Olivet's driving "into cross fire." [16] When the Red Cross asked for an official investigation into this matter, the United Nations—which had launched an extensive investigation of Lumumba's death—denied the request on the basis that it did not have "adequate legal or technical resources." [17]

The Roman Catholic bishop of Elisabethville accused the United Nations of "sacrilegious profanities" and revealed that their troops had deliberately destroyed and looted churches and had wantonly murdered innocent civilians.[18]

More than ninety percent of the buildings bombed by UN aircraft were strictly civilian structures with no possible military value. As briefly described in the opening passages of this book, the operation rapidly assumed the aspect of full-scale war. With all utilities cut and no refrigeration, civilians rushed about frantically trying to find something to eat and drink. A light rain brought thankful Katangans to every rain spout to collect the

[15] *46 Angry Men*, pp. 48-51.
[16] *Ibid.*, pp. 20-24. Also, Hempstone, p. 195.
[17] Hempstone, p. 224.
[18] The *Tidings* (Los Angeles, January 11, 1963), p. 1.

life-saving drinking water. The stench of rotting food hung over the city and mingled with the smell of death.

The Communist press around the world was jubilant. Even in Rome the Social Democratic *La Guistizia* said that the UN had succeeded "in bringing back peace," and the Communist newspaper *L'Unità* called Operation Morthor "a hard defeat for the colonialists and their agents." [19]

Miraculously, Katanga held the UN at bay. News correspondent Peter Younghusband gave the following eyewitness report in an article datelined Elisabethville, September 15, 1961:

> Katanga Province President Tshombe said yesterday that he and his people will fight "to the last drop of blood" to keep Katanga independent. I spoke to Tshombe in a small villa situated in the grounds of his official residence. Mortar shell explosions and machine-gun fire could be heard throughout the city. I was astonished when a Belgian settler told me that Tshombe was not in hiding as reported Tuesday, but was still in his residence—and offered to take me there. I went and found the residence heavily defended by troops with machine guns in the gardens and armored cars in the road outside.
>
> The president, haggard and eyes bloodshot from lack of sleep, said, "Did you think I would run away when my soldiers are fighting and dying for their country? We will fight to the bitter end and, if necessary, the last battle will be here in my home, and I will be part of it." President Tshombe said he was prepared to negotiate with the UN for a cease-fire if they would withdraw from the center of the city and refrain from attacking his troops and leave him to settle his affairs with the central Congo government in his own time. "They have lied to me and have murdered my people," he said. "I appeal to the free world —to Britain, to France, to America—to all nations who treasure the principles of freedom and the right of a people to self-determination to bring this terrible thing to an end." . . . Elisabethville is a terror town of shattered buildings and deserted streets, where bullets whine and ricochet. . . . Belgian settlers who armed themselves to the teeth and joined the Katanga army in the fight for Katanga's freedom include former war veterans and police officers. Other civilians organized food and water supplies to the

---

[19] "UN Action in Katanga Stirs Dismay in Europe," London newspaper article entered in the *Congressional Record* by Senator Thomas Dodd (September 16, 1961).

President Moise Tshombe of Katanga, a Christian, a college graduate, and an admirer of the American system, was anathema to the United Nations.

Wide World Photo

Conor Cruise O'Brien (right), chief United Nations representative in the Congo, is shown with fellow Irishman Lt. Gen. Sean McKeown, commander of UN forces there.

Colonel Joseph Mobutu (left) and Congolese President Joseph Kasavubu (right, saluting) review troops after they ousted Lumumba and began to restore law and order to the region.

Patrice Lumumba, Communist puppet in the Congo, travels from bar to bar in Leopoldville drumming up support.

One of the many anti-Communist demonstrations that greeted Lumumba on his return to the Congo. The signs call for the expulsion and death of the Communist traitors.

Cyrille Adoula, who appointed Communists to key spots in his government, was sold to the American people as a "moderate."

Antoine Gizenga, a Prague-trained Communist, established a Communist regime in opposition to Kasavubu and Mobutu. The UN swung its support behind Gizenga.

Wide World Photo

Greeting Dag Hammarskjold (right) and other UN representatives at the Elisabethville airport, Katanga's President Moise Tshombe (center) has the honor guard present the Katangese colors while a band plays the newly written Katangese national anthem.

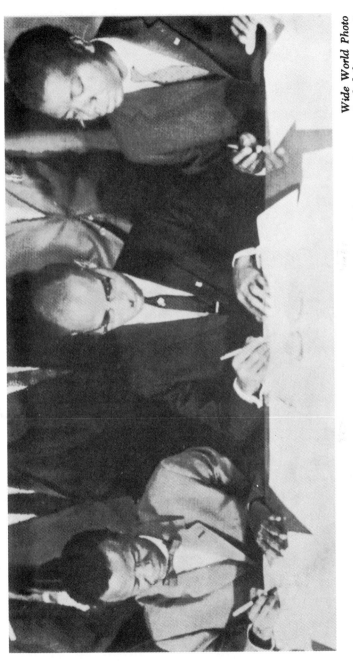

Wide World Photo

Delegates from the central government and Kasai province join Tshombe (right) in signing a mutual defense pact against what they referred to as a United Nations "regime of tyranny." The Congo was well on its way back to unity and stability; but the UN had other plans.

"Our people have a different history, traditions, and outlook from those of the Congo. Every people has the right to its own self-determination. There is no reason why we should be exploited by the Congo." Moise Tshombe.

UPI Photo

When United Nations forces move in, citizens find themselves expelled from their homes and country.

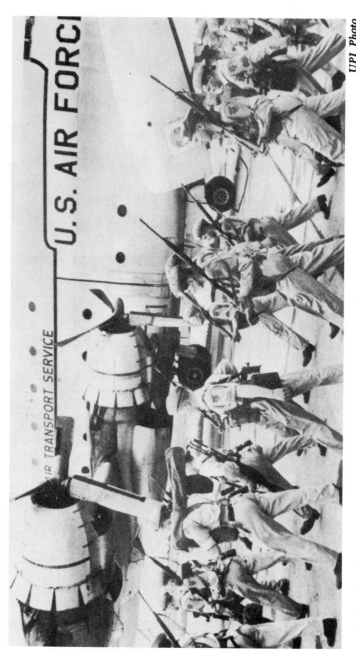

UPI Photo

At the height of the sacking of Katanga, Tshombe personally appealed to the United States to use its influence to put an end to the destruction of Elisabethville. In reply, U.S. Globemasters air-lifted additional UN troops, artillery and armored cars right into the heart of the city.

Seventh Day Adventist church. *UPI Photo*

Spes Nostra Church.

A dress shop in Elisabethville. *UPI Photo*

Lubumbashi hospital.

"Over ninety percent of the buildings bombed and shelled by the United Nations were strictly civilian structures with no military value."

United Nations "peace-keepers" bring war to **Katanga**.

UN officials Michel Tombelaine (white shirt) and Conor **O'Brien**
ride through Elisabethville in a UN armored car. Tombelaine **has been**
identified as a member of the French Communist party.

The ambulance in which Red Cross delegate Georges Olivet was killed by UN bazooka and machine gun fire.

Father Alexandre Ferdinando Gagna (known as Father Michel) met his death when his Lancia was burned out by bazooka fire from a UN Swedish armored car.

President Tshombe struggles to regain his composure during his farewell speech at Kolwezi. Standing in the rain, he said: "You have fought bravely. . . . The odds have been against you."

troops. All Elisabethville's hospitals are filled with wounded. I visited the Katanga radio station, which is now nothing more than a blackened shell of a building, doorless and windowless with smashed radio equipment, furniture, telephones, steel helmets and boots all lying in a jumbled mess. Outside, I counted thirteen corpses still lying in the grass nearby, all Katanga police and all, inexplicably, shot in the back. UN troops yesterday again fired on a Katanga army ambulance displaying Red Crosses, seriously wounding the African driver and two white nurses.[20]

Tshombe, speaking to his people over a hidden transmitter that identified itself as "Radio Free Katanga," called for total resistance—"a fight to the last round of ammunition." Five thousand Baluba warriors responded by joining the Katangese soldiers. Several hundred Bayeke warriors also came into the fight. White residents took up arms and fought side-by-side with their African neighbors. They were not mercenaries. Nobody paid them. They volunteered to fight for the simple reason that the United Nations was destroying their homes and killing their loved ones.

Finally, the tide began to turn. The UN had prematurely announced to the world that the secession was over. It was now in serious danger of having its forces completely annihilated because of the unexpected determination of the Katangese people to maintain their independence. As supplies and morale began to run low, it became obvious that the UN had made the fatal mistake of believing its own propaganda. It had asserted that Tshombe was a mere puppet of the Belgians and that he was supported in power only by a few mercenaries against the true will of his people. It maintained that his government would collapse at the first blow. It was now paying the price of self-deception. Things were going so badly for the United Nations that by September 17 its whole company A was cut off, badly beaten, and forced to surrender. With Operation Morthor on the verge of total collapse, the UN finally agreed to a face-saving cease-fire. On September 20, just one week after the United Nations had launched its unprovoked attack, peace once again returned to Katanga; its green and white flag still fluttered proudly to proclaim that Katanga remained free.

[20] "All Out War in Katanga," newspaper article entered in the *Congressional Record* by Senator Thomas Dodd (September 16, 1961).

The only thing more incredible than the United Nations military action in Katanga is the way in which it tried to justify that action. If things had gone according to schedule there would have been little trouble. Press releases would have simply stated that Tshombe had been replaced by "moderate" Bochely-Davidson and that after a light exchange of gunfire "secessionist" Katanga had been brought back under the central government. The United States President would have sent his congratulations to Dag Hammarskjold and State Department officials would have expressed great satisfaction with this victory over Communism. But as it turned out, the situation had "escalated," and there were just too many newspaper reporters willing to make that hundred-mile trek to Northern Rhodesia to get the true story out to the world.[21]

At one point, the UN explained that it had initiated military action "at the request of the central government." An official spokesman elaborated: "The UN motive in complying with the request was to avoid the alternative—invasion of northern Katanga by central government troops and a prolonged civil war." [22] In other words, the central government was preparing to attack Katanga; but that would have been civil war. Therefore, the UN attacked Katanga to save the central government the trouble!

As the fighting spread, it became apparent that the United

[21] In addition to news reporters, of course, there were many prominent individuals who independently came to Katanga to conduct their own personal investigations. One such observer was Lord Bertrand Russell, a strong supporter of the United Nations. Not only did he confirm the stories of UN atrocities, but the following excerpt from his report presents an interesting sidelight on the way in which UN officials were becoming overwhelmed by the dilemma of so many impartial observers: "Next day by appointment I saw General Yakub . . . I told the general that I had been collecting evidence regarding the alleged reports of murder of innocent civilians in Elisabethville by United Nations troops, and that I wanted to ask him some questions. He said that 'No offense has been committed; there are only rumors.' I told him that I had not come to argue whether such offenses had been committed, but merely to ask whether any inquiry had been set on foot to find out whether there was any foundation to such an allegation. . . . The general would say nothing; he just sat and stared at me." As quoted by Sturdza, p. 26.

[22] "UN Troops Seize Katanga in an Eight Hour Street Battle," New York Times (September 14, 1961). Also, Senator Thomas Dodd, Congressional Record (September 16, 1961). Also, Visa Procedures of Department of State, report to the Senate Committee on the Judiciary (August 6, 1962), p. 16.

Nations needed another story. As a result, it was decided to announce that the UN had nothing to do with starting the action at all—that it was merely defending itself against Katangese aggression. And so, on September 16, three days after the United Nations had stated it had initiated the action "at the request of the central government," Dag Hammarskjold, at a press conference, told this fantastic story:

> In the early hours of September 13th . . . an alert was set since arson was discovered at the UN garage. As the UN troops were proceeding toward the garage premises, fire was opened on them from the building where a number of foreign officers are known to be staying. UN troops were subsequently also resisted and fired at as they were deploying toward key points or while they were guarding installations in the city.[23]

In the words of Conor O'Brien, the man who helped plan the attack:

> I have no idea what the source for the "arson" statement may be. No such fire was ever reported by me, or to me, or ever referred to in my presence. Nor is there any reference to such a phenomenon in the military "situation report." . . . Some days before, an empty UN vehicle was upset and damaged by the "spontaneous demonstrators" outside a garage in the town (properly speaking, there was no "UN garage"). This incident, the nearest known to me to the "arson alarm," was no longer present to our minds on the morning of September 13th.[24]

Just for the record, Operation Morthor comes from a Hindi word. *Morthor* does not mean "Sound the alarm; there is arson in the garage" or "Let us now assist the authorities to prevent civil war." It means *smash!*

[23] UN document S/4940. Also, O'Brien, p. 264.
[24] O'Brien, pp. 265-266.

They make desolation which they call peace.
Tacitus (54-119 A.D.)

AH, PEACE

The defeat of the United Nations in Katanga was met with anguished cries from the world Communist press. Tass, the Soviet news agency, said that the cease-fire agreement with "colonialist puppet Tshombe" evoked only a feeling of "indignation." The Tass writer, V. Kharokov, complained that what had been a promising UN operation to end Katanga's secession had turned out to be "a total flop." [1]

The Communists, however, were unduly concerned, for the UN was not giving up yet. It was using the cease-fire merely as a means of building up its strength for a renewed attack. Immediately, additional troops began to arrive on the scene: The first four of fourteen UN jets landed at Leopoldville. The buildup was both extensive and rapid. Finally, on November 24, 1961, the Security Council swung into action once again. It passed another resolution strongly condemning Katanga for its continued use of mercenaries and then authorized the further use of force to bring it under the control of the central government. The velvet glove was now completely off. This amounted to a declaration of war against Katanga. Tshombe was quick to realize this and, addressing a crowd of eight thousand cheering Africans two days later, he said that the United Nations would soon "undertake war on our territory. . . . Tomorrow or the day after, there will be a trial of strength. Let us prepare for it. Let Katanga fighters arise at the

[1] "Moscow Scores Capitulation," New York *Times* (September 21, 1961). Entered in the *Congressional Record* by Senator Thomas Dodd (September 22, 1961).

given moment in every street, every lane, every road and every village. I will give you the signal at the opportune time." [2]

Minister of the Interior Munongo later echoed Tshombe's sentiment when he proclaimed: "We are all here, resolved to fight and die if necessary. The UN may take our cities. There will remain our villages and the bush. All the tribal chiefs are alerted. We are savages; we are Negroes. So be it! We shall fight like savages with our arrows." [3]

While the UN military buildup was taking place, troops of the central government began to move into position to invade the regions of northern Katanga. Since this would be civil war, and since the UN said it was in the Congo to prevent civil war, one might expect the peace-keepers to do something about it. They did. They provided large quantities of supplies and helped transport the central government troops into Katanga. The UN referred to this as a "police action." The chief UN representative in the Congo, Sture Linner, further explained that any move on the part of Tshombe to secure his defensive military position along Katanga's borders would be considered an act of civil war and that the UN would take action to prevent it.[4]

The central government was getting impatient to nail Tshombe's hide to the wall. Justin Bomboko, the Congolese foreign minister who had previously brought charges of high treason against Tshombe, later revealed the prevailing mood of his government when he said: "Tshombe only understands the language of force and pressure. . . . We can negotiate for 100 years with Tshombe, but it will be in vain. There is no hope of solving this problem by peaceful means. We lose our time, and this is the reason why we went to the UN and Washington." [5]

What kind of troops were these that the UN brought into Katanga and sustained with supplies and jet air cover? They were mostly the same mutinous bunch that had been on the rampage for many months. Their numbers included several thousand of those whom Tshombe had kicked out of his army and who had

[2] Hempstone, p. 182.
[3] *Ibid.*, p. 188.
[4] *Ibid.*, p. 149.
[5] Katanga Information Service news bulletin (New York, March 22, 1963).

since reenlisted in Leopoldville. The rest were from Gizenga's former Communist stronghold of Stanleyville.

A few weeks earlier, Gizenga's soldiers seized and brutally beat thirteen Italian airmen serving the United Nations at Kindu. After the beating the men were shot and cut up into tiny pieces. According to witnesses parts of the bodies were thrown into the Congo River. Others were sold in the market place. A human hand was presented to a United Nations doctor by a giggling Congolese soldier. Colonel Alphonse Pakassa, commander of these soldiers, when questioned on the subject of the massacre simply shrugged his shoulders and replied, "You know how soldiers are." [6]

The world was shocked at the news. But, as usual, memories were short. These were the very same soldiers that just six weeks later were transported by the United Nations into northern Katanga.[7] After their arrival, they proceeded to slaughter a group of twenty-two Roman Catholic missionaries. This time, however, since the victims were not wearing UN uniforms, there was practically no publicity.[8]

Turning southward, these soldiers put whole villages to the torch, slaughtered women and children, and sent over ten thousand families fleeing in panic. Anyone, black or white, who was found to be armed with even a penknife was killed on the spot. Risking her life to visit the terror zone, newswoman Philippa Schuyler reported:

> As this story goes to press, the wild, chaotic Congolese National Army is advancing from the north into Katanga, moving ever southward, ravaging wherever they go, like a diabolic visitation of locusts. The UN is not stopping their advance. These are wild barbarians, like the fifth century Gauls advancing on Rome, determined to annihilate the bastion of civilization that remains in Katanga. Sacked by the barbarians, the remainder of the Congo has already entered the Dark Ages; helped by the UN, these barbaric hordes wish also to plunge Katanga into desolation, ignorance and misery.[9]

[6] Hempstone, pp. 178-179.
[7] Senator Thomas Dodd, *Congressional Record* (January 25, 1962).
[8] Hempstone, pp. 184-185.
[9] Philippa Schuyler, *Who Killed the Congo?* (New York, The Devin-Adair Company, 1962), pp. 295-296.

In the wake of this imported terror, the entire region began to revert to its primitive origin. With no local authority to keep peace and order, the natives—afraid and confused—revived ancient and suppressed rituals. Cannibalism was reintroduced. Smoldering tribal feuds broke out into full-scale tribal wars. Even the beloved missionaries who were once reasonably safe in the area were terrorized and murdered as a result of the mass hysteria that had been unleashed.[10]

The Katangese forces that previously had been responsible for law and order were now fighting for their very lives. A ten-man Katangese patrol led by a local administrative officer, Gregoire Kulu, was ambushed by about one hunderd wild savages who cut off Kulu's legs, jammed sticks into the stumps and forced him to run on them before burning him alive.[11] As a result of atrocities of this kind and the onslaught of the central government troops, Tshombe's gendarmes in the area urgently sent for reinforcements and additional ammunition. Their plea was denied by the United Nations, however, on the basis that this would enhance civil war and thus would be in violation of the cease-fire agreement.

But once again, Katanga overcame the impossible odds and finally pushed the invaders back. Order was restored to the territory. By November the invaders were in full retreat—looting and pillaging as they went.

By now the UN had completed its own military buildup for a renewed assault on Elisabethville. Seeing that the central government could not subdue Tshombe, the United Nations issued a few more promises not to intervene in the internal affairs of Katanga and began to draw up plans for its next attack. It came on December 5, just three weeks before Christmas. United Nations troops assaulted a Katangese roadblock, and when the smoke cleared thirty-eight Katangans lay lifeless in the street. The war was on!

From this point the story becomes tragically monotonous.

[10] Conor O'Brien admitted that since in many regions of Katanga the missionaries cannot live in safety unless Katangese gendarmes are present, and since the UN was expelling these law enforcement contingents, the missionaries were, in reality, being driven out by the UN. See O'Brien, p. 162.

[11] Hempstone, pp. 117-119.

Once again the United Nations unleashed a reign of terror, death and destruction on peaceful Elisabethville. Once again the primary targets were hospitals, churches, homes, ambulances and shops. Once again the victims were civilians—men, women and children. And, once again, the Secretary-General insisted that the United Nations was merely fighting back as the innocent victim of Katanga's aggression. The only changes were that Conor O'Brien had been recalled and U Thant was now issuing the contradictory statements instead of Dag Hammarskjold. Thant stated on December 12 that the goal of the United Nations military operations in Katanga was merely to "regain and assure our freedom of movement to restore law and order, and to insure that, for the future, UN forces and officials in Katanga are not subject to attacks." Yet, just five days later, when Tshombe was calling for a cease-fire, Thant declared, "For us to stop short of our objectives at the present stage would be a serious setback for the UN." [12]

While the United Nations was pursuing its objectives, the forty-six civilian doctors of Elisabethville sent an electrifying telegram to President Kennedy, Pope John, and some fourteen other leading dignitaries around the world:

> SOS TO THE MORAL CONSCIENCE OF THE WORLD
> —stop—IMPLORE YOU TO INTERVENE WITH ALL YOUR
> AUTHORITY TO STOP THE TERRORIST BOMBARDMENT
> OF HOSPITALS AND CIVILIAN POPULATIONS BY UNO.
> . . . ON OUR HONOUR AS PHYSICIANS WE DECLARE AS
> LIES THE DENIALS OF UNO SECRETARY-GENERAL—stop
> —INSIST UPON INQUIRY HERE BY HIGH MAGISTRATES
> AND PRESIDENTS OF MEDICAL ORDERS OF ALL CIVI-
> LISED NATIONS—stop—ONLY MEANS OF CONVINCING
> THE WORLD OF INCONCEIVABLE ACTIONS OF UNO
> ALAS DISHONORED—stop—INSIST UPON CREATION IN-
> TERNATIONAL TRIBUNE COMPETENT JUDGE CRIMES
> AND MISDEEDS UNO PERSONNEL WHO BENEFIT FROM
> IMMUNITY CONTRARY TO NATURAL LAW.[13]

At the height of the sacking of Elisabethville, Tshombe personally appealed to the United States to use its influence to put an end to the destruction of the city. U.S. Ambassador to the

[12] *Ibid.*, p. 206.
[13] *46 Angry Men*, pp. 91-92.

United Nations Adlai Stevenson replied that "the U.S. is very pleased with the plans of the Secretary-General to bring Katanga under control." [14] Secretary of State Dean Rusk explained to the unsuspecting public that the U.S. was backing the UN action "to save the Congo from the Communists." [15] And on December 13, twenty-seven U.S. Globemasters flew additional UN troops, artillery and armored cars right into Elisabethville.[16] The next day Mr. Jules Cousin, administrative director for one of Katanga's largest mining companies, sent a bitter message to President Kennedy describing the United Nations' blind "killing and wounding —even in the hospitals." He stated that since the United States had continued to finance and support this carnage he was returning with disgust the Medal of Freedom awarded to him by the United States in 1946.[17]

That same day, December 14, a full-page advertisement was run in the New York *Times* protesting the bombing of Katanga, which had "committed no aggression except wanting to be free of a Communist-controlled central government." The State Department replied by accusing the sponsors of the ad of taking bribes from the Katanga Information Service in New York.[18] Adlai Stevenson said further: "The object of the United States in supporting the United Nations during this long and trying period has been to advance American policy in Africa. . . . It seems to me that our policy and UN policy have coincided exactly in the Congo. I wish many Americans would think of that when they complain about what has been done there." [19]

And so it went. The great and powerful United Nations— the "last best hope for peace," the "moral conscience of the world"—pitted against tiny Katanga, a country that would not give up. Again and again, Katanga held firm. Finally another cease-fire was called.

[14] Congressman Donald C. Bruce, *Congressional Record* (September 12, 1962).

[15] "Rusk Says Congo Unity Is Goal," Chicago *Tribune* (December 9, 1961). Also, Schuyler, p. 294.

[16] Hempstone, pp. 189, 194.

[17] "Mining Aid in Katanga Hands Back U.S. Medal," New York *Times* (December 14, 1961).

[18] Schuyler, p. 293.

[19] "Stevenson Answers Critics on Congo," Los Angeles *Times* (February 10, 1963).

Almost a year went by while the United Nations went through the motions of conciliation and pondered its next move. Matters were complicated by the Congo war lasting longer and costing far more than expected. It put the United Nations into debt. A further financial complication arose when Soviet Russia refused to pay its share of the cost. This, of course, made it appear as if the Communists were really quite unhappy over the UN Congo policy. They knew full well, however, that their friends in Washington would put up enough "dirty capitalist" money to cover the whole operation. They were right, as was proved by subsequent events.

The American taxpayer was simply told that the Congo operation was anti-Communist while he was being relieved of several hundred million more dollars.[20]

On October 12, 1962, the American Committee for Aid to Katanga Freedom Fighters revealed a highly confidential memorandum which had been circulated among top United Nations

[20] This was in addition to the 100 million dollars worth of United Nations bonds that the United States purchased. The average voter did not realize that President Kennedy quietly used over 200 million dollars of his own personal "slush fund" (officially referred to as the President's "foreign aid contingency fund") to help the UN get out of the red ink resulting from its military operation in the Congo. The UN, in turn, applied some of this money against the back dues and special assessments of several countries that were in arrears with payments. Needless to say, most of the countries that received the benefit of this donation of American tax dollars were those that consistently vote against the United States. These included Cuba, Yugoslavia, Poland, Albania, and Bulgaria—all of which are openly Communist—as well as Brazil, Burma, Ghana, Indonesia and many others that are, for all practical purposes, just as much Soviet satellites as the rest. Naturally the State Department emphatically denied that this had happened. Through the miracles of bookkeeping, they explained that the money was used only to pay the costs of the Congo operation. But this is what enabled the UN, in turn, to cancel off the assessments of the above countries—so it all adds up to the same thing. According to Article 19 of the United Nations Charter, the member nation that is more than two years in arrears in its payments loses its vote. President Kennedy's generosity with American tax dollars out of his slush fund and other foreign aid grants actually saved these countries that consistently vote against us from losing their votes! See congressional debate on budget request, *Congressional Record* (September 12, 1962). Also, *Purchase of UN Bonds*, hearings before the Senate Committee on Foreign Relations (February 6-9, 1962), pp. 1-180. Also, report of the House Committee on Foreign Relations regarding the purchase of UN bonds, House report #2176 (August 10, 1962), pp. 14-22. Also, Congressman Otto Passman, *Congressional Record* (September 20, 1962), p. 20156; and (October 6, 1962), pp. 22712, 22715.

officials. The memorandum put forth a very precise and intricate timetable for renewed military aggression against Katanga. It also predicted that the United States would go along with these plans in spite of rising public opposition at the grass roots. It declared:

> The U.S. will judge itself bound, as in the past, by UN decisions and will supply the necessary transport aircraft and, later on, helicopters. . . . Washington would like to work out a compromise; but the State Department has based its policy on the UN and will in no circumstances disregard its obligations to the UN decision.

United Nations officials and State Department spokesmen immediately charged that the memorandum was fictitious. Events since then, however, have proved that it was one hundred percent accurate, even to the timetable.

Suddenly, the UN released a press report describing a letter said to have been signed by eight important tribal chiefs in Katanga. The letter branded Tshombe as a traitor, asked for his immediate arrest, demanded that troops be sent to crush Tshombe's resistance, and highly praised the United Nations. While most newsmen took the report at face value, Michael Padev of the daily *Arizona Republic* thought that the whole matter seemed too slick and decided to check further. As a result, it was revealed that the whole story was completely fabricated by the United Nations. After giving assurances that the letter was authentic and promising to provide the press with photostatic copies, UN press officers later backed down and admitted that they did not have the letter but that it had been seen. Finally, when word reached Katanga all but one of the chiefs who supposedly signed the letter telegraphed angry denials saying, "Everything the UN published was a campaign of lies." One chief, Kasengo Nyembo, stated that he had been recently approached by the UN to make an anti-Tshombe statement but had refused. The United Nations quietly dropped the issue.[21]

Finally, on December 29, 1962, the United Nations delivered its second annual Christmas present to Katanga. As *Time* magazine described it:

[21] "Charges UN Hit Tshombe with Big Lie," Chicago *Tribune* (January 20, 1963).

The sound of Christmas in Katanga Province was the thunk of mortar shells and the rattle of machine-guns. . . . Blue-helmeted UN soldiers swarmed through Elisabethville, seized roadblocks on the highways. Swedish UN Saab jets swooped low over Katanga's airfield at Kolwezi, destroying four planes on the ground and setting oil tanks ablaze. . . . From Manhattan UN headquarters, orders were flashed to the 12,000 man UN force in Katanga: "Take all necessary action in self-defense and to restore order." . . . Secretary-General U Thant says he is convinced that unless Tshombe is subdued soon, Premier Cyrille Adoula's Central Government in Leopoldville will collapse.[22]

With a fresh supply of American money and military support Robert Gardner, the new UN chief officer in the Congo, confidently declared: "We are not going to make the mistake this time of stopping short. . . . This is going to be as decisive as we can make it." [23]

One month later, after having captured control of Elisabethville, Kamina and Kipushi, the United Nations finally seized Kolwezi—a city of seventy thousand and Tshombe's last stronghold. An hour before UN troops entered the center of the city, Tshombe made a dramatic farewell speech to his soldiers. About two thousand of them gathered in the market square. Standing in a drizzling rain, Tshombe told his men: "You have fought bravely against the enemy three times in the past two and one-half years. The odds have become overwhelming against you." [24]

A few minutes later Katanga's independence was ground into the mud by United Nations boots. The last flame of freedom in the Congo flickered and died.

[22] *Time* (January 4, 1963), p. 12.
[23] New York *Times,* west. ed. (December 31, 1962), p. 1.
[24] New York *Times,* west. ed. (January 22, 1963), p. 1.

PART II

THE MASTER PLANNERS
Communist Control
of the United Nations

*What will be left of the American experiment
when we have been integrated with the political
system of France, the economic system of Turkey,
the social system of Italy? I do not know—but
SOMEONE knows. . . .*

Senator William E. Jenner, June 1956

CHAPTER

SEVEN | BABY CARRIAGES

Speaking before the Senate on February 23, 1954, Senator William Jenner told the story of a young married man working in a baby-carriage factory in Germany during the early days of the Nazi regime. Since his wife was soon expecting their first child, the young man began to save his money to purchase one of the baby carriages he was helping to build. But for some reason the Nazi government refused to let anybody buy them. So he decided to collect secretly the parts—one from each department—and do the assembly himself at home. Finally, when all the parts had been gathered, he and his wife began to put them together. To their utter astonishment, they wound up with, not a baby carriage at all, but a *machine gun!* And, as Senator Jenner observed:

> The pattern . . . was divided into separate parts, each of them as innocent, safe and familiar looking as possible. The leaders did not intend to assemble the parts until they needed machine guns. But let's keep in mind that when the parts of a design are carefully cut to exact size to fit other parts with a perfect fit in final assembly, the parts must be made according to a blueprint drawn up in exact detail. This does not happen by chance. The men who make the blueprints know exactly what the final product is to be. They have planned the final assembly years ahead. They do not think they are making baby carriages.[1]

[1] Senator William Jenner, *Congressional Record* (February 23, 1954).

The United Nations operation in the Congo was no accident. When all the component parts are put together and viewed in their entirety, they mesh so neatly and consistently over a period of time as to reveal a pattern far too obvious to ignore. Nor did this machine gun come into existence overnight. Actually, the planners, who knew what the end product was to be, had been working feverishly for years. Their job was to get the individual pieces properly designed and then manufactured by as many unsuspecting souls as could be enticed to the assembly line. The baby carriages had been described to these workers with such appealing phrases as "peace," and "security," "world brotherhood," and "international cooperation." But when the pieces were assembled in Katanga they brought death, destruction and Communism. The only people who were surprised at the final product were those who had taken the United Nations at face value and who had never closely examined either the blueprint or the planners who drafted it.

The first rough sketches for this blueprint were drawn up by Nikolai Lenin. They were expanded by Joseph Stalin and refined by Nikita Khrushchev. Subtle changes and variations are still added from time to time, but the basic plan remains essentially the same.

Stalin laid down five intermediate goals of Communism as necessary steps toward the ultimate goal of global conquest. Summarized, they are as follows:

1. Confuse, disorganize and destroy the forces of capitalism around the world.
2. Bring all nations together into a single world system of economy.
3. Force the advanced countries to pour prolonged financial aid into the underdeveloped countries.
4. Divide the world into regional groups as a transitional stage to total world government. Populations will more readily abandon their national loyalties to a vague regional loyalty than they will for a world authority. Later, the regionals [such as the present NATO, SEATO, and the Organization of American States] can be brought all the way into a single world dictatorship of the proletariat.[2]

[2] Joseph Stalin, *Marxism and the National Question* (New York, International Publishers, 1942).

For those who may be puzzled at why the Communists are concerned over raising the level of underdeveloped countries, it should be noted that this not only helps to "bring all nations together into a single world system of economy," but also serves to bleed dry the capitalist countries that will be paying the bill. In addition there is the fact that underdeveloped countries are more difficult for the Communists to take over than the more advanced ones. This will undoubtedly come as quite a shock to those who have been told that our massive giveaway program to foreign countries is keeping the Communists at bay. But, as Nikolai Lenin explained to his comrades:

> The more backward the country . . . the more difficult it is for her to pass from the old capitalist relations to socialist relations. To the tasks of destruction are added new, incredibly difficult tasks, vis. organizational tasks . . . the organization of accounting, of the control of large enterprises, the transformation of the whole of the state economic mechanism into a single huge machine, into an economic organization that will work in such a way as to enable hundreds of millions of people to be guided by a single plan.[3]

In 1928 and again in 1936 the Communist International formally presented a three-stage plan for achieving world government:

1. Socialize the economies of all nations.
2. Bring about regional unions of various groupings of these socialized nations.
3. Amalgamate all of these regional groupings into a final worldwide union of socialist states.

The following is taken directly from the official 1936 program of the Communist International:

> Dictatorship can be established only by a victory of socialism in different countries or groups of countries, after which the proletariat republics would unite on federal lines with those already

[3] Nikolai Lenin, *Selected Works,* vol. 7, pp. 285-287. As quoted by Joseph Stalin, *Problems of Leninism* (Moscow, Foreign Languages Publishing House, 1947), pp. 130-131.

in existence, and this system of federal unions would expand . . .
at length forming the World Union of Socialist Soviet Republics.[4]

The blueprint was further developed by William Z. Foster, national chairman of the Communist Party, U.S.A., from 1933 to 1957, when he wrote:

> A Communist world will be a unified, organized world. The economic system will be one great organization, based upon the principle of planning now dawning in the USSR. The American Soviet government will be an important section in this world government. . . .
>
> Once the power of the bourgeoisie is broken internationally and its States destroyed, the world Soviet Union will develop towards a scientific administration of things, as Engels describes. There will be no place for the present narrow patriotism, the bigoted nationalist chauvinism that serves so well the Capitalist warmakers.[5]

By 1945 the blueprint was being drafted into its final form. Delegates from countries all over the world were preparing to participate in a conference at San Francisco which was to mark the creation of something to be called the United Nations. Earl Browder, well known past leader of the United States Communist party, in his book *Victory and After,* stated: "The American Communists worked energetically and tirelessly to lay the foundations for the United Nations, which we were sure would come into existence." The April 1945 issue of the Communist periodical *Political Affairs* explained to its readers the importance of getting the capitalist countries committed to this international body. It pointed out that since Russia would be one of the dominant voices in the UN, it could be used to prevent other countries from acting independently against Communism. The magazine stated:

> Victory means more than the military defeat of Nazi Germany. It means the collapse of anti-Soviet policies and programs as dominant tendencies within the capitalist sector of the world. It means that the policy predominant during the interwar years of attempting to solve the world crisis at the expense of the

[4] Hearings before the Senate Committee on Foreign Relations (July 11, 1956), p. 196.

[5] William Z. Foster, *Toward Soviet America* (Balboa Island, Calif., Elgin Publications, 1961), pp. 326-327.

Soviet Union is replaced by the policy of attempting to solve the crisis *through cooperation with the Soviet Union.*[6] [Italics added.]

Five months later the Communists printed a pamphlet entitled *The United Nations* which further explained what function they had in mind for the United Nations. To be sure, it was *not* the function of "peace" that Americans anticipated. The pamphlet said: "It [the San Francisco conference] met to outlaw war. But everyone knows that war cannot be abolished until imperialism [i.e. capitalism] is abolished." It went on to explain that there were four primary reasons why Communists should support the United Nations:

1. The veto will protect the USSR from the rest of the world.
2. The UN will frustrate an effective foreign policy of the major capitalist countries.
3. The UN will be an extremely helpful instrument in breaking up the colonial territories of non-Communist countries.
4. The UN will eventually bring about the amalgamation of all nations into a single Soviet system.[7]

In 1953 Colonel Jan Bukar, a former Czechoslovakian army intelligence officer, testified before the House Committee on Un-American Activities that a General Bondarenko delivered a lecture at the Frunze Military Academy in Moscow and declared:

From the rostrum of the United Nations, we shall convince the colonial and semi-colonial people to liberate themselves and to spread the Communist theory over all the world. We recognize the UN as no authority over the Soviet Union, but the United Nations serves to deflect the capitalists and warmongers in the Western World.[8]

One final and extremely revealing glimpse of the blueprint was offered by Dr. Marek Stanislaw Korowicz, a member of the United Nations delegation from Communist Poland who defected

---

[6] "The World Assembly at San Francisco," *Political Affairs* (April 1945), pp. 293, 295.

[7] Mohan Kumaramangalam, *The United Nations* (Bombay, India, Peoples Publishing House, 1945), pp. 3-14.

[8] Testimony of Jan Bukar before the House Committee on Un-American Activities (May 13, 1953), committee report entitled *Soviet Schedule for War—1955*, p. 15.

in 1953 and sought political asylum in this country. Testifying before the House Committee on Un-American Activities, Dr. Korowicz said:

> We were all indoctrinated strongly with the Russian master plan to reach the working masses of the various countries in the Western World over the heads of their governments. . . . The organization of the UN is considered as one of the most important platforms for Soviet propaganda in the world. I wish to underline the following comment: Not only Russia, but its satellites attach a primary importance that the members of their bloc of satellite powers maintain their relations with the Western World. It is emphasized at all times that, in the acts of real democracy, socialist democracy, they should seek a direct channel over the heads of their governments to the great popular masses of the U.S. and the other western countries. The UN organization offers a parliamentary platform to the Soviet politicians, and from this platform, they may preach to the populations of the entire world and do their subversive propaganda.[9]

It is no mere coincidence that the United Nations headquarters was located in the United States. Most Americans think that this was a victory for us in the cold war. Nothing could be further from the truth. Not only has this made it much easier for the Communists in the United Nations to "reach directly to the American masses" with their propaganda, but their spies and espionage agents posing as delegates and staff can gain entry into this country under full diplomatic immunity. Matt Cvetic, former undercover agent for the FBI, has testified that

> . . . representatives of the Soviet bloc governments in the UN do not only operate as propaganda ministers in the UN, but also, whenever possible, carry on in this country to further the revolutionary aims of the Communist International by working in close proximity with members of the American Communist party and alien Soviet agents.[10]

In confirmation of Cvetic's testimony, J. Edgar Hoover, head of the FBI, stated that Communist diplomats assigned to the

[9] Hearings before the House Committee on Un-American Activities (September 24, 1953), pp. 2596, 2607.
[10] SISS hearings (July 9, 1951).

United Nations "represent the backbone of Russian intelligence operations in this country."[11]

A former employee of the Czechoslovakian consulate testified before a committee of the United States Senate in 1951 that UN officials from her country routinely took large amounts of baggage with them on their frequent trips home. She said that this meant usually less than 30 large bags per person, but on at least one occasion to her knowledge a returning UN official took 97 bags. She said that this baggage, which has diplomatic immunity and cannot be inspected, contained electronic devices, "equipment which was very secret," literature and secret communications.[12]

It should not come as a surprise, therefore, to learn that it was the Soviet Union, not the United States, that insisted that UN headquarters be located on our soil. Trygve Lie, the first secretary-general of the United Nations, revealed this fact in his book *In the Cause of Peace*. Describing the debates over the future location of the permanent headquarters, Lie said:

> The Americans declared their neutrality as soon as the Preparatory Commission opened its deliberations. The Russians disappointed most Western Europeans by coming out at once for a site in America. . . .
>
> Andrei Gromyko, of the USSR, had come out flatly for the United States. As to where in the United States, let the American Government decide, he had blandly told his colleagues. Later, the Soviet Union modified its stand to support the East Coast.[13]

Let us now put these scattered pieces of the master plan together and see what it looks like in its entirety. Briefly summarized, the Communist blueprint for world conquest via the United Nations is as follows:

1. Consolidate total working control of the United Nations into Communist hands as rapidly as possible.
2. Use the United Nations to break up the colonial territories of non-Communist countries.

[11] "FBI Chief Finds Red Spies 'Potent Danger,'" Los Angeles *Times* (May 4, 1963).

[12] SISS hearings (July 9, 1951).

[13] Trygve Lie, *In the Cause of Peace* (New York, The Macmillan Company, 1954), pp. 58-60.

3. Use the United Nations as a vehicle for subversion, espionage and propaganda within the non-Communist member nations.
4. Induce the non-Communist member nations to abandon any strong independent foreign policy of their own by turning over this function to the United Nations.
5. Maneuver the non-Communist member nations into establishing socialism at home as the necessary transition stage to Communism and to become dependent economically on the overall international socialist control and direction of the UN.
6. Induce the stronger non-Communist member nations to transfer full control of their military forces to the United Nations. After this, no resistance will be possible. The world will be Communist.

Since the United States is, at the present time, the only nation on earth that offers the potential of real resistance to the Communist plan of world conquest, the UN blueprint has been primarily designed for us. The Communists know that if they can just get America to step completely into the cage, the rest of the world will be theirs. And so, in practical terms, the master plan can be further simplified and condensed into just one simple objective: to gain full working control of the UN and, at the same time, to entice the United States to gradually surrender its sovereignty to this world government.

With the blueprint clearly before them, the Communists next launched a massive propaganda campaign to sell the UN to the American people. The April 1945 issue of the Communist periodical *Political Affairs* set the pace with the following directive:

> The major question for us in connection with the San Francisco Conference is to assure the adherence of the United States to the World Security Organization, in the spirit of the policies formulated in the Crimea Declaration [at which time it was decided to form the UN]. We have come a long way along this path. But the final battle has not yet been won, although we are in an extremely favorable position to destroy the remaining bridgeheads of opposition. In his address to the National Committee of the Communist Political Association in March 1945, Earl Browder [head of the Communist party in the U.S.] signalized the struggle for complete national adherence to the Crimea policies as "America's decisive battle." At the time of the Moscow Conference in October 1943, the Senate voted 85 to 5 in favor of United States

participation in a World Security Organization, even changing the phraseology of its resolution to accord with the Moscow Declaration. Only the diehard obstructionists voted against the resolution. . . . Building up vast popular support of the Crimea policy would create the best atmosphere for the United Nations meeting and for routing the opposition. After the Charter is passed at San Francisco, it will have to be approved by two thirds of the Senate, and this action will establish a weighty precedent for other treaties and agreements still to come. But the victory cannot be won in the Senate alone; it must emanate from the organized and broadening national support built up for the President's policy, on the eve of the San Francisco gathering and after. . . . Great popular support and enthusiasm for the United Nations policies should be built up, well organized and fully articulate. But it is also necessary to do more than that. The opposition must be rendered so impotent that it will be unable to gather any significant support in the Senate against the United Nations Charter and the treaties which will follow.[14]

Elsewhere in the same issue of *Political Affairs*, the Communists received detailed instructions on how to capture this great popular support.

It is necessary to show convincingly that, in criticizing or directly opposing the decisions of Crimea, these elements are opposing not only London and Moscow, but also, and in the first place, Washington—our Nation's foreign policy; that they are jeopardizing and obstructing America's national interests. . . . In fact, around this single proposition, it is now possible to enlist the active and coordinated support of every major organization and group in the United States, ranging from national, state, and local governmental bodies, the U.S. Chamber of Commerce, the Farm Bureau, and the American Legion, to the AFL, the CIO, and all other people's organizations. . . . This will be achieved if this vital battle is fought out in an uncompromising manner so as to reject all amendments and reservations, and if it is waged in behalf and on terms of America's national interests, as well as those of the common needs and the unity of action of all of the United Nations.[15]

---

[14] "The World Assembly at San Francisco," *Political Affairs* (April 1945), pp. 289-300.
[15] "Yalta and America's National Unity," *Political Affairs* (April 1945), pp. 304-305.

That this campaign was overwhelmingly successful hardly needs mentioning. The opposition was, indeed, rendered so impotent that it was unable to gather any significant support in the Senate against the United Nations Charter. Americans, jubilant at the idea of a peace organization which was in their national interest, unhesitatingly pledged their unlimited cooperation and support.

By 1954, however, the United Nations began to lose some of its initial luster in American circles. A rising tide of opposition was clearly on the horizon. Once again, the Communists went into high gear, this time to throw up a wall of protection around their pet creation. For instance, the July 1954 issue of the Communist *Daily Worker,* in an article headed "U.S. Labor and the UN," said:

> Both AFL and CIO have consistently given verbal support to the UN. Their conventions unfailingly adopted resolutions to this effect since the establishment of the world organization in 1945. Now the time has come when it is more than ever necessary to match the words with deeds. For the UN is in danger of going the way of the old League of Nations.[16]

A few months later, the same newspaper offered its Communist readers several tips on what arguments to use to overcome any criticism of the United Nations' dismal record. It answered the critics this way:

> So you see, its not the UN that merits your scorn and active opposition, but the policies that have undermined the UN and turned it into the opposite kind of an organization than was envisioned in San Francisco and provided in the Charter.[17]

A further indication of the Communists' interest in maintaining the United Nations can be found in the Preamble to the constitution of the Communist party:

> The Communist party of the United States . . . fights uncompromisingly against . . . all forms of chauvinism. . . . It holds further that the true national interest of our country and

[16] "U.S. Labor and the UN," *Daily Worker* (July 15, 1954), p. 5.
[17] "Policies that Undermine the UN," *Daily Worker* (December 21, 1954), p. 5.

the cause of peace and progress require . . . the strengthening of the United Nations as a universal instrument of peace.

This, then, is the "baby carriage" that has been sold to the American people—sold, but not yet delivered. When the day comes that the planners feel ready to assemble the parts on our soil, our innocence and good intentions will be of small comfort.

The plan is both simple and brilliant. But have the Communists succeeded in conquering one third of the world through stupidity? Did they do it with brute force? Was it luck? The answers to these questions are obvious. One thing for which the Communists must be given credit is that they are master strategists. They know full well that they could never hope to conquer the world through military might alone. But through trickery and deception, they have developed a formula whereby they can take over America, and thus the rest of the world, without firing a single shot. Khrushchev has said that when the Red flag flies over America, it will be Americans who will put it there. And in that simple boast lies the key to everything the Communists and their allies are trying to accomplish through the United Nations.

As Abraham Lincoln predicted, "If destruction be our lot, we must ourselves be its author and finisher. As a nation of free men, we must live through all time, or die by suicide."

Let none but Americans stand guard tonight!
George Washington

| UNDER EVERY BED

It is a sad commentary on contemporary America that when any-one tries to call attention to the fact that known Communists have succeeded in penetrating into key positions within our govern-ment, he is usually met with a barrage of wild accusations and condemnations from the anti-anti-Communists who now seem to dominate our opinion-molding channels of mass communications. Anyone who tries to arouse his fellow citizens to the terrible danger of allowing Communists and fellow travelers in high places runs the risk of becoming the object of public scorn. He will be labeled "extremist," "radical right," "crackpot." He will be contemptuously dismissed with the observation, "Oh, he sees a Communist under every bed." This phrase has almost become the national slogan of that great army of Americans who, being afraid to examine the evidence closely lest they discover a truth too unpleasant to bear, loudly repeat over and over again, as though saying it made it so, "It can't happen here; it can't happen here."

As a former head of the U.S. Communist party, William Z. Foster, put it:

> American imperialism is now strong. Its champions ridicule the idea of a revolution . . . they console themselves with the thought that "it could never happen in this country," and they scorn the at-present weak Communist party. But they overlook the detail that the same attitude was taken toward the pre-revo-lution Bolsheviki.[1]

[1] Foster, pp. 342-343.

There is, of course, no law that offers us eternal immunity from a Communist take-over. It can and *will* happen here unless enough of us do something to prevent it. To act intelligently, however, we must first know how the enemy is operating and then appraise his progress and the strength of his present position. We have already studied his master strategy. Let us now examine the extent to which he has succeeded in carrying it out.

Since a major Communist objective is to consolidate total working control of the United Nations, and since all else depends on that single accomplishment, we shall begin with that part of the record.

The casual observer might conclude that the degree of Communist control over the United Nations can be measured by the number of votes they have from satellite countries. On this basis the Communists could only come up with about 12 out of the total of 113. The record shows, however, that a substantial number of countries classified as neutral consistently vote with the Communist bloc. The Afro-Asian bloc, for instance (which now has over half the total number of votes in the entire organization), and much of the Latin American bloc almost never vote on the same side as the United States unless the United States happens to be voting on the same side as the Soviets—as is often the case. Not all of these countries, of course, are under the full control of Moscow; but they are, without exception, fiercely socialist and anti-U.S. in their orientation. Many of them consist of little more than primitive areas of the world ruled by tribal chiefs and petty despots. Kenya, for instance, is now run by Jomo ("Burning Spear") Kenyatta, former leader of the terrorist Mau Mau uprisings of the 1950's.

Many nations in the United Nations are dictatorships with hardly a pretense at representative government. Few of them share values and traditions similar to ours. There is widespread contempt for the rich Yankee who thinks that his money can buy friendship. And we should not deceive ourselves. Most of what apparent support we do get in the UN is the result of financial bribery, nothing more. Conor O'Brien inadvertently confirmed this when he wrote:

> Delegations from countries receiving aid from the United States would be warned in a friendly way that "Congress might

find it hard to understand" a given vote. Such countries rarely allowed to their delegates the luxury of an incomprehensible, and therefore potentially expensive voting position.[2]

Shocking as this situation is, it should not be surprising. After all, how does one go about enlisting the support of feudal princes, tribal chieftains, despots and cannibals? With moral suasion? The Soviets are perfectly content to let us spend ourselves silly buying the illusion of temporary leadership while they work behind the scenes consolidating their control of the UN. It is frightening to ponder what will happen when Uncle Sam's money runs out.

The voting delegates, however, are not nearly as important in the ultimate control of the United Nations as are the permanent staff members of the Secretariat. The resolutions and edicts that are ground out by the General Assembly and the Security Council are, as we have seen, purposely vague to leave "wide margins of latitude" for implementation by the Secretary-General and members of the Secretariat. It is in the Secretariat that the United Nations becomes the reality of world government. It is here among the faceless thousands of international bureaucrats that ultimate control resides. These men and women can effectively neutralize any resolution and prevent it from being realistically carried out; or they can put teeth into those that were never intended to bite.

When Conor O'Brien was transferred from his position as a delegate from Ireland to the staff of the Secretariat, he was so impressed at the greater importance of his new role that he was prompted to write:

> What produced the sense of shock was the growing impression that neither the General Assembly nor the Security Council had the full materials necessary for an adequately informed discussion and adequately motivated decisions, on the UN operation in the Congo. The only people who had these materials were the people who saw the actual telegrams—the inner circle of the Secretariat. . . . As for the Congo Advisory Committee, "advising" the Secretary-General on the basis of the information with which the Secretary-General saw fit to supply it, it seemed, in the light of the telegrams, much less like an advisory body than like a

[2] O'Brien, p. 24.

group of innocent outsiders being taken for a guided tour. . . .

. . . the Secretariat—rather than the half-paralysed Security Council or the amorphous General Assembly—was the reality of the United Nations, the advancing edge of the sense of international community. If the Secretariat played its cards remarkably close to its chest, as it now seemed that it was in the habit of doing, it was justified in this, because it was tremendously important, for the hopes it represented, that it should win.

Much of this was implicit in my attitude of mind . . . rather than fully thought out. What I was actually most conscious of was the more primitive feeling of pleasure at now being, as I thought, "on the inside" of this major international operation, combined with a sense of deflation, on realizing how very much "on the outside" one had been as an ordinary delegate in the corridors of the Assembly and at the Advisory Committee.[3]

What kind of person does it take to be a desirable member of this "inner circle"? First of all, like Conor O'Brien, he must have sufficient loyalty to the United Nations that he is willing to place it well above any loyalty to his own native land. All members of the United Nations Secretariat must take the following oath upon employment:

I solemnly affirm to exercise in all loyalty, discretion and conscience the functions entrusted to me as a member of the international service of the United Nations, to discharge those functions and regulate my conduct with the interests of the United Nations only in view, and not to seek or accept instructions in respect to the performance of my duties from any government or other authority external to the organization.[4]

Many of the American employees in the Secretariat who gladly took this loyalty oath to the UN refused to answer when questioned by a committee of the Senate regarding their Communist activities. Oath or no oath, any Communist who may be employed by the United Nations will never be loyal to anything except Communism. They will be loyal to the UN only as long as the UN is serving the purposes of the Kremlin—not one minute longer. Of course everyone knows this, yet the non-Communists at the United Nations have learned that whenever this fact is

[3] *Ibid.*, p. 50.
[4] Lie, p. 53.

brought up it enrages the Soviets. Consequently, they no longer discuss it lest it upset the cause of peace. This absurd ostrich complex has even gone so far that, while it is officially forbidden for the UN to hire anyone "connected with fascism" on the plausible basis that no one wants a potential Mussolini or Hitler to show up in the Secretariat, it is perfectly all right to hire persons connected with Communism. Apparently no one is worried about harboring a potential Stalin.

J. Edgar Hoover, director of the FBI, has disclosed that between 70 and 80 percent of the iron curtain diplomatic representatives in this country have "some type of espionage assignment." [5] Since it is only logical to assume that these people are dedicated Communists and that they will be exerting their maximum influence to channel the efforts of the United Nations toward Communist objectives, we will not waste a lot of time belaboring the point. There are several factors, however, that need to be emphasized. The first is that these people are not just run-of-the-mill international servants. They are carefully screened and professionally trained in the art of espionage. Once inside the United States their mission is to gather secret material and to serve as a communications link between Moscow and American-based Communists.

Hardly a month goes by without our reading in the newspaper of another United Nations delegate being nabbed by the FBI for espionage. It happens so often that it is hardly newsworthy any longer. The frustrating part of it, however, and the second point to be emphasized, is that since these enemy agents are officially accredited to the United Nations, they can operate under complete diplomatic immunity. If the FBI catches them red-handed, all they have to do is flash their UN passes and they are free again. Our State Department usually dashes off a stiff note of protest to the Soviet delegation asking that the individual be sent home, but a few days later, the exposed spy is replaced by another highly trained espionage agent from behind the iron curtain and the whole operation continues without missing a stroke. As *U.S. News and World Report* summarized it:

[5] "Red Spies Swarm U.S. Says Hoover," Los Angeles *Herald-Express* (October 18, 1960).

Agents of Russia, Czechoslovakia and Poland, as employees of a world organization, face little or no surveillance of the type Americans face in Communist countries. They can talk to anyone. They can communicate with Moscow by secret radio code; they can travel back and forth between New York and their home capitals freely, carrying secret documents with immunity. They are even free from arrest for minor crimes. And, if one is caught red-handed with secret U.S. documents, as was Velentin Gubitchev in the Judith Coplon case, he can count on merely being sent home, his passage paid by the UN.[6]

This diplomatic immunity makes it possible for UN Communists on our soil to go much further than acts of espionage. In fact, there is no limit to the extent of their activities—even to the point of kidnapping, murder and terrorism. For instance, Arkady Sobolev, who was at the time chief of the UN Soviet delegation, sent members of his staff to forcibly repatriate nine Soviet sailors who had sought sanctuary in America. The UN delegates who were members of the Soviet secret police went into the homes of these seamen (in New York and New Jersey), beat them into submission, kidnapped them and sent them back to Russia. American law enforcement officials knew what was happening but were powerless to do anything about it because of the diplomatic immunity of the UN personnel.[7] These same international servants later spirited away two-year-old Tanya Romanov, a little girl born in America—legally an American citizen—whose parents were Soviet refugees.[8]

In 1953 Dr. Marek Korowicz, a UN delegate from Communist Poland, took advantage of his presence in New York to escape to freedom in the United States. This is much riskier than it sounds, for, as the Chicago *Tribune* reported:

> The possibility that Communist secret police may try to shoot down Dr. Marek Korowicz, escaped Polish alternate representative to the UN, who has asked asylum in the U.S., has posed another problem for New York police, it was learned today. Their apprehension was dramatized by the fact that the FBI is standing

[6] Congressman Fred Busbey, *Congressional Record* (August 3, 1953).
[7] Chicago *Tribune* (May 4, 1956), pp. 1, 10. Also, *The Episode of the Russian Seamen*, SISS report (May 12, 1956).
[8] *Soviet Political Agreements and Results*, SISS publication (1959), p. VII.

24-hour guard over Dr. Korowicz, and the disclosure that at least 18 known agents of Russia or Red satellite nations carry guns in this area. These agents . . . go about claiming diplomatic immunity, and police say they do not have the authority to disarm them.[9]

But let us return to the main issue which is the degree of Communist control over the United Nations itself. While these agents are actively engaged in espionage against the United States, they are also busy within the structure of the UN doing their part to influence all that goes on there. They may be high-ranking administrative officials overseeing the work of hundreds of employees, or they may be merely innocuous statisticians, researchers or translators. But regardless of their particular assignment, they are part of those unseen hands that can change a word here, interpret a report there, bury important statistics, delay progress on research projects, and in a hundred other ways paralyze the whole organization when it comes to a clear-cut issue involving real opposition to Communism. But, for the most part, these agents are not relegated to the lesser posts within the United Nations. They are smart enough to get themselves into the key spots where they can exert maximum influence. For instance, for many years a Mrs. Jugolova, a Russian Communist from the Soviet ministry of education, has been head of the secondary education department of UNESCO.[10] Many will recall that as recently as July 1963 two UN employees fled the country after being exposed by the FBI as secret officers of the Soviet military intelligence. One of these, Dmitrievich Egorov, was a key personnel officer at the United Nations and was involved in the critical task of hiring and placing other employees in the Secretariat.[11] Another Soviet official by the name of Permogorov was one of the chiefs of UN radio broacasts.[12] Mr. Katz-Suchy, a

[9] "Fear Attempt by Red Police to Kill Envoy," Chicago *Tribune* (September 21, 1953), sec. 1, p. 2.

[10] V. Orval Watts, *Should We Strengthen the UN?* (Colorado Springs, The Freedom School, 1960), p. 24. Also, Frank Denke, "The UN and the Catholic Conscience," the *Wanderer* (St. Paul, October 10, 1963), p. 7. Dr. Watts earned his Ph.D. in economics and history at Harvard. Formerly a college professor, he is now an economics consultant and lecturer.

[11] UPI dispatch, Los Angeles *Times* (July 2, 1963), sec. 1, p. 1.

[12] Syndicated column, *Freedom Press* (Santa Barbara, Calif., January 9, 1963), sec. 1, p. 1.

Communist from Poland, was president of the Sixth Commission of Jurists, one of the principal standing committees of the United Nations. (His only qualification for this post, by the way, in addition to the fact that he was a Communist, was just one year of study of law at the University of Krakow.)[13]

These are just samples picked at random to show that these people are not only present within the heart of the UN mechanism, but they are often placed in extremely important policy-making positions. One of the most important positions within the entire United Nations—if not *the* most important—is that of undersecretary-general for political and security council affairs. Most Americans have never even heard of this position, much less anything about the man who holds the job. The undersecretary-general for political and security council affairs has three main areas of responsibility. They are:

1. Control of all military and police functions of the United Nations peace-keeping forces.
2. Supervision of all disarmament moves on the part of member nations.
3. Control of all atomic energy ultimately entrusted to the United Nations for peaceful and "other" purposes.

In view of the fact that these three functions may soon constitute the ultimate power of life and death over every human being on the face of the earth, there would appear to be some minor justification for us to be more than passingly curious over who will wield this power. Since the United Nations was created in 1945 there have been eight men appointed to the position of undersecretary-general of political and security council affairs. They are:

1. Arkady Sobolev—USSR (Resigned April 1949)
2. Konstantin Zinchenko—USSR (Resigned May 1953)
3. Ilya Tchernychev—USSR (Finished above term to 1954)
4. Dragoslav Protich—Yugoslavia (Resigned July 1958)
5. Anatoly F. Dobrynin—USSR (Resigned February 1960)
6. Georgi Petrovich Arkadev—USSR (Resigned March 1963)

[13] Hearings before the House Committee on Un-American Activities (September 24, 1953), pp. 2593-2594.

7. Eugeny Dmiterievich Kiselev—USSR (Died April 17, 1963)
8. Vladimir Pavlovich Suslov[14]—USSR (Appointed May 21, 1963) [15]

Some observers feel that eight Communists out of eight appointees constitutes a trend of sorts. But whatever you call it, Trygve Lie, the first secretary-general of the United Nations, revealed that this pattern was no mere coincidence. In his book *In the Cause of Peace* Lie wrote:

> Mr. Vyshinsky [of the USSR] did not delay his approach. He was the first to inform me of an understanding which the Big Five had reached in London on the appointment of a Soviet national as assistant secretary-general for political and security council affairs. . . .
>
> Mr. Stettinius [U.S. secretary of state] confirmed to me that he had agreed with the Soviet delegation in the matter. . . .
>
> The preservation of international peace and security was the organization's highest responsibility, and it was to entrusting the direction of the Secretariat department most concerned with this to a Soviet national that the Americans had agreed.[16]

[14] According to the Hungarian refugees, in 1956 Suslov was head of the Soviet secret police. They say he is the one who was responsible for the betrayal of General Pal Maleter, the representative of the Hungarian Freedom Fighters who met with the Soviets under their promise of protection. When Maleter arrived for the talks he was arrested by Suslov and executed a few months later.

[15] *United Nations Yearbook,* published annually in New York by Columbia University Press in cooperation with the United Nations. Also, *Statesman's Yearbook,* published annually in New York by St. Martin's Press. Also, *Facts on File: World News Digest* (119 West 57th Street., New York 19, N.Y., Facts on File, Inc.). These men are the individuals who held this office on a long-term appointment basis. Occasionally, other men have temporarily held the position during short periods to cover a brief leave of absence, vacation, etc. Researchers must be careful not to be led astray or confused by this fact.

[16] Lie, pp. 45-46.

An open foe may prove a curse;
but a pretended friend is worse.

Benjamin Franklin,
Poor Richard's Almanac

CHAPTER

NINE | THE HOME TEAM

In 1950 the State Department issued a volume entitled *Post-war Foreign Policy Preparation, 1939-45.* It described in detail the policies and documents leading up to the creation of the United Nations and named the men who shaped these policies. This and similar official records reveal that the following men were key government figures in UN planning within the U.S. State Department and Treasury Department: Alger Hiss, Harry Dexter White, Virginius Frank Coe, Dean Acheson, Noel Field, Laurence Duggan, Henry Julian Wadleigh, John Carter Vincent, David Weintraub, Nathan Gregory Silvermaster, Harold Glasser, Victor Perlo, Irving Kaplan, Solomon Adler, Abraham George Silverman, William L. Ullman and William H. Taylor. With the single exception of Dean Acheson, *all of these men have since been identified in sworn testimony as secret Communist agents!*

It is truly fantastic, but here is the record:

Alger Hiss: In 1950 Hiss was convicted and sent to prison for perjury involving statements relating to his Communist activities. Since the second Hiss trial evidence has continued to be amassed through other congressional investigations that is even more incriminating than that used for his conviction. As it was, the FBI had solid evidence of Hiss's Communist activities as far back as 1939 and had even issued numerous security reports to the Justice Department and executive branch dealing with this fact.[1] In

[1] *Interlocking Subversion in Government Departments,* SISS report (July 30. 1953), pp. 8-10.

addition, a parade of former Communists testified that they personally had known and worked with Alger Hiss as a fellow member of the party.

It is worth noting that Alger Hiss was very influential with the leaders of the Institute of Pacific Relations, which a Senate committee found to be infiltrated at the top by Communists. Hiss was one of the trustees of the IPR and was very active in its affairs.[2]

Mr. J. Anthony Panuch, who had been assigned the task of supervising the security aspects of the transfer of large numbers of personnel from various war agencies to the State Department in the fall of 1945, testified that as a security officer he had access to conclusive information on Hiss's Communist activity; but when he tried to do something about it, it was he, not Hiss, who was dismissed.[3]

In 1944 Hiss became acting director of the Office of Special Political Affairs which had charge of all postwar planning, most of which directly involved the creation of the United Nations; and in March 1945, in spite of all the FBI reports and other adverse security information circulating among the top echelons of government, he was promoted to director of that office.

It is more than a little ironic that Alger Hiss was the man who traveled with FDR to Yalta as his State Department advisor. It was at the Yalta meeting that the decision was made to give the Soviets three votes in the General Assembly to one for the United States. Giving votes to the Russians for the Ukrainian SSR and Byelorussia SSR made as much sense as giving extra votes to the United States for Texas and California. At any rate, even if Roosevelt had been inclined to protest this absurd agreement, he was up against the demands of Joe Stalin and the advice of Alger Hiss.

The Dumbarton Oaks Conference was held in 1944 to determine the future form that the United Nations would take. It was an extremely important meeting since most of the really critical decisions were made there. This meeting was so hush-hush that the public and even the press were excluded from the proceedings. Alger Hiss was the executive secretary of this conference.

[2] *Ibid.*
[3] *Ibid.*

Hiss's role at the San Francisco conference, where the United Nations was finally taken off the drawing board and put on the assembly line, is better known to most Americans. He was the chief planner and executive of the entire affair. He organized the American delegation and was the acting secretary-general. Visitor passes bore his signature. According to the April 16, 1945, issue of *Time* magazine:

> The Secretary-General for the San Francisco Conference was named at Yalta but announced only last week—lanky, Harvard trained Alger Hiss, one of the State Department's brighter young men. Alger Hiss was one of the Harvard Law School students whose records earned them the favor of Professor (now Justice) Felix Frankfurter and a year as secretary to the late Justice Oliver Wendell Holmes. He was drafted from a New York law firm by the New Deal in 1933, joined the State Department in 1936, accompanied President Roosevelt to Yalta. At San Francisco, he and his Secretariat of 300 (mostly Americans) will have the drudging, thankless clerk's job of copying, translating and publishing, running the thousands of paper-clip and pencil chores of an international meeting. But Alger Hiss will be an important figure there. As secretary-general, managing the agenda, he will have a lot to say behind the scenes about who gets the breaks.[4]

Hiss was not only the acting secretary-general at the San Francisco conference, but also served on the steering and executive committees which were charged with the responsibility of actually writing the new Charter.[5] In such a position, he undoubtedly wielded a tremendous amount of influence on the drafting of the Charter itself. He did not do it single-handedly, however, as some critics of the United Nations have claimed. For instance, Andrei Gromyko was asked during a press conference in 1958 whether he considered it a violation of the Charter for a country to send its forces into the territory of another. He replied: "Believe me, I sit here as one who helped to draft the UN Charter, and I had a distinct part in drafting this part of the Charter with my own hands."[6]

[4] *Time* (April 16, 1945), international section.

[5] *Insignia,* conference issue (1801 Broadway, San Diego, Calif., 1945), vol. 6, no. 1, p. 67.

[6] "Russia Keeps Up Pressure on Withdrawal," London *Daily Telegraph* (August 23, 1958). As quoted by Mark Ewell, *Manacles for Mankind* (London, Britons Publishing Company, 1960), p. 50.

At the conclusion of the conference Alger Hiss personally carried the freshly written document back to Washington by plane for Senate ratification. The Charter traveled in a black water-tight box with a parachute. The master planners were taking no chances.

Knowing that Alger Hiss was a Soviet agent, the FBI had prepared an extensive surveillance of his activities during the San Francisco conference. Shortly after Hiss learned of this through his contacts in the Justice Department, however, the FBI received orders from the top to cancel its plans.[7]

An entire book could be written on the single subject of Alger Hiss and his influence over the United Nations during its formative phase. But, as important as he was, he was only one man. Had Hiss never been born, or had he spent his entire life in a monastery, the UN would still be what it is today, for Hiss was not alone.

Harry Dexter White: White was the assistant secretary of the United States Treasury Department under Henry Morgenthau. As such, he had complete control over our foreign policy dealing with treasury matters. The following Treasury Department directive indicates the influence that White had:

> On and after this date [December 15, 1941], Mr. Harry D. White, assistant to the secretary, will assume full responsibility for all matters with which the Treasury Department has to deal having a bearing on foreign relations. Mr. White will act as liaison between the Treasury Department and the State Department, will serve in the capacity of advisor to the secretary on all treasury foreign affairs matters, and will assume responsibility for the management and operation of the stabilization fund without change in existing procedures. Mr. White will report directly to the secretary.[8]

Elizabeth Bentley testified that while she was a Communist supervising the liaison between various espionage rings in Washington, Harry Dexter White was a member of one of these groups. It was known as the Silvermaster cell. She also revealed that

---

[7] Statement by Senator Edwin Mechem, a former FBI agent assigned to cover Alger Hiss and other Russian spies, Chicago *Tribune* (May 26, 1963), sec. 1, p. 4.

[8] SISS report (July 30, 1953), p. 29.

White, acting on instructions from Moscow, pushed hard for what was later known as the Morgenthau plan and which was designed to destroy Germany's industry after the war so Germany could never again pose a serious obstacle to the Soviet plans for future expansion in Europe.[9]

J. Edgar Hoover testified before a Senate investigating committee that "from November 8, 1945, until June 24, 1946, seven communications went to the White House bearing on espionage activities wherein Harry D. White's name was specifically mentioned."[10] In spite of all this, White stayed on in his government post, as did Alger Hiss. After being sent to the San Francisco conference to represent the Treasury Department, White served as chairman of the important committee that established the United Nations multi-billion-dollar International Monetary Fund. Only a few months after being thoroughly exposed as a secret agent, White was appointed to the post of executive secretary of this International Monetary Fund which he helped create with large injections of United States tax money. When he turned in his resignation to the Treasury Department to accept this new position, President Truman sent him the following letter:[11]

> Dear Mr. White:
>
> I accept with regret your resignation as assistant secretary of the Treasury. My regret is lessened, however, in the knowledge that you leave the treasury only to assume new duties for the government in the field on international economics as the U.S. executive director of the International Monetary Fund. In that position, you will be able to carry forward the work you so ably began at Bretton Woods and you will have increased opportunity for the exercise of your wide knowledge and expertness in a field that is of utmost importance to world peace and security. I am confident that in your new position you will add distinction to your already distinguished career with the Treasury.
>
> Very sincerely yours,
> (signed) Harry S. Truman

[9] Hearings before the Senate subcommittee investigating the Institute of Pacific Relations, p. 403.

[10] SISS hearings (November 17, 1953).

[11] *Interlocking Subversion in Government Departments*, SISS report (July 30, 1953), p. 31.

Virginius Frank Coe: Coe was another American who moved from a high position with the United States Government to accept a key post within the United Nations. He had been an assistant to Harry Dexter White in the Treasury Department and, as such, was the technical secretary at the Bretton Woods Conference. He, too, had been identified under oath by Elizabeth Bentley as a member of one of her Communist cells. When questioned about these activities, Coe found it necessary to invoke the Fifth Amendment to avoid incriminating himself. Consequently, Coe was appointed as the $20,000 a year secretary of the United Nations International Monetary Fund, a post which he held for many years. He is now working as an economic expert for the Red Chinese government.[12]

Dean Acheson: As mentioned earlier, Secretary of State Dean Acheson is the only one in this list of State Department and Treasury Department personnel active in UN planning who has not been identified as active with the Communist party. In this connection, however, it is interesting to note the following facts. Early in his political career, Acheson was praised by the Communist *Daily Worker* "as one of the most forward looking men in the State Department." [13] In November of 1945 he was one of the principal speakers at a Madison Square Garden rally sponsored by the National Conference of Soviet-American Friendship. The other speakers were Corliss Lamont and Paul Robeson.[14] While undersecretary of state, Acheson promoted a loan of ninety million dollars to the Communist-controlled government of Poland. The loan was negotiated by Donald Hiss, Alger Hiss's brother. Donald Hiss was a member of Acheson's law firm.[15]

When former Assistant Secretary of State Adolph Berle, Jr., testified before the House Committee on Un-American Activities, he described Dean Acheson as heading up a pro-Russian group

[12] Senator Thomas Dodd, *Congressional Record* (March 22, 1962).

[13] *Daily Worker* (June 7, 1945). As quoted by Felix Wittmer, "Freedom's Case Against Dean Acheson," *American Mercury* (New York, April 1952).

[14] Felix Wittmer, "Freedom's Case Against Dean Acheson," *American Mercury* (New York, April 1952).

[15] Victor Lasky, "The Case Against Dean Acheson." Entered in the *Congressional Record* (December 6, 1950).

in the United States State Department "with Mr. [Alger] Hiss as principal assistant." [16]

In June of 1947, a Senate appropriations subcommittee addressed a confidential memorandum to George Marshall, the new secretary of state. This memorandum read, in part, as follows:

> It becomes necessary, due to the gravity of the situation, to call your attention to a condition that developed and still flourishes in the State Department under the administration of Dean Acheson. It is evident that there is a deliberate, calculated program being carried out, not only to protect Communist personnel in high places, but to reduce security and intelligence protection to a nullity. On file in the department is a copy of a preliminary report of the FBI on Soviet espionage activities in the U.S. which involves a large number of State Department employees, some in high official positions. . . . Voluminous files are on hand in the Department proving the connection of the State Department employees and officials with the Soviet espionage ring.[17]

Marshall reacted to this information by doing exactly what Acheson had done—nothing.

Laurence Duggan: Duggan was head of the Latin American division of the State Department. Hede Massing, a former Soviet agent, identified Duggan as a member of a spy ring under her direction. While his case was being investigated, he mysteriously fell from a window of his New York office and was killed.

Noel Field: Field was a high official in the West European division of the State Department and was a close friend of Duggan. When Field was also identified by Hede Massing as a secret Communist, he disappeared behind the iron curtain.

Henry Julian Wadleigh: Wadleigh was in the trade agreements division of the State Department. During the Hiss trial he admitted that he had been working for a Soviet spy ring.

John Carter Vincent: As chief of the Chinese affairs division of the State Department, Vincent was a member of the American

---

[16] Testimony before House Committee on Un-American Activities (August 30, 1948).

[17] Victor Lasky, "The Case Against Dean Acheson." Entered in the *Congressional Record* (December 6, 1950).

delegation at the San Francisco conference. He was also identified in sworn testimony as a member of the Communist party.

David Weintraub: Weintraub, who was in the Office of Foreign Relief and Rehabilitation Operations, became the key figure in 1952 of a Senate investigation of Communist infiltration into the American quota of United Nations employees. As the Senate committee stated in its report *Interlocking Subversion in Government Departments:* "David Weintraub occupied a unique position in setting up the structure of Communist penetration of government agencies by individuals who have been identified by witnesses as underground agents of the Communist party." [18]

Nathan Gregory Silvermaster: As a high-ranking officer of the Treasury Department, Silvermaster was also head of one of the secret Communist cells under Elizabeth Bentley's direction.

Harold Glasser: Glasser also came from the Treasury Department where he succeeded Virginius Frank Coe as director of the division of monetary research. Glasser was the Treasury spokesman on the affairs of United Nations Relief and Rehabilitation Administration (UNRRA, the UN's first giveaway program of American money) and had a predominant voice in determining which countries should receive aid and which should not. Elizabeth Bentley and Whittaker Chambers both revealed that Glasser was known to them as a Communist agent.

Victor Perlo: Perlo was closely associated with Hiss in the Ware cell in the early days of the New Deal. He later became the head of his own Communist cell under the direction of Elizabeth Bentley.

Irving Kaplan: Kaplan was appointed to the Treasury Department by Virginius Frank Coe. Later, he became a high-level official in the UN office of the assistant secretary-general for economic affairs. When called to the witness stand to testify during the Senate investigation of the Institute of Pacific Relations, Kaplan sought refuge behind the Fifth Amendment 244 times. David Weintraub helped him get his UN job.

William L. Ullman: A captain in the Air Force at the time, Ullman testified that he had been borrowed by Harry Dexter White and taken as White's assistant to both the Bretton Woods

[18] *Interlocking Subversion in Government Departments,* SISS report (July 30, 1953), pp. 10-12.

and San Francisco conferences. When asked whether or not he had ever been a Communist or a spy, Ullman claimed the Fifth Amendment to avoid self-incrimination.

Lauchlin Currie: Currie was not included among the list of names at the beginning of this chapter because he was in neither the State nor the Treasury departments. Nevertheless, as a personal assistant and advisor to President Roosevelt he played a major role in helping to formulate United States policy leading to the creation of the United Nations. He was thoroughly exposed as a fellow traveler by both Elizabeth Bentley and Whittaker Chambers.

The whole ugly story of these men and their actions can be found in the Senate report on the investigations of the IPR, the transcript of the Senate hearings on *Activities of United States Citizens Employed by the United Nations,* and the report entitled *Interlocking Subversion in Government Departments.*[19] It adds up to a clear pattern of deliberate Communist penetration into key positions within our own government and the use of these positions to generate a Communist-inspired United States foreign policy. The major feature of this policy has centered around getting the United States to gradually give up its independence to the authority and control of the United Nations, which was created by the Communists for just this purpose. As security officer J. Anthony Panuch summarized it:

> It was World War II which gave the Soviet plan its impetus. During this period, a massive infiltration of sensitive agencies of the government took place. Pro-Communist and personnel of subversive and revolutionary tendencies were able to establish themselves in strategic slots . . . to shift the center of gravity in the process of U.S. foreign policy from a national to an international orientation via the supra-national UN organization. Furthermore, if working control of the U.S. foreign policy were focalized in the UN organization, the role of Congress in our foreign affairs could be bypassed.[20]

Postwar foreign policy planning and the San Francisco conference of 1945 seem so far in the past that it is difficult for many

[19] Two of these documents are now out of print, but can be located still in many large metropolitan public libraries.

[20] *Interlocking Subversion in Government Departments,* SISS hearings, pt. 8, pp. 904-905.

to find a correlation between then and now. Yet events in Katanga were shaped as much by these now forgotten hands as they were by the O'Brien's and the Hammarskjold's of more recent memory. Needless to say, however, 1945 was just the beginning. When it came time to begin the actual hiring of the UN administrative staff, secret American Communists were among the first in line.

Trygve Lie, the United Nations' first secretary-general, said that in the first year members of the Secretariat had to be recruited very rapidly; about three thousand were hired between March and December of 1946 and hundreds more were hired in 1947. Lie was well aware of the possibility of their being secret Communists among the American job applicants, but this caused him little concern. As he put it: "Nothing in the Charter or in the staff regulations bars a Communist from being a member of the UN Secretariat; nor could there be in an organization that embraces both Communist and non-Communist members." [21]

This is, of course, one of the reasons why the United Nations can never work to promote freedom, justice or anything else the Communists wish to suppress. But that is another subject and one with which we shall deal at some length further along. For now, the important point is that the immediate demand for thousands of people to fill out the United Nations' original staff provided a golden opportunity for the agents of Communism to get in on the ground floor and to swarm into the key positions. The record shows that this is precisely what they did.

Since the new world-government organization needed men and women with skills and experience similar to those acquired in the service of national government agencies, it was only natural that most of the original applicants were people who had been working for the United States Government in one capacity or another. It was natural, too, that these people should have the approval or recommendation of their former employer. There are two kinds of recommendations, however: official and unofficial. An official recommendation would naturally be entered into the record and might contain, among other things, a security check. An unofficial recommendation would have no such drawbacks; a simple telephone call from an influential person in the State Department is all that would be required.

[21] Lie, p. 388.

It is not surprising that the State Department elected to follow what it called the "no recommendation rule." The reason offered for this policy was that it would avoid making the U.S. look as if it overly influenced the selection of UN personnel.[22] According to the testimony of Carlisle Humelsine, deputy undersecretary of state, the "no recommendation rule" was formulated in the department that was under the direction of Alger Hiss, and Hiss had much to do with it.[23]

Apologists for the United Nations have often attempted to deny or minimize Hiss's part in influencing the selection of employees for the initial United Nations staff. State Department officials have insisted that most of these people were merely on loan from various branches of the U.S. Government. But the record is unmistakably clear and speaks for itself. As the 1954 report of the SISS revealed, Alger Hiss was "unofficially" influential in the employment of 494 persons by the United Nations on its initial staff.[24]

During the Korean War, a New York grand jury accidentally stumbled across evidence of Communist penetration into the American staff of the United Nations. One piece of evidence led to another and so alarmed the grand jury that it proceeded to conduct a full-scale inquiry into the matter. The publicity attracted a great deal of attention and prompted the Senate Committee on the Judiciary to initiate a parallel investigation of its own. Shortly after these investigations began, some two hundred Americans employed by the UN resigned, apparently to avoid testifying.[25] Those that did testify, however, provided more than

[22] Chesly Manly, *The UN Record* (Chicago, Henry Regnery Company, 1955), p. 110. After serving for two years on the staff of the Milwaukee *Journal,* Chesly Manly went to work for the Chicago *Tribune* in 1929. In the intervening years he has become one of the country's top news reporters. During his varied career he has covered the Al Capone trials in the prohibition era as well as major political events in Washington. Since 1946 he has reported the proceedings at the UN and other international conferences for the Chicago *Tribune.*

[23] *Activities of U.S. Citizens Employed by the UN,* SISS hearings (December 17, 1952), p. 332.

[24] *Activities of U.S. Citizens Employed by the UN,* second report of the SISS (March 22, 1954), p. 12.

[25] SISS hearings (September 24, 1953), pt. 3, p. 503. Also, "Is the United Nations Anti-U.S.?" *U.S. News and World Report* (December 12, 1952), pp. 32-34.

ample evidence for the grand jury to issue the following present-
ment:

> This jury must, as a duty to the people of the United States,
> advise the court that startling evidence has disclosed infiltration
> into the UN of an overwhelmingly large group of disloyal U.S.
> citizens, many of whom are closely associated with the interna-
> tional Communist movement. This group numbers scores of indi-
> viduals, most of whom have long records of federal employment,
> and at the same time have been connected with persons and or-
> ganizations subversive to this country. Their positions at the time
> we subpoenaed them were ones of trust and responsibility in the
> UN Secretariat and in its specialized agencies.[26]

The Senate investigations produced exactly the same con-
clusions. Senator Eastland, chairman of the committee, made the
following statement at the conclusion of the hearings:

> I am appalled at the extensive evidence indicating that there
> is today in the UN among the American employees there, *the
> greatest concentration of Communists that this Committee has
> ever encountered.* Those American officials who have been called
> represent a substantial percentage of the people who are repre-
> senting us in the UN. . . . These people occupy high positions.
> They have very high salaries and almost all of these people have,
> in the past, been employees in the U.S. government in high and
> sensitive positions. I believe that the evidence shows that the
> security officers of our government knew, or at least had reason
> to know, that these people have been Communists for many years.
> In fact, some of these people have been the subject of charges
> before Congress before and during their employment with the UN.
> It is more than strange that such a condition existed in the gov-
> ernment of the U.S., and it is certainly more than strange that
> these people should be transferred to the UN and charged to the
> American quota.[27] [Italics added.]

It takes the better part of a day to read through the transcript of the hearings that led up to that conclusion, but for those
who have the time, it is well worth the effort. There is no better
way to get an accurate perspective on how the Communists have

---

[26] *Activities of U.S. Citizens Employed by the UN,* hearings before the
Senate Committee on the Judiciary (1952), pp. 407-408.
[27] *Ibid.,* pp. 181-182.

secretly captured complete working control of the American staff positions within the United Nations. The following are just a few examples taken at random to give an idea of the scope of this control.

Frank Carter Bancroft: Bancroft was editor of the documents control division. A minister of the Episcopal church on the inactive list, he has a long record of joining Communist fronts and sought refuge behind the Fifth Amendment when asked if he was a Communist.

Ruth Crawford: A publications officer of the United Nations International Children's Emergency Fund, Ruth Crawford admitted that she had been at one time a member of the Communist party and was still in sympathy with it.

Abraham H. Feller: Feller was general counsel for the United Nations. When called before the New York grand jury which was investigating United States Communists in the United Nations, he avoided testifying by jumping to his death from a window of his apartment. He had been closely associated with Alger Hiss and other Soviet agents. Trygve Lie said that "Feller was a victim of the witch hunt, of the awful pressure of the hysterical assault upon the United Nations that reactionaries were promoting and using for their own ends." [28] Eleven months later, Lie dedicated the Abraham Feller memorial room in the UN library "in memory of a loyal American."

Joel Gordon: As chief of the trade analysis division, Gordon's salary was $13,000. He had been with UNRAA. He invoked the Fifth Amendment to avoid self-incrimination when asked if he was a member of the Communist party.

Irving P. Schiller: Schiller was scheduled to be the next registrar of the United Nations' European office in Geneva. When asked by an investigating committee if he was presently (at the time of questioning) a member of the Communist party, he loudly proclaimed, "No!" But when the investigator asked him if he had been a member of the Communist party on the preceding day, Schiller invoked the Fifth Amendment.

Alexander H. Svenchanski: A naturalized American citizen born in Russia, Svenchanski's job at the United Nations was information officer. He broadcast news and other items to the

⁑ Lie, p. 399.

Soviet Union. When asked if he was a Communist, he invoked the Fifth Amendment to avoid incriminating himself.

Alfred J. Van Tassel: As chief of the economics section, special projects division of the technical assistance administration, Van Tassel's salary was $12,840. He organized and coordinated UN training seminars and demonstration centers around the world. He invoked the Fifth Amendment to avoid self-incrimination when asked about membership in the Communist party.

Eugene Wallach: Wallach was simultaneously a steno-type reporter at the UN and part of the New York security organization of the Communist party.

David Zablodowsky: Zablodowsky was in charge of the publishing division of the United Nations with a salary of $14,000. He admitted that he had transmitted secret messages between Whittaker Chambers and J. Peters knowing that they were both Communists. At one time he was president of a union which was later revealed to be Communist dominated. He also had been editor of the publication put out by the League Against War and Fascism, a Communist united front organization.

Herman Zap: Zap was a training officer in the technical assistance administration and he coordinated government training programs all around the world. His specialty was economic development and social welfare. He also coordinated the exchange of persons between the United States and other countries. He invoked the Fifth Amendment.

Shortly after the results of these hearings were made known, Trygve Lie attempted to calm the waters of rising public concern by dismissing eleven of the Fifth Amendment pleaders. The "Red eleven," as they were called in the newspapers, appealed the dismissal to the UN administrative tribunal which promptly declared that they must be either reinstated or be awarded substantial cash indemnities. As a result, seven of them were put back into their jobs with full back pay, and the others each received cash awards up to $40,000. (American taxpayers paid the lion's share, needless to say.) The UN administrative tribunal which reinstated and indemnified these security risks to America was composed completely of non-Americans. Seven nations were represented but at the time the U.S. was not even entitled to a voice in the decision.

Shortly afterward, Senator Pat McCarran introduced legislation requiring that all American citizens seeking employment at the United Nations receive a security clearance from the attorney general's office. This was certainly a reasonable policy and one which most Americans assumed had been in operation all along. Nevertheless, Trygve Lie was alarmed at the suggestion and declared: "To my dismay, the only precedent I could discover for such a law was the edict promulgated by fascist Italy in 1927. . . ." [29] Washington was equally alarmed. Just two days after the McCarran bill was introduced, President Truman signed an executive order stipulating that the United States would not undertake to instruct the Secretary-General as to American citizens he may not employ, nor would it penalize any citizens that he might employ contrary to the attorney general's judgment.[30] In other words, Hiss's "no recommendation rule" was to remain unchanged.

When the Eisenhower administration took over, there was a great deal of loud talk and breast-beating about cleaning out the Communists, not only from Washington, but from the United States staff at the United Nations as well. It was a fine campaign promise but turned out to be just as sincere as the proverbial two chickens in every pot. Professing to be anti-Communist is always good for votes. Since many Americans are perfectly willing to accept a sincere face, a warm smile, and a little political oratory as a substitute for action, the politicians know that they will seldom be called upon by their constituents to produce what they have promised. When he was seeking our votes Eisenhower promised to clear out the subversives. But he never did. The worst of the security risks stayed right where they were, or were promoted. Senator Joseph McCarthy, who was actually trying to do what candidate Eisenhower promised *he* was going to do, received the full wrath of the new administration. Eisenhower even went so far as to issue an executive order which became the basis for what was later called the gag rule. This injected so much red tape into the proceedings of congressional committees investigating Communist penetration into our government that it soon became quite impossible to obtain meaning-

[29] *Ibid.*, p. 401.
[30] *Ibid.*, p. 402.

ful testimony. Consequently, since 1954 there have been few attempts to investigate Communist penetration of the U.S. Government. Apparently we are to assume that after Alger Hiss, Lauchlin Currie, Harry Dexter White, etc., were exposed, the Communists suddenly lost interest in trying to infiltrate the United States Government!

At any rate, part of this great pretense centered around cleaning up the mess at the United Nations. Eisenhower set up a widely publicized international organizations employees loyalty board to hold hearings and review FBI reports on all United States employees at the United Nations. As the first step, all Americans at the United Nations were instructed to fill out loyalty questionnaires. The public once again relaxed with satisfaction that at last something was being done. The whole thing, of course, was a fraud. The net catch of the entire operation was one woman clerk by the name of Eda Glaser. She was employed in the Security Council reference library where she clipped articles out of newspapers.[31]

Eisenhower's loyalty board gave clearance to people with blatant backgrounds of Communist activities and sympathies. For example, the board cleared Henry S. Block, director of the UN statistical division. Block's record was so bad that even the United States State Department had described him as a person "believed to be Communist or under Communist discipline." [32]

The most revealing clearance of all, however, was that of Ralph Bunche.

Ralph J. Bunche: As undersecretary-general of the United Nations and one of the three most influential men in that organization, Ralph Bunche may well be the best-known Negro in the entire world. Consequently, many people shy away from discussing his pro-Communist record for fear they will be branded as anti-Negro or racist. But the record speaks for itself.

Bunche was on the editorial board of the openly Communist magazine *Science and Society* for over four years. Even after the Communists themselves officially stated that *Science and Society* had as its function "to help Marx-ward moving students and intellectuals to come closer to Marxism-Leninism; to bring

[31] Manly, pp. 137-138.
[32] *Ibid.*, p. 138. Also, SISS hearings (December 17, 1952), p. 385.

Communist thought to academic circles," Bunche continued to write for the magazine.[33]

In 1936 Bunche authored a pamphlet entitled *A World View of Race* which presented the Communist propaganda line so well that the October 1937 issue of the *Communist* declared: "A fresh breeze is blowing through the classrooms of American colleges, carrying with it elements of Marxist and progressive thought. One of the welcome fruits of the renaissance is a world-embracing study of race attitudes by Dr. Bunche, professor of political science at Howard University."

In his pamphlet, Bunche wrote: "And so class will some day supplant race in world affairs. Race war will then be merely a side-show to the gigantic class war which will be waged in the big tent we call the world." [34]

In 1943 Bunche went to the State Department where he became associate chief of the division of dependent area affairs under Alger Hiss. He became, with Hiss, one of the leaders of the IPR which, according to a congressional investigating committee, was "considered by the American Communist party and by Soviet officials as an instrument of Communist policy, propaganda and military intelligence." [35]

On August 19, 1948, after Hiss had been exposed as a Communist agent, Bunche sent him a letter in which he stated: "I want you to know that I am in your corner." [36]

Bunche tried to line up employment in the State Department for a Jack S. Harris. But Harris' pro-Communist background was so blatant that even the State Department had to turn him down. Bunche finally got Harris a job at the United Nations. Harris was one of those to whom the UN administrative tribunal awarded forty thousand dollars indemnity after dismissal. One of the factors cited by the tribunal as justification for this award was "the fact that he joined the UN at the special request of Mr. Ralph Bunche." [37]

In spite of all this Dwight D. Eisenhower, while president of

---

[33] Congressman James B. Utt, *Congressional Record* (January 15, 1962).
[34] *Ibid.* (April 11, 1962).
[35] Hearings before the Senate subcommittee investigating the Institute of Pacific Relations, p. 223.
[36] As quoted by Manly, p. 143.
[37] *Ibid.*, p. 141.

Columbia University, praised Ralph Bunche as "the greatest statesman this country has produced." [38] The Eisenhower appointed loyalty review board, likewise, found no reason to question the loyalty of Ralph Bunche. He was routinely cleared along with a host of others with similar backgrounds.

On May 31, 1954, just three days after Bunche received his security clearance, the Communist *Daily Worker* ran an article which boasted:

> The UN was getting ready to appoint Dr. Ralph J. Bunche to a new high post when certain racist "anti-Communist" forces moved to stop this. . . . And so Dr. Bunche again had to solemnly prove his "loyalty"—meaning that he had to prove he is innocent of the "crime" of Marxism and is a reliable supporter of the "anti-Communist" policy. The plans of the "anti-Communists" who could not stomach the idea of a Negro in a top UN post couldn't be carried through. The same enormous anti-racist pressure which, in the U.S.A. and throughout the world, compelled the Supreme Court to declare segregated schools and housing un-Constitutional, also blocked this scheme. But what was revealed again was the un-American machinery of the "anti-Communist" frame-up mill. Bunche, thanks to the new anti-racist upsurge, escaped.[39]

Philip Jessup: Philip Jessup is the man who represents the United States as one of the fifteen justices on the United Nations World Court. His past is studded with affiliations with groups officially designated as Communist fronts. One of these, the Institute of Pacific Relations, has already been discussed. However, since Jessup was probably the most prominent and influential of all the leaders of this organization, it warrants recalling that the Senate Internal Security Subcommittee found that:

> The IPR has been considered by the American Communists and by Soviet officials as an instrument of Communist policy, propaganda and military intelligence. . . . A small core of officials and staff members carried the main burden of IPR activities and directed its administration and policies. Members of the small core of officials and staff members who controlled the IPR were either Communists or pro-Communists.

[38] *Ibid.*, p. 144.
[39] "Dr. Bunche's Case," *Daily Worker* (May 31, 1954), p. 5.

Jessup was chairman of the IPR American council from 1939 to 1940 and chairman of its Pacific council from 1939 to 1942. Both councils were high-level policy-making bodies.[40]

Jessup, both in and out of the IPR, was closely associated with Alger Hiss, Harry Dexter White, Frederick Vanderbilt Field and Lauchlin Currie. And, like Ralph Bunche, he came to the defense of Hiss as a character witness at Hiss's trial.

When Frank Coe, secretary of the United Nations International Monetary Fund, testified before the Senate Internal Security Subcommittee in 1952, he inadvertently put Jessup in rather strange company. After readily answering questions about his associations with sundry individuals who had never been implicated in the Communist conspiracy, he suddenly found it necessary to invoke the Fifth Amendment when asked if he knew Philip Jessup.

Jessup served as assistant secretary-general of the UNRRA conference in 1943 and the Bretton Woods Conference in 1944. He was a member of the American delegation to the San Francisco conference in 1945. He was also the United States representative on the fifteen-man United Nations committee of jurists that had drafted the World Court statute. Continuing as a technical expert and advisor to various important UN commissions, Jessup prepared the State Department's infamous "White Paper" on China. Written at the very time when the Communists were overrunning the mainland of China, this report lavishly praised the Reds and condemned the anti-Communist Nationalist forces. Jessup later became one of the early advocates for the admission of Red China to the United Nations.

President Truman was so impressed by this record that he appointed Jessup as United States delegate to the United Nations in 1951. When the appointment came before the Senate, however, it was not approved because of Jessup's pro-Communist record. At the United Nations, Soviet delegate Vyshinsky reacted by praising Jessup during a meeting of the General Assembly's political committee. Vyshinsky said he had "learned with dismay"

[40] Hearings before the Senate subcommittee investigating the Institute of Pacific Relations. Also, Congressman James B. Utt, *Congressional Record* (January 15, 1962).

the Senate's decision.[41] Equally dismayed, of course, was President Truman who proceeded to circumvent the Senate action by assigning Jessup to the United Nations on an "interim appointment." [42]

Shortly after the Eisenhower administration came in on the promise of cleaning the United States security risks out of the United Nations, the State Department approved the appointment of Philip Jessup as our candidate for the UN World Court—an infinitely more important position than the one denied him by the Senate. This time, however, neither Congress nor the Senate had any voice in the selection.

Even though each country is allowed to nominate two of its own nationals and two from other countries, the United States elected to nominate three foreigners with Philip Jessup as the only American—making it very clear to all that he was the man!

In the final voting, Jessup was elected by an overwhelming majority. With both the United States *and* the USSR voting for him, how could he miss?

[41] Manly, pp. 157-158.
[42] "Jessup Nomination Stirs Controversy," Los Angeles *Examiner* (November 8, 1960).

> *The hottest places in hell are reserved for those who, in a period of moral crisis, maintain their neutrality.*
>
> Alighieri Dante, 1300

CHAPTER

TEN

NEUTRALS AND NON-COMMUNISTS

> Anyone who doubts the potent, if intangible, force of the United Nations should consider the eagerness even of Communist regimes to join a club which is, and will continue to be, managed predominantly by its non-Communist members.[1]

This statement by United Nations Ambassador Adlai Stevenson is a classic example of the technique of combining an observable fact with an absurd conclusion. The eagerness of Communist regimes to join the United Nations is a fact that cannot be concealed. But since the obvious implications of this fact are not in accord with the image which the internationalists wish to present to the American people, we are told that (1) the Communists are eager to join the United Nations because it is a "potent, intangible force," and (2) the United Nations is, and will continue to be, managed by non-Communists.

As for the potent-intangible-force argument, little needs to be said. Anyone who is familiar with even the bare rudiments of Communist strategy and tactics knows that the Communists do not join or support an organization merely because it is a potent force. They join organizations either to destroy them or to take them over and use them for their own purposes; they support an organization only if it advances the cause of Communism. But how can this be if the organization is, as Mr. Stevenson says, managed predominantly by its non-Communist members?

[1] *United Nations Guardian of Peace,* Department of State publication #7225 (September 1961), p. 2.

107

Part of the answer became painfully obvious during the investigation of United States "non-Communist" employees at the United Nations. The other part is the subject of this chapter.

At the time of this writing, the United Nations has approximately six thousand employees in the Secretariat. About one fourth of these are classified as professional, which means that they hold top supervisory and policy-making positions. These are filled according to the geographical origin of the member nations and in proportion to the various contributions to the total UN budget. The United States, therefore, is entitled to approximately one third of the "professional" appointments. The two-thirds balance comes from other nations—Communist as well as non-Communist.

Theoretically, the United States bars Communists from holding government jobs. But as we have seen, this has been only a minor inconvenience to the party faithful. For years, secret underground Communist agents have moved with ease throughout our entire governmental structure where they have been protected and promoted. The exposures of a few years ago were the result of congressional investigations which now have been, for all practical purposes, completely discontinued.

In France the Communist party is the biggest political party in the entire country, and it holds the balance of power in the French Assembly. The French constitution even goes out of its way to make it illegal to discriminate against Communists in government jobs. A Communist is head of the French atomic energy agency and was recently made advisor to the European center of nuclear research.[2] It would be absurd not to expect the Communists to be well represented among France's quota of employees *and delegates* at the United Nations.

Italy is in almost the same position. At each election for the past eight or nine years the Communists, posing as a legitimate political party, have gained a larger and larger vote at the polls to the point where today they hold the balance of political power in that country. Much of this power in Italy comes from the influential labor unions, the largest of which is completely Communist dominated.

[2] *U.S. News and World Report* (October 22, 1954), p. 53. Also V. Orval Watts, *The United Nations: Planned Tyranny* (New York, The Devin-Adair Company, 1955), p. 32.

As the *Wall Street Journal* observed:

> The Italian government can't legally keep Communists out of the government. Further, the laws there provide that questionable characters have the same right to government jobs as anybody else, even if the job is a "classified" position. Also, there are no statutes the Library of Congress can find to protect military secrets.[3]

Even Great Britain allows Communists to hold government jobs so long as they are not classified as sensitive positions. The British do not consider United Nations employment as sensitive.[4]

A Senate subcommittee investigating this situation reported that certain UN delegates from foreign countries have been invited to Communist party headquarters in New York to lecture local party leaders. One of these was from the French delegation who gave a speech on the problems of the French Communist party in relation to the situation in Indochina. The other was from the Indian delegation who lectured on the problems faced by the Communist party in India with the dissemination of propaganda.[5]

Mr. Joseph Z. Kornfeder, a former Communist who trained in Moscow and who specialized in methods of Communist political warfare in this country, spoke before the Congress of Freedom in 1955 and told his audience:

> How many Communists, fellow travelers and sympathizers there are among the UN employees, no one seems to know, but judging by their number among the American personnel, there can be no doubt that the Communists control the UN and its staff association, and use it for all its worth; which means that most of the special agencies at UN headquarters are, in fact, operated by them and coordinated through the Communist cell in the UN staff association.[6]

[3] *Wall Street Journal* (December 23, 1957).

[4] *U.S. News and World Report* (October 15, 1954), p. 86. Also, Watts, *UN: Planned Tyranny*, p. 32.

[5] Testimony of former Communist John Lautner before the Permanent Subcommittee on Investigations, Senate Committee on Government Operations (September 11, 1953), p. 42.

[6] "The Communist Pattern in the UN," speech by Joseph Z. Kornfeder before the Congress of Freedom, Veterans War Memorial Auditorium (San Francisco, April 1955).

The situation was summarized by the *U.S. News and World Report* in 1952 when it stated:

> U.S. authorities have no power to dig into the backgrounds of UN employees from other nations, although they have information indicating heavy Communist infiltration among these employees. Some UN employees who come from Great Britain, France, Mexico, Canada and other non-Communist countries are known or suspected Communists. . . . *An informed estimate suggests that as many as one-half of the 1,350 administrative executives in the UN are either Communists or people who are willing to do what they want.*[7] [Italics added.]

Note that the date of this estimate was 1952. Communist influence within the governments of the world has greatly expanded during the intervening years.

Since the United Nations was first launched in 1945 the secretary-general has traditionally been portrayed to the American people as the epitome of neutralism, the ideal non-Communist (as distinguished from an anti-Communist)—the truly impartial man. If the secretary-general had been portrayed as openly anti-American and pro-Communist, we Americans would have withdrawn our support long ago. Knowing this, the strategists decided from the very beginning to select men with obscure pasts; men who were not actual party members but who were ideologically so compatible that they could be relied upon to carry the ball for the party. A brief look at the record will illustrate the wisdom of this strategy.

Trygve Lie: Politically, Trygve Lie, the first United Nations secretary-general, was a dedicated socialist, a labor lawyer, and a high ranking member of the Social Democratic Labor party in Norway—an offshoot of the early Communist International.[8] According to Leon Trotsky, one of the founders of the worldwide Communist apparatus: "The Norwegian Workers' party had the reputation of being a radical party. . . . In the past, it belonged to the Third [Communist] International."

Trotsky further revealed that Trygve Lie was no stranger to the Communists in those early days. Lie had visited Moscow

---

[7] "Is the United Nations Anti-U.S.?" *U.S. News and World Report* (December 12, 1952), p. 32.

[8] Lie, pp. 11, 16, 17.

in 1921 and, as Trotsky put it, had been identified with the Comintern at that time.

When Trotsky—the archenemy and rival of Stalin—was exiled in Norway, Trygve Lie was the minister of justice of that country. Acting in accordance with the wishes of Stalin, Lie confronted Trotsky with an ultimatum of choosing between either ceasing all criticism of the Communist regime in Moscow or going to jail. Trotsky continued to write exposes of the ruthlessness of Stalin and his henchmen. Lie, consequently, had him thrown in prison and later deported him to Mexico.[9]

Commenting on the desirability of admitting Red China to the UN, Lie revealed an almost unbelievable naivety about the nature of Communism when he wrote:

> Once before, the world had seen a Communist state—the USSR—isolated by the West after a successful revolution. I had always believed that this was a great mistake and that the West, instead, should have sought every means to fuller intercourse with Russia in the 1920's. Such a policy might well have influenced the development of the Soviet state in a direction other than the one it took.[10]

One of the first items on the agenda of the newly created United Nations was the election of the president of the General Assembly. At first the United States delegation considered nominating Lie for the position but later shifted its support to Henri Spaak, a Belgian socialist. What happened next is described by Lie:

> On the morning of the 10th—the day on which the president of the assembly was to be elected—Feodore T. Gousev, the Soviet ambassador in London, sought me out. His delegation, he said, had been informed by the Americans of my withdrawal; neverthe-

[9] Isaac Don Levine, *The Mind of an Assassin* (New York, Farrar, Straus and Cudahy, Inc., 1959), pp. xvii, 8, 9. Levine, a lifelong student of Communism, draws upon a wealth of personal experience dating back to his first-hand knowledge of the Russian revolution and his close association with the early leading Bolsheviks, including Leon Trotsky. When Trotsky was the supreme chief of the Red Army during the civil war, Levine personally accompanied him to the front as a foreign correspondent. Also, "A Letter from Trotsky," the *Nation* (October 10, 1936), p. 431. Also, Preliminary Commission of Inquiry (held in Mexico City), *The Case of Leon Trotsky* (New York, Harper and Brothers, 1937), pp. 32, 405.

[10] Lie, p. 254.

less the USSR, together with its Eastern European associates, wanted to nominate me. . . . His delegation had conferred with the United States delegation upon hearing of my withdrawal and, as a result of the meeting, the Americans had agreed to revert to their original support of my candidacy. The Soviet Union would nominate me, he added, and the Americans would vote for me. . . .

Mr. Gromyko strode to the rostrum and declared:

"Weighing the candidatures which have recently been mentioned in connection with the election of the president . . . the Soviet delegation has come to the conclusion that the most appropriate candidature would be that of the foreign minister of Norway, Mr. Trygve Lie." . . .

Wincenty Rzymowski of Poland then rose in dutiful support of the nomination, and spoke of Norway and of me in generous terms. He was followed by Dimitri Manuilsky, the "old Bolshevik" from pre-Stalin days who was then foreign minister of the Ukrainian SSR. . . .

Spaak won the election by just three votes, but, as Lie reminisced: "There is no doubt that the results of that election were felt long after, and clearly influenced the subsequent election of the secretary-general." [11]

The post of secretary-general is infinitely more important than that of president of the assembly. So when the time came to fill this post, Washington and Moscow once again moved in unison. Lie wrote:

I recall something that Andrei Vyshinsky said in the course of a conversation in London just before my election as Secretary-General. It was a most friendly talk in which Vyshinsky said that both the Soviet Union and the United States warmly advocated my nomination, and that Mr. Bevin [of Great Britain] could be "brought around." [12]

As mentioned previously, Trygve Lie was outspoken in his advocacy of the admission of Red China to the United Nations. He had even taken the initiative in trying to drum up sufficient votes to make this possible. He further took the stand that Chiang Kai-shek should be ousted from Formosa.[13]

[11] *Ibid.*, pp. 5-10.
[12] *Ibid.*, p. 26.
[13] *Ibid.*, p. 265.

It is no wonder, then, that the Communists were well pleased at having such a "non-Communist" at the head of the United Nations. But Americans were led to believe just the opposite. During the Korean War, for instance, the Soviet delegation put on an impressive performance of pouting in public, supposedly over the way in which Lie was standing firm against their aggression. It was corny acting but good enough to fool the American public—which is all it was intended to do. How the Communists really felt about Trygve Lie is best revealed by Lie himself. When Lie first threatened to resign as secretary-general (he threatened to do so on several occasions), he went to discuss the matter with his good friend Gromyko.

> . . . I went to see Mr. Gromyko. . . . I announced the feeling that I should resign in protest at the American shift of position, and I have never found Ambassador Gromyko more friendly. His melancholy features lit up with sympathy. But he seemed half alarmed at my idea. "Speaking for myself," he said, "I hope you will not resign, and I advise you against it. What good will it do? How will it change American policy? In any case, I would be grateful if you would take no action before I have time to consult my government."
>
> Tuesday, Mr. Gromyko took me aside. He had cabled Moscow, he reported, and Moscow's reply was "No, definitely not!" [14]

Much later, at the height of the controversy over Communist penetration into the American quota at the United Nations, Trygve Lie finally did resign and was soon replaced by Dag Hammarskjold.

Dag Hammarskjold: The rape of Katanga was primarily the result of his planning and direction. Although portrayed to the American people as a great humanitarian, one need only recall his policy of deliberate deception, outright lying and utter disregard for human suffering to fully appreciate the absurdity of such an image. In this regard Conor O'Brien unintentionally indicted himself, Hammarskjold, and the whole United Nations when he wrote:

> The greater the ambiguity in a Security Council decision, the wider was the Secretary-General's margin of interpretation.

[14] *Ibid.,* p. 171.

Through ambiguities resolved, through margins skillfully used, the office of Secretary-General had grown in stature and authority far beyond what the framers of the Charter seem to have envisaged at San Francisco. This was quite widely recognized; someone, I know not who, had even jested that the motto of the Secretary-General ought to be *Per Ambigua ad Astra* [ambiguity unlimited]. To most good "United Nations people," like myself, this growth seemed entirely healthy. . . . As for Mr. Hammarskjold himself, we had complete confidence in him as being—I quote the words used about him, in private, by a Russian member of the Secretariat—"an integritous man." We even, I think, found something slightly intoxicating in the paradox of equivocation being used in the service of virtue, the thought of a disinterested Talleyrand, a Machiavelli of peace.[15]

Aside from that, however, Hammarskjold was almost a political rubber stamp of Trygve Lie. He was an outspoken socialist, was openly sympathetic toward world Communism, and pushed hard for the admission of Red China to the United Nations. It was while Hammarskjold was in charge of UN affairs in the Swedish foreign office in 1951 that his government refused to support a mild UN resolution condemning Red China as an aggressor in Tibet.

The kind of people a man chooses for his closest assistants and advisors is a good indication of the man himself. A glimpse at the Congo executive advisory committee affords a fairly typical view. As we have seen, Conor O'Brien and Ralph Bunche held key positions in this committee. As for other members, O'Brien gave us an interesting insight when he wrote: "Nobody said out loud, 'keep Communism out of Africa' . . . and indeed most people round that table would have been genuinely shocked, and for a moment even puzzled, if such language had been used." [16]

Shortly after the Hungarian uprising the United Nations sent a small team of investigators to Europe to interview as many of the refugees as possible in an attempt to document the tragedy. This was a far cry from the vigorous action they took against the anti-Communists in Katanga, but it was a nice gesture just the same which, while it did not help the Hungarian Freedom Fight-

[15] O'Brien, p. 47.
[16] O'Brien, p. 59.

ers, was offered to the American people as evidence that the United Nations did do *something*.

Active in this committee was Povle Bang-Jensen. Determined to do a conscientious job, he found that the only way he could get the refugees to testify was to personally promise them that their names would not be disclosed to anyone else—especially anyone at the United Nations.

Most of these people still had relatives inside Hungary and they feared that if their identities were known their loved ones would be executed or imprisoned. This seemed fair enough, but not for Dag Hammarskjold. He insisted that Bang-Jensen turn over the list of names in spite of Bang-Jensen's promise to the refugees. Rather than break his word or endanger the lives of innocent people, Bang-Jensen burned the list on the roof of the United Nations building. Hammarskjold was furious. Bang-Jensen was fired amidst a barrage of sweeping accusations, including insanity. No UN tribunal demanded reinstatement or cash indemnification.

To further complicate the situation, Bang-Jensen had been approached in confidence by a potential Soviet defector who pleaded with him to help arrange for asylum in the United States. The defector told Bang-Jensen that the thirty-eighth floor of the United Nations, where the top administrative offices are located, was actually under Communist control and that the Soviet secret police had successfully penetrated even the American intelligence services. This shocking information was then dispatched to Allen Dulles, head of our Central Intelligence Agency, who, instead of moving resolutely to acquire the full details from this vital source of information, let Bang-Jensen and the Soviet defector cool their heels for seven long and agonizing months before even expressing any interest. By this time the defector had been sent back to Russia. The CIA never did ask Bang-Jensen for details.

Shortly afterward, Bang-Jensen's body was found in a park in New York. Although it appeared to be a suicide, the surrounding evidence as presented by the Senate Internal Security Subcommittee strongly indicates that he was murdered by the Soviet secret police for knowing too much.

But the most interesting part of all is the fact that several of the Hungarian refugees interviewed were formerly officials of the Hungarian Communist party. When testifying, they *specifically* wanted assurances that their names *would not be made known to the Secretary-General.*[17] One can only wonder why.

U Thant: One of the strongest political groups in Burma today is the Anti-Fascist Peoples Freedom League, an organization that leans considerably to the left. U Thant was at one time the press and publicity director for this group.[18] But it was U Nu, then prime minister of Burma, who really brought Thant into politics. U Nu regarded U Thant as his personal friend and advisor, made him his first secretary and also appointed him to the United Nations. In short, Thant was the protégé of U Nu. It is certain that Thant's political beliefs and basic orientation could not have strayed too far from those of his tutor without disrupting the close working relationship and mutual confidence so obviously shared by them for many years. What, then, is the political philosophy of U Nu?

In a speech delivered on May Day, 1948, U Nu declared:

> When I moved that the draft constitution of the Burma Union should be approved by the Constituent Assembly, I stated clearly that Burma was to be a leftist country. . . . In such a leftist country, the production of commodities is not for the purpose of profit. . . . Briefly, leftism is the policy by which the world is being turned from the wrong path to the right path. . . . Lenin and Stalin, when building up Russia, did not use everything which they found in the writings of Karl Marx. They adopted what was suitable for Russia. In [Red] China also leftist leaders adopted what was suitable for that country. Not very long ago when my friend Ko Ohn went to [Communist] Poland, he was advised by Polish leftists thus: "We don't go wrong because others go wrong. We do what is suitable for Poland and we advise Burma to do what is suitable for Burma."
>
> See what Stalin did to build up Russia's own strength. In 1939, in order to bring additional strength to Russia, he entered into a non-aggression treaty even with Hitler. . . . When Trotsky was trying to bring about a world revolution, he accused Stalin and his followers, who were endeavoring to strengthen Russia, of

[17] *The Bang-Jensen Case,* SISS report (September 14, 1961), p. 9.
[18] Vera Micheles Dean, *West and Non West—New Perspectives* (New York, Holt, Rinehart & Winston, Inc., 1963), introduction.

Wide World Photo
This Red Cross worker was machine-gunned by UN troops as he was stepping out of an ambulance.

UPI Photo
A wounded policeman is transferred to a car after the ambulance was disabled by UN snipers.

UPI Photo
Katangans run for shelter as UN forces open fire on them.

"It is inconceivable that the United Nations troops could commit atrocities against civilians." Spokesman for U Thant, New York, December 14, 1962.

A Soviet propaganda pamphlet with Khrushchev's picture lies amid the debris following the ouster of Communist diplomats from the Congo by Mobutu and Kasavubu. The pamphlet says, "Hands off the Congo."

UN Photo

M. Khiary, chief of UN civilian operations in the Congo, is shown at a press conference in Leopoldville. He was described by Conor O'Brien as "a man who knows that all official versions are . . . worded to deceive the enemy and appease the clamor of the ignorant."

Wide World Photo

Protected from arrest by United Nations troops, Patrice Lumumba
(arrow) stands at the balcony of his residence.

His car machine-gunned by UN troops, Albert Verbrugghe sits stunned behind the wheel of the car.

"Why . . . why did you shoot? You said we could pass!"

Verbrugghe hysterically embraces the dead body of his wife as a UN soldier examines the car.

With a bandage covering his facial wounds, Verbrugghe comforts his dog, also wounded by UN fire.

UN Gurkha troops in the Congo. Apparently on the alert for enemy aircraft, these men are actually posing for the photographer. At the time this picture was taken, Tshombe's "air force" of two rebuilt propeller-driven trainer planes had long since been destroyed.

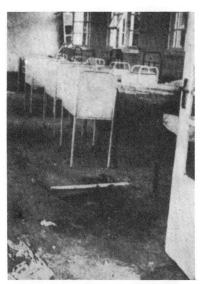

Shinkolobwe hospital, after United Nations bombardment on December 12, 1961.

Maternity ward of Shinkolobwe hospital. "The blood from the wounded makes the buildings look like a battlefield."

Direct hit on a ward of the Shinkolobwe hospital by a rocket fired from UN aircraft. ". . . the UNO [UN] prefers to aim at the hospitals."

Communist Patrice Lumumba and U.S. Secretary of State Christian
Herter stand under an umbrella in the rain during ceremonies held in
Lumumba's honor.

United States Ambassador to the United Nations Adlai Stevenson
and Congolese Premier Cyrille Adoula stand before a portrait of George
Washington in Stevenson's Waldorf-Astoria hotel suite.

Secretary of State Stettinius holds up the first draft of the United Nations Charter. Seated are Andrei Gromyko, Russian ambassador and head of the USSR delegation, and Alger Hiss.

Alger Hiss, secretary-general of the San Francisco conference (where the UN was born), addresses the delegates. Seated (left) is Soviet Foreign Minister Molotov.

Alger Hiss shakes hands with President Truman as Truman and Secretary of State Edward Stettinius cross the speakers' platform during a San Francisco conference meeting.

The San Francisco conference ended June 26, 1945. This photo shows the delegates as they unanimously adopt the United Nations Charter. Secretary of State Stettinius, at the rostrum, became the chief United States representative to the UN. The secretary-general of the conference, Alger Hiss, is standing to the left of the speakers' area.

Alger Hiss is shown here before the House Committee on Un-American Activities as former Communists testify that he was known to them as a secret member of the Communist party.

Harry Dexter White (left) and Lauchlin Currie helped formulate the United States policy on the United Nations. White was promoted in the Treasury Department by Truman after the FBI exposed him as a Soviet agent. Currie, aid to FDR, passed secret wartime information to the Russians.

USSR emblem.

The man in charge of the U.S. government department which designed
the UN emblem was a secret member of the Communist party.

UN Photo
Trygve Lie, the first secretary-general of the UN, was a dedicated socialist and a high ranking member of the Social Democratic Labor party in Norway—an offshoot of the early Communist International.

Dag Hammarskjold chats with Chou En-lai during Hammarskjold's 1955 trip to Peiping to plead for the release of the American soldiers and flyers who were still imprisoned in direct violation of the Korean armistice agreements. The mission was unsuccessful.

After the Senate refused to ratify Philip Jessup's appointment as delegate to the UN because of his notorious background, he became the U.S. representative on the UN World Court.

Ralph Bunche, undersecretary-general of the UN, in academic regalia. After Alger Hiss was exposed as a Soviet agent, Bunche sent Hiss a letter in which he said, "I want you to know that I am in your corner."

Combat-armored personnel carriers speed a wounded Marine to a waiting helicopter on Vegas Hill on the western front in Korea. Until the UN-managed Korean War, United States troops had never fought a war that ended in less than victory.

Three American boys who lost their lives in Korea are buried in foreign soil while the UN flag flutters over them in place of their own Old Glory.

In Korea, over five thousand American boys, defenseless prisoners of war, were murdered by Communist forces. Most were shot in the head and dumped into mass graves. The UN General Assembly refused to condemn the Communists for these acts.

UPI Photo

In 1952 it was brought to the UN's attention that the Red Chinese had committed between 14- and 20-million political murders. The UN listened but took no action.

UPI Photo

In North Korea thousands of helpless families who refused to embrace Communism were stripped and put out to die in the sub-zero weather. Few Americans can imagine the horror of life under Communism.

U.S. Army Photo

Displaying white flags, United Nations and American negotiators went to these buildings in Kaesong, Korea, in July 1951 to work on terms for a cease-fire with the Communist North Koreans and Chinese. Two years later a formal armistice was signed at Panmunjom, and the Korean War ended.

When Russian tanks moved in to crush the Hungarian revolution, the United Nations suddenly ceased its talk about "self-determination," and "anti-colonialism." In fact, even four years later "the press of other business prevented the assembly's consideration of the item on Hungary."

UPI Photo

The UN Charter proclaims respect for treaties. Yet Russia continues to violate almost every treaty entered into. One brazen example was the building of the Berlin wall. The UN said nothing.

Famous in death, Peter Fechter failed in a try for freedom over the
Berlin wall. The United Nations rarely speaks out against Communist
violations of human rights.

The revolutionary rulers of Zanzibar, a new member of the United Nations.

Jomo (Burning Spear) Kenyatta is the former leader of the terrorist Mau Mau. He is now head of Kenya, one of the new member nations of the UN.

This illustration, taken from a UNESCO-recommended book designed to teach children about the UN, is supposed to depict our forefathers drafting the U.S. Constitution and is symbolic of UNESCO's policy of subtly undermining a child's respect for his national heritage.

United Nations and NATO flags have replaced the American flag in this U.S. Air Force recruiting poster.

The U.S. pays one third of all UN costs directly. Indirectly, through voluntary contributions and foreign aid which enables other nations to pay their dues, we pay almost the entire bill.

being traitors to the revolution. . . . If we now look back to history, we find that Stalin followed the right path.[19]

U Nu then went on to advocate the following program: Strengthen ties with Soviet Russia; confiscate all capitalist enterprises in Burma; abolish private ownership of land; form a league for the propagation of Marxist doctrine; and create a peoples democratic army.

Knowing what kind of political views were held by U Nu, we are now better able to appreciate the full impact of the following rather innocuous news item that appeared in the November 16, 1961, issue of the *Burma Weekly Bulletin*:

> Before Burma became independent soon after the Second World War, U Thant entered the political field upon call by General Aung San and U Nu. On September 1, 1947, he was made deputy director (press), information department. As a public servant, U Thant earned reputation and rapid promotion because of his ability, hard work, simpleness and good nature. U Thant was promoted as secretary in the same ministry before becoming the prime minister's secretary on January 7, 1954. In the year 1952, U Thant went to the seventh session of the UN General Assembly as a member of the Burmese delegation. *Since then, he has traveled widely and generally in the company of Prime Minister U Nu as a trusted advisor and friend.*[20] [Italics added.]

In March of 1962 U Nu was ousted by General Ne Win. This was hardly an anti-Communist or anti-socialist coup. The new government merely speeded up the machinery which U Nu had set in motion. All commercial banks were taken over by the state, all private industry was declared illegal, and the entire economy was put under "total state control."[21]

After Thant was elected Secretary-General he immediately began to exercise his special brand of Burmese impartiality. One has almost grown accustomed to the kind of headlines which

[19] *Toward Peace and Democracy* (Burmese Ministry of Information, 1949).

[20] "U Thant Appointed Secretary-General of United Nations," *Burma Weekly Bulletin* (Rangoon, November 16, 1961).

[21] "Where Reds May Take Over a Key Country," *U.S. News and World Report* (April 1, 1963), p. 69. Also, "Left Full Rudder," *Newsweek* (March 11, 1963), p. 46. Also, "Army Socialism," *Time* (February 22, 1963), p. 32.

appeared on the front page of the Chicago *Tribune* on December 3, 1962: "Thant Asks U.S. To Meet Reds at UN: Chides West and Lauds Nikita." [22] Thant blasted the United States for resuming nuclear testing: "A manifestation of a very dangerous psychosis," he called it. He said nothing about Russia's series of tests.[23] It was U Thant who tried to tone down the UN resolution against the brutal Soviet suppression of Hungary. It was Thant who was so alarmed and disturbed over United States sanctions against Communist Cuba and who proposed UN control posts in the Caribbean and in the United States to prevent an American invasion.[24] After UN troops had conducted themselves like barbarians in the Congo, it was U Thant who sent them these accolades of praise: "Their loyalty to the United Nations, their team spirit and comradeship have been an inspiration to all those who value the peace-keeping role of the UN. . . . In truth I have every reason to be proud of their discipline and their conduct." [25]

Since U Thant is the present Secretary-General of the United Nations and is very much involved in what that organization does, let us enter one more piece of evidence into the record—Thant's views expressed in his own words. Speaking in 1958 before the annual meeting of the American Academy of Political and Social Science in Philadelphia, he said:

> Let me be candid. When American foreign policy did concern itself with what was happening in the rest of the world, it did so out of fear and suspicion—fear of Communism and suspicion of Communist motives. Fear and suspicion are very undesirable states of mind. They breed hatred, and hatred in turn breeds cruelty and intolerance. Fear of Soviet Communism has led the United States, and those who follow her lead, to take a distorted view of the world situation and of the forces that are at work in modern society. . . .
>
> The U.S. policy toward China is unreal. It needs a thorough reexamination and reappraisal. . . . The refusal of the United States to support the admission of China to the United Nations

[22] Chicago *Tribune* (December 3, 1962).

[23] "Thant Blasts A-Testing in Space by U.S." Chicago *Tribune* (June 6, 1962), sec. 2, p. 10.

[24] Richmond *News-Leader* (March 7, 1963).

[25] *United Nations Review* (July 1963), pp. 55-56. Also, *46 Angry Men*, p. 14.

is based on two assumptions—that the Chinese government's behavior unfits it for membership in the world organization; that the Peiping government's grip on China may be broken at any moment. No one, however, believes this. . . .

It can be argued, however, that though the Soviet Union has not as yet attempted to impose its will on any state outside the Communist cordon, the Soviet has had and still has the intention to do so whenever the circumstances are favorable. But it is very difficult to arrive at an objective appraisal of such suppositions. Suspicions are not proof, and it is doubtful whether any proof has been established to sustain this charge.[26]

If the above quotation does not speak for itself, there is little that could be added here to make it any plainer.

When the Soviet demand for a *troika* was defeated at the United Nations, it was hailed as a great victory for the West. But was it? Or was it another one of those apparent Soviet defeats which in reality was a strategic victory for them. In this case the Communists were demanding that the single position of secretary-general be replaced by a group of three men. U Thant held out for the status quo. The status quo was maintained but note the men that Thant appointed as his two principal assistants: G. P. Arkadev of the Soviet Union and Ralph Bunche of the United States. In reality, the Soviets *did* obtain their *troika*. In fact, they were so pleased with the arrangement that, in spite of all their fiery oratory to create the public impression that they were not getting their way, they never even bothered to introduce a formal proposal for their *troika* in either the Security Council or the General Assembly. It was all for propaganda value, nothing more.[27]

These, then, are the non-Communists that Mr. Stevenson says keep the United Nations out of Communist hands; the "citizens of the world" who place loyalty to every nation above loyalty to their own native land; the neutral men who spend their lives advocating Communist causes.

Several years ago, Mr. Joseph Z. Kornfeder, a former member of the Communist party, summarized all that we have been

[26] As quoted by Congressman James B. Utt, *Congressional Record* (April 11, 1962).

[27] *United Nations Guardian of Peace,* Department of State publication #7225 (September 1961), p. 25.

trying to demonstrate in this section of the book. His words deserve serious consideration by all Americans:

> Now, as to the United Nations. If you were, let's say, a building engineer, and someone were to show you a set of blueprints about a certain building, you would know from those blueprints how that building was going to look. Organization "blueprints" can be read the same way. I need not be a member of the United Nations Secretariat to know that the UN "blueprint" is a Communist one. I was at the Moscow headquarters of the world Communist party for nearly three years and was acquainted with most of the top leaders, and, of course, I was also a leading party worker. I went to their colleges; I learned their pattern of operations, and if I see that pattern in effect anywhere, I can recognize it.
>
> The UN idea was sold to us on the basis that a setup of that sort was needed to keep the peace in this world. Nothing was said about the UN being a world government in the making. I need waste no time about the UN peace-keeping qualities. With an aggressive Communist world empire on the loose and sitting right inside the UN, that idea was definitely unrealistic in the first place; unrealistic and disastrous as many of the New Deal's foreign policies.
>
> From the point of view of its master designers meeting at Dumbarton Oaks and Bretton Woods, and which included such masterful agents as Alger Hiss, Harry Dexter White, Lauchlin Currie, and others, the UN was, and is, *not* a failure. They and the Kremlin masterminds behind them never intended the UN as a peace-keeping organization. What they had in mind was a fancy and colossal Trojan horse under the wings of which their smaller agencies could more effectively operate. And in that they succeeded, even beyond their expectations. . . .
>
> The United Nations is the sole great survivor, the grand monument, as it were, to the greatest folly of all time; namely, the illegitimate marriage between the New Deal and Communism. Its internal setup, Communist designed, is a pattern for sociological conquest; a pattern aimed to serve the purpose of Communist penetration of the West. It is ingenious and deceptive.[28]

---

[28] "The Communist Pattern in the UN," speech by Joseph Z. Kornfeder before the Congress of Freedom, Veterans War Memorial Auditorium (San Francisco, April 1955).

PART III

PSYCHOLOGICAL WARFARE

United Nations Capture
of the American Mind

On a dark scene in a dark time of troubles, New York's guest, the UN is proclaiming, by deed as well as word, that men can live not by violence and brute strength, but, at last, by reason and law.

Adlai Stevenson, March 2, 1961

ANIMAL FARM

Some years ago George Orwell wrote a brilliant satire on twentieth-century collectivism entitled *Animal Farm*. It is the story of a revolution staged by the animals on Farmer Jones's place. The animals considered themselves workers being exploited by non-productive humans—the capitalists. They reasoned that once the entire farm was turned over to the workers they would all live better and not have to work so hard.

As with all revolutions, there were leaders and there were followers—mostly the latter. On Animal Farm, the leadership was cheerfully provided by the pigs who hastened to point out that they were, through no fault of the others, a little smarter than the rest.

One of the first official acts of the new regime was to draft a statement of seven great principles which were then painted on the back wall of the barn for all to see. These principles became the basis of the new order and were designed to protect the animals from any future injustice or infringement on their rights. There were such noble pronouncements as, "No animal shall drink alcoholic beverages"; "No animal shall sleep in a bed"; and "No animal shall kill another animal." But the greatest and wisest of all was the seventh great principle which read: "All animals are equal."

As the months slowly turned into years, however, things did not turn out quite the way the "workers" had expected. They were working twice as hard and eating half as well as they had when they were "exploited" by Farmer Jones. The one significant exception, of course, was the ruling clique of pigs who were now living very well indeed. In fact they had moved right into Jones's house where they had been seen drinking Jones's ale and sleeping in Jones's bed! When the puzzled workers went to the rear of the barn to see if there was not something in the seven great principles prohibiting this kind of conduct, they found that a few changes had been made: "No animal shall drink alcoholic beverages . . . *to excess*"; "No animal shall sleep in a bed . . . *with sheets*." Even the important sixth principle now read, "No animal shall kill another animal . . . *without cause*." But by far the worst shock came when the poor creatures turned with hope to the seventh and greatest of all the principles, which now declared, "All animals are equal . . . *but some animals are more equal than others*"!

In this allegory, Orwell has exposed one of the universal devices of demagoguery—the use of high-sounding phrases to appeal to the noble aspirations of well-intentioned but unenlightened followers. It has been used with success from the very beginning of recorded history. But the device has been expanded and refined during recent years to the point where it is now perhaps the most important single item in the Communist bag of tricks. Without the appearance of being motivated by noble causes, the Communist conspiracy would have collapsed long ago.

For example, Article 4 of the Soviet constitution calls for the abolition of "exploitation of man by man." Nothing is said about the exploitation of man by government.

Communism is generally thought to be based on the doctrine "From each according to his ability, to each according to his need." However, Article 12 of the Soviet constitution says:

> Work in the USSR is a duty and a matter of honor for every able-bodied citizen in accordance with the principle: he who does not work, neither shall he eat. . . . From each according to his ability, to each according to his *work*. [Italics added.]

Article 124 of the Soviet constitution speaks of freedom of religion; but Article 122 of the Soviet penal code makes it a crime to teach religion to small children. In other words, it is recognized that everyone has freedom of religion *except as provided by law*, and the Soviets have such a law.

Article 103 of the Soviet constitution states: "In all courts, cases are tried with the participation of peoples assessors [juries] *except in cases specially provided for by law.*" Article 111 states: "In all courts of the USSR, cases are heard in public unless *otherwise provided for by law. . . .*" [Italics added.]

This "except as provided by law" gimmick is at the heart of practically all the high-sounding phrases which constitute UN declarations, covenants and conventions. If we read these phrases rapidly, listening to them only with our emotions, we will find in them expressions of man's noblest aspirations. But if we read them with just half as much care as we would a sales contract, they will fall apart under the sheer weight of their own demagoguery.

For example, Article 14 of the United Nations Covenant on Human Rights begins with the statement: "Everyone shall have the right to freedom of expression." A little further along, however, we find: ". . . but it carries with it special duties and responsibilities . . . and is, therefore, subject to certain penalties, liabilities and restrictions . . . as are provided by law. . . ."

Article 15, Section 3 says: "Freedom to manifest one's religion or beliefs may be subject only to such limitations as are prescribed by law. . . ."

Article 19 promises liberty of opinion and then cancels it immediately by stating that it may be subject to certain unspecified restrictions "as provided by law. . . ."

Article 20 states: "The right of peaceful assembly shall be recognized. No restriction may be placed on the exercise of this right other than those imposed in conformity with the law. . . ."

In fact, every single right outlined in the United Nations Covenant on Human Rights may be legally denied if in the opinion of the politicians it is "necessary to protect national security, or public order, or public safety, or public health, or public morals, or the rights, freedoms or reputations of others." What better excuse could any tyrant hope for? Most wars and national crimes are committed in the name of one of these. In the Reign of Terror in France during the 1789 revolution, unspeakable atrocities were perpetrated in the name of the committee of public safety. Hitler did the same in the name of national security. The United Nations followed suit in Katanga in the name of restoring public order.

"No animal shall kill another animal . . . *without cause*"!

What a far cry this is from the American Constitution which says that Congress shall pass *no* law abridging the people's right of free speech, religion, peaceful assembly, and so forth. Not "except as provided by law," but "*no* law"! What a difference this makes.

According to Marxist doctrine, a human being is primarily an economic creature. In other words, his material well-being is all important; his privacy and his freedom are strictly secondary considerations. The United Nations Declaration of Human Rights clearly reflects this philosophy in its emphasis on social security: food, clothing, housing, medical care, unemployment compensation. In this connection, the UN declaration closely parallels the Soviet constitution. The following comparison should be studied carefully:

SOVIET CONSTITUTION	UNITED NATIONS DECLARATION
Article 118: Citizens of the USSR have the right to work.	Article 23: Everyone has the right to work.
Article 120: Citizens of the USSR have the right to maintenance in old age and also in case of sickness or disability. This right is insured by the extensive development of social insurance of industrial, office and professional workers at state expense; free medical service for the working people; and the provision of a wide network of health resorts for the use of the working people.	Article 25: Everyone has the right to . . . medical care and necessary social services, and the right to security in the event of unemployment, sickness, disability, widowhood, old age, or other lack of livelihood.
Article 119: Citizens of the USSR have the right to rest and leisure.	Article 24: Everyone has the right to rest and leisure.

Article 122: [Guarantees] State protection of the interests of mother and child, State aid to mothers of large families and to unmarried mothers, maternity leave with full pay, and the provision of a wide network of maternity homes, nurseries, and kindergartens.

Article 25 (2): Motherhood and Childhood are entitled to special care and assistance.

Article 126: Citizens of the USSR are guaranteed the right to unite in . . . trade unions.

Article 23 (4): Everyone has the right to . . . join trade unions.

Article 121: Citizens of the USSR have the right to education.

Article 26: Everyone has the right to education.

There are a great many other similarities between the Soviet constitution and the United Nations Declaration of Human Rights, but the foregoing comparison is sufficient to reveal a common inspiration. The basic concept embodied in both of these documents is that the government has full responsibility for the welfare of the people and, in order to discharge that responsibility, must assume control of all their activities. How different this is from the traditional American concept of limited government.

It is significant that in actuality the Russian people have few of the rights guaranteed to them in their constitution while the American people have them in abundance even though they are not guaranteed. The reason, of course, is that material gain and economic security cannot be guaranteed by any government. They are the reward of hard work and industrious production. Unless the people produce one loaf of bread for each citizen, the government cannot guarantee that each will have one loaf to eat. Constitutions can be written and laws can be passed, but unless the bread is produced, it can never be distributed. As Benjamin Franklin put it, "An empty bag cannot stand upright."

Why, then, do Americans bake more bread, manufacture more shoes, and assemble more TV sets than Russians? They do so precisely because our government does *not* guarantee these things. If it did, there would be so many accompanying taxes, controls, regulations and political manipulations that the productive genius that is America's would soon be reduced to the floundering level of waste and inefficiency now found behind the iron curtain. If Americans ever reach the point where the government is powerful enough to give them all they want, they will find that they also have a government powerful enough to take from them all that they have.

In 1801 Thomas Jefferson said:

> With all these blessings, what more is necessary to make us happy and a prosperous people? Still one thing more, fellow citizens—a wise and frugal government which shall restrain men from injuring one another, shall leave them otherwise free to regulate their own pursuits of industry and improvement, and shall not take from the mouth of labor the bread it has earned.[1]

The principle behind this American philosophy can be reduced to a rather simple formula:

1. Economic security for all is impossible without widespread abundance.
2. Abundance is impossible without industrious and efficient production.
3. Such production is impossible without energetic, willing and eager labor.
4. This is not possible without incentive.
5. Of all forms of incentive (fear, altruism and material compensation) the most sustaining and productive for most people is material compensation.
6. This profit motive diminishes as government controls, regulations and taxes increase to deny the fruits of success to those who produce.
7. Therefore, any attempt to artificially create or redistribute economic security *through governmental intervention* can only result in eventually destroying the productive base of society, without which real security for more than the ruling elite is quite impossible.

On the surface, this may sound heartless and unmindful of the needs of those less fortunate individuals who are found in any society. What about the lame, the sick and the destitute? is

[1] *American Historical Documents* (New York, Barnes & Noble, Inc., 1960), p. 152.

an often-voiced question. Every other country in the world has confused real charity with the giving of *other* people's money, and has attempted to use the power of government to meet this need. Yet, in every one of these cases, the improvement has been marginal at best and has resulted in the long run in more misery, more poverty and certainly less freedom than when government first stepped in. By comparison, America has traditionally followed Jefferson's advice of relying on individual action and charity and of keeping the hand of government out of such matters. The result is that the United States has fewer cases of genuine hardship per capita than any other country in the entire world or throughout all history. Even during the depression of the 1930's, Americans ate and lived better than most people in other countries do today.

In the United Nations concept, even those rights not related to material things, such as freedom of religion and speech, are presumed to be granted by government. In America, government cannot grant rights for the simple reason that they are presumed to be God-given. The Declaration of Independence says that men are "endowed *by their Creator* with certain inalienable rights." [Italics added.] Our Bill of Rights does not pretend to grant rights; it is merely a list of restrictions and limitations on government to make sure that no future government officials will ever violate the God-given rights of each citizen. The United Nations Declaration of Human Rights also refers to these as inalienable but the articles themselves clearly reveal that such words are quite meaningless and serve only as window dressing.

This is by no means an insignificant distinction. If we accept the premise that human rights are granted by government, then we must be willing to accept the corollary that they properly can be denied by government. Few Americans would be willing to accept this premise if they took the time to think it through. Yet, that is exactly the premise upon which the United Nations is building its world government and under which all Americans may someday have to live.

There is still another and even more important reason why the distinction between God-given and government-given rights is important. It lies at the very center of the present gigantic struggle between the forces of freedom and the forces of slavery.

To overlook this factor is to miss the dominant meaning of the whole contest. Atheism is *the* basic tenet of Communism. If even the *possibility* of God is accepted, the entire superstructure of Communist ideology crashes into a heap of contradictions and absurdities. Conversely, an acknowledgment of dependence on God is *the* basic tenet of Americanism (recent Supreme Court decisions notwithstanding). As George Washington said in his farewell address in 1796:

> Of all the dispositions and habits which lead to political prosperity, religion and morality are indispensable supports. . . . Let it simply be asked, where is the security for property, for reputation, for life, if the sense of religious obligation desert the oaths which are the instruments of investigation in courts of justice? And let us with caution indulge the supposition that morality can be maintained without religion. What ever may be conceded to the influence of refined education on minds of peculiar structure, reason and experience both forbid us to expect that national morality can prevail in exclusion of religious principles.[2]

It should be no comfort to Americans that the United Nations has elected to adopt the Communist approach to this most basic issue. During the final United Nations debates on the Declaration of Human Rights in 1948, the representative from the Netherlands rose and said:

> I only want to stress one particular aspect which, to our great regret, has not obtained due recognition in this document. I am referring to the origin of these rights. The fact that man's rights and freedoms are based on his Divine origin and immortal destiny, the fact that there is a Supreme Being who is the fount of these rights, increase their value and importance. To ignore this relation would mean the same thing as breaking a plant from its roots, or building a house and forgetting its foundations.[3]

It is to our everlasting shame that the United States delegation remained silent on this matter.

The Communist master planners have seen to it that nowhere in the Charter, in the covenants, in the declarations, or anywhere

[2] *Ibid.*, p. 144.
[3] *Our Rights as Human Beings. A Discussion Guide on the Universal Declaration of Human Rights,* UN publication, third revision (1953), p. 18.

else does the United Nations grant even the slightest acknowledgment of God. To create an acceptable public image, the meetings are opened each day, not with silent prayer, but with a "minute of silence." The choice of terms is precise and deliberate. In the legislative chambers in Washington one can find a chapel for the use of our elected representatives in seeking Divine guidance in their work. At United Nations headquarters we find instead a huge statue of the mythological Greek god Zeus, whc was known for his ferocity and cruelty. Rather than a chapel, there is a "meditation" room, the inside of which resembles a nightmarish cross between an ancient pagan temple and a Picasso modern art exhibit. Completely devoid of religious symbols, there is only a lighted panel of bizarre geometric design, a few oriental benches, and a huge block of polished iron ore under a small shaft of light from the darkened ceiling.

*   *   *

There are two ways of "legally" denying the rights of citizens: One is to write into the law certain escape clauses, prolific qualifications and vague terminology, which can later be interpreted any way the politicians desire. The second way is far simpler: The assumption is merely that rights do not exist and no reference is made to them in the first place. The United Nations knows all about this second approach, as the following clearly reveals.

Abraham Lincoln said: "Property is the fruit of labor; property is desirable; it is a positive good in the world. That some should be rich shows that others may *become* rich, and hence is just encouragement to industry and enterprise." The *Communist Manifesto,* on the other hand, says: "The theory of the Communists may be summed up in the single sentence, 'abolition of private property.'" It seems strange, then, that the Communist master planners should have allowed Article 17 of the UN Declaration of Human Rights to mention specifically the right to own property. Does it not seem likely that the Communists would delete this provision? The answer is that this is precisely what they have done.

Reference has been made to both the *declaration* and the *covenants* when talking about United Nations pronouncements on human rights. The declaration is a broad outline of principle, a public statement of general good intentions. It has no other meaning. The covenants, on the other hand, correspond to legislation and would, if ratified by the member nations, become legally binding upon us. They would completely `override and replace our own Bill of Rights. It is not surprising, therefore, to discover that there is often quite a substantial difference between the wording of the Declaration of Human Rights and the draft covenants on human rights. The sweet-sounding, vague terminology of the declaration has been replaced by far more precise and enforceable language in the covenants. But in the case of the right to own property, the provision which appeared in the declaration vanished altogether in the covenant!

Dr. Charles Malik of Lebanon was the chairman of the United Nations Human Rights Commission. Writing in the *United Nations Bulletin* of September 1, 1952, he said:

> I think a study of our proceedings will reveal the amendments we adopted to the old text under examination, responded, for the most part, more to Soviet than to western promptings. . . . The concept of property and its ownership is at the heart of the ideological conflict of the present day. It was not only the Communist representatives who riddled this concept with questions and doubts; a goodly portion of the non-Communist world had itself succumbed to these doubts. A study of this particular debate will reveal the extent to which the non-Communist world has been communistically softened or frightened.

He further stated that a "quiet revolution" had occurred with the emphasis shifting "with a vengeance" from personal liberty to "the adequate standard of living."

It was nine years later, after this trend had gone even further, that United States Ambassador Adlai Stevenson said:

> The United Nations—as an idea and as an institution—is an extension of western ideas; of western belief in the worth and dignity of the individual; of western ideology. It is based on a western parliamentary tradition. Its roots are in the western ideal of representative government. When one stops to consider the philosophical foundation of the UN, it is easier to understand why Premier Khrushchev pounds the desk in frustration.[4]

[4] *United Nations Guardian of Peace,* Department of State publication #7225 (September 1961), p. 1.

That sound you just heard was George Washington and Thomas Jefferson turning over in their graves.

In 1948 the United Nations subcommittee on information and of the press issued a proposed international convention supposedly to protect the right "to seek, receive and impart" information by word of mouth and by publication. It then proceeded to state that government has the right to impose "penalties, liabilities and restrictions" as well as the "right of correction" whenever it felt that news had been reported falsely.[5] More recently, the Preamble of the United Nations Convention on Freedom of Information was altered to contain this significant qualification: ". . . freedom of information and opinion *accurate, objective and comprehensive.*" [6] [Italics added.]

An excellent example of the kind of freedom of information the world could expect under future United Nations management was provided at a meeting of "psychiatrists and scientific authorities" held under the auspices of the UN World Health Organization (WHO) in November of 1957. This group discussed the "deplorable" free and public discussion among scientists of questions which are controversial. They declared: "The publicizing of disagreements and contradictions among scientists, for example, about polio vaccine, or the cancer-producing effects of tobacco" has contributed to public mistrust of scientists and has caused science to lose "the infallibility with which it was credited in the nineteenth century." [7]

What kind of information would United Nations officials decide is "accurate, objective and comprehensive?" Conor Cruise O'Brien gave us a hint when he wrote:

> . . . I referred [UN] headquarters to statements which I had indeed made during the fighting [in Katanga], but in the latter days of it, when it had already been impressed on me, by the telegrams from Leopoldville, that talk about ending the secession was frowned on. These statements were naturally more guarded and *nuancé* than my first statements. . . . I also referred

[5] Harold Courlander, *Shaping Our Times* (Dobbs Ferry, N.Y., Oceana Publications, Inc., 1962), p. 54. Also, Manly, pp. 119-120.

[6] Ewell, p. 34.

[7] J. B. Matthews, "The World Health Organization," *American Opinion* (May 1958), p. 10. Dr. Matthews is a former chief investigator for the House Committee on Un-American Activities.

them to an interview I had given Keith Kyle, for the BBC. Khiary [UN official], who was in Elisabethville at the time, asked whether it was an "orthodox" interview. . . . And smiled the smile of a man who knows that all official versions are, have been from the beginning of time, and will forever be, worded to deceive the enemy and appease the clamor of the ignorant.[8]

And, if there is any lingering doubt as to what the United Nations has in mind when it says it may impose "penalties, liabilities and restrictions" on the right to transmit information, ponder the following news item that appeared in the New York *Times* during the United Nations December 1961 attack on Katanga:

> Asked why a UN jet attacked the post office in Elisabethville with rockets yesterday, General McKeown replied that the air strike had been ordered because the building had been used to transmit anti-United Nations propaganda.

If it were not so tragically serious, the following extracts taken from a recent issue of the *United Nations Review* would certainly be good for a laugh:

> A United Nations Regional Human Rights Seminar was held in Canberra from April 29 to May 13. Several speakers termed wire-tapping a "dirty business," and the seminar agreed that it was a serious infringement on human rights—in particular, the right to privacy. Indiscriminate and uncontrolled wire-tapping was unanimously condemned [apparently discriminate and controlled wire-tapping is not objectionable]. . . . Wire-tapping for criminal investigations should be permitted *only by law,* and only to combat particularly heinous crimes committed so clandestinely that such a practice was absolutely necessary. . . .
>
> A majority at the seminar agreed that national compulsory fingerprinting of all citizens did not infringe any human rights. . . . The seminar view was that *human rights could not be violated when action was taken for the good of all.*[9] [Italics added.]

Since the United Nations claims that one of its purposes is to put an end to aggression, it is interesting to note the United Nations' definition of aggression. At the fifth session of the Gen-

[8] O'Brien, pp. 299-300.
[9] *United Nations Review* (June 1963), pp. 33-34.

eral Assembly, in 1950, the International Law Commission inserted a paragraph into the draft code of offenses against the peace and security of mankind which declared the following as the UN definition of aggression: "The employment by the authorities of a state of armed force against another state, for any purpose other than national or collective self-defense *or in pursuance of a decision or recommendation by a competent organ of the United Nations.*" [10] In other words, if it is a UN military action, such as in Katanga, it simply cannot be considered aggression!

During the attempted Communist take-over of Greece in 1948, the Soviet satellites bordering on the north abducted approximately 25,000 Greek children. The children were never returned to their parents and they have since grown to adulthood, many of them not even aware of their national origin.[11] Yet a few years later, delegates from all over the world traveled to Communist Poland for a UN seminar on the rights of the child and, with the participation of representatives from Communist countries, they piously drafted the declaration of the rights of the child. Adopted by the General Assembly in 1960, the declaration provides that the child must be protected, not only from all forms of neglect, cruelty and exploitation, but also from practices which may foster "religious or other forms of discrimination." This would authorize the United Nations to dictate to parents everywhere, including America, how they may raise their own children. After all, any parent who inculcates in his child a reverence for a particular religion is discriminating against all other religions. The only way to avoid religious discrimination in rearing children is to teach them none at all.

And so it goes. The master planners and their unsuspecting helpers have been busy for years concocting poisonous pills with candy coating and offering them to the American public as the elixir for human suffering. They have covered every possible sphere of man's activities. There is a genocide convention, a declaration of the rights of women, and even proposals for legislation to protect the rights of animals! And lest anyone take these "great

[10] *Issues Before the 12th General Assembly: International Conciliation* (Carnegie Endowment for International Peace Foundation, September 1957), p. 173.
[11] Courlander, p. 78.

principles" too seriously and make the fatal mistake of believing that they are any different from the ones painted on the barn in Orwell's *Animal Farm*, let them examine the record.

The United Nations Charter says: "Membership in the United Nations is open to other peace-loving states which accept the obligations contained in the present Charter, and in the judgement of the organization, are able and willing to carry out these obligations." Yet, the greatest peace-destroying force the world has ever seen sits in its tribunals and commands the unquestioning acceptance and respect of all other members.

The Preamble to the Charter states: "We the peoples of the United Nations, determined . . . to establish conditions under which justice and respect for the applications arising from treaties and other sources of international law can be maintained. . . ." But Russia continues to violate every agreement she enters into. When, in violation of one such treaty, she builds a wall through the center of Berlin, denies access to the western sector, and murders in cold blood scores of civilians trying to escape over the wall, the United Nations says nothing—nothing!

In 1952 the free trade union committee of the AFL brought to the attention of the UN the fact that the Communists in Red China had committed between *fourteen- and twenty-million political murders*. The United Nations listened but took no action. It was apparently too busy drafting the code of offenses against the peace and security of man to be much concerned with twenty million murders.

In 1953 the United Nations Economic and Social Council was asked to discuss the rise of slave labor in the USSR. The council would not discuss the matter and removed it from the agenda.

When Red China conquered the independent nation of Tibet, set about systematically destroying its race and its culture, and proceeded to murder over fifty thousand Buddhists, the United Nations looked the other way. Years afterward it passed a vague resolution which started off by praising the principles of its own Charter and then called for "respect for the fundamental human rights of the Tibetan people and for their distinctive cultural and religious life." The resolution did not even mention the name of the aggressor!

When Soviet tanks moved in to crush the Hungarian Revolution, the UN suddenly ceased its talk about "self-determination," "anti-colonialism" and "the peace and security of man." As a matter of fact, throughout the blood bath, the Hungarian delegates from the Communist regime continued to attend United Nations meetings, to vote, and to enjoy all the respect and privileges of membership without one word of protest from the other countries. When the UN committee which had investigated the Communist suppression of freedom in Hungary finally submitted its report to the General Assembly, the United Nations was suddenly too busy to consider it. When the item came up on the 1960 agenda, we find the following official explanation of what happened: "The press of other business prevented the Assembly's consideration of the item on Hungary." [12] As the *Wall Street Journal* editorialized on September 19, 1960: "Abdication of the UN's professed moral purpose is looming; it follows logically from the prevailing double standard at the UN which indicted the West for Suez and Lebanon, but was indifferent to the Communist rape of Tibet and Hungary."

The United Nations has always loudly professed the right of self-determination as a basic right. The Charter proclaims "respect for the principles of equal rights and self-determination." In 1955 the social commission of UNESCO declared: "All peoples and all nations shall have the right of self-determination— namely, the right freely to determine their political, economic and cultural status." But when anti-Communist Katanga applied for some of that self-determination, the UN suddenly ran out—or did it? At the very time that it was denying this right to Katanga, the United Nations admitted Communist-controlled Outer Mongolia to the ranks of peace-loving nations. It recognized Syria's independence and admitted it to the UN when it seceded from the United Arab Republic. It did the same when Senegal broke away from the Mali Federation; Pakistan from India; Sudan from Egypt. While the United Nations was insisting that the Congo could not function economically without Katanga, it cut up an area about one tenth the size of Katanga and created two whole

[12] *U.S. Participation in the UN: Report by the President to the Congress for the Year 1960,* p. 68.

new nations; the Kingdom of Ruanda and the Republic of Burundi.

At the very time that the Security Council was condemning Portugal for defending its citizens against Communist-inspired atrocities in Portuguese Angola, it refused to take any action whatsoever in a clear cut case of unprovoked aggression against Portuguese Goa by pro-Communist Nehru of India.[13] All animals may be equal, but some are obviously more equal than others.

The list is endless. The United Nations' actions speak so much louder than its words that one can only wonder in amazement at the number of otherwise observant Americans who have fallen for all its propagandizing about human rights. But the above item regarding Nehru suggests a good place to end this part of the story. The London *Daily Telegraph* a few years ago reported that a young recruit in India's army was asked during a written examination to define "fundamental rights." His answer? *"Big rules done by the great people like Lenin, Nehru and Karl Marx."* [14]

---

[13] Nehru's representative at the UN was frank and defiant in his statement to the General Assembly that India would have her way "Charter or no Charter; Council or no Council!" In the Security Council, a resolution condemning India for her aggression was promptly vetoed by the Soviets; and in the General Assembly less than one third of the members (thirty-five, to be exact) were willing to go on record as opposing Nehru. Also, speech by former Secretary of State James F. Byrnes, entered in the *Congressional Record* by Congressman James B. Utt (May 1, 1962). Also, "Goa, UN and Nehru," Chicago *Tribune* (December 19, 1961), sec. 1, p. 20.

[14] Ewell, p. 92.

Breathes there a man with soul so dead,
Who never to himself hath said,
"This is my own, my native land!"

The Lay of the Last Minstrel,
Sir Walter Scott

CHAPTER

TWELVE | POISON IN THE AIR

In 1955 Congressman Lawrence H. Smith of Wisconsin described the United Nations and UNESCO (the United Nations Educational, Scientific and Cultural Organization) as "a permanent international snake pit where Godless Communism is given a daily forum for hate, recrimination, psychological warfare against freedom, and unrelenting moral aggression against peace." [1]

That same year, at its annual national convention in Miami, the American Legion formally passed the following resolution:

> *Resolved,* that the American Legion urges Congress to repeal the law creating the United States Commission for UNESCO and its Secretariat; and that Congress deliver mandates to all administrative departments of the United States Government to desist from further dissemination of UNESCO and U.S. Commission for UNESCO materials, reports and programs within the territorial jurisdiction of the United States.

As the true nature of UNESCO became better understood by more and more Americans, popular opposition began to rise against it. Patriotic organizations and service clubs all over the nation began to speak up and demand corrective action. To stem the tide, the State Department issued a series of lengthy bulletins which asserted that a few people had been "making some

[1] Congressman Lawrence H. Smith, *Congressional Record* (April 18, 1955).

misstatements about UNESCO, some of them attaining the proportions of deliberate misrepresentation. Many of these statements repeat irresponsible charges which were long ago shown to be groundless." [2] And, a few days after the American Legion passed its resolution condemning UNESCO, President Truman told newspaper reporters: "The Legion doesn't know what it is talking about. They have gone haywire in the last few years. They don't know what they are doing." [3]

The purpose of this chapter is to examine some of the "groundless, irresponsible charges and misrepresentations" that have led the American Legion, the Daughters of the American Revolution and many other patriotic societies to go "haywire" against UNESCO.

Friedrich Engels wrote that under Communism the youth of the world "will grow up in new, free social conditions and will be in a position to cast away all this rubbish of state-ism." [4]

William Z. Foster amplified this by stating:

> The studies will be revolutionized, being cleansed of religious, patriotic and other features of the bourgeois ideology. The students will be taught on the basis of Marxian dialectical materialism, internationalism, and the general ethics of the new Socialist society. . . .
>
> Our teachers must write new school textbooks, and rewrite history from the Marxian point of view. . . .
>
> There will be no place for the present narrow patriotism, the bigoted nationalist chauvinism that serves so well the capitalist warmakers.[5]

And in 1936, speaking before the ninth national convention of the Communist party in the United States, Earl Browder declared: "Who wins the youth, wins the future of America." [6]

---

[2] Undated seven-page memorandum on the official letterhead of the U.S. National Commission for UNESCO, Washington 25, D.C., released approximately January 1, 1962.

[3] "Legion—Truman—UNESCO," Washington *News* (October 14, 1955).

[4] As quoted by Leon Trotsky, *The Revolution Betrayed* (Garden City, L.I., Doubleday, Doran & Company, Inc., 1937), p. 161.

[5] Foster, pp. 316, 327. Also, as quoted in the 6th report of the California Senate Investigating Committee on Education (1949), p. 36.

[6] As quoted in the 6th report of the California Senate Investigating Committee on Education (1949), p. 36.

In these three brief statements, the Communists themselves have fully explained what UNESCO in America was designed to accomplish:

1. Achieve effective control of the educational system of our country. If the Communists can condition the minds of the youth of a nation for just one generation, that nation will be theirs within that generation.
2. Deride, ridicule and ultimately destroy any feelings of patriotism or loyalty to our country among the youth.
3. Instill in our youth an outlook of so-called internationalism and world-mindedness. This can easily be reconciled at a later date with the concept of a one-world Communist empire.
4. Indoctrinate the youth to embrace Marxian socialism (not under that name, of course) as the correct political and social viewpoint.
5. Neutralize the youth against the religious influences of the home and all other concepts of rigid morality which might interfere with the acceptance of Marxian and Communist doctrine.

As former Communist Joseph Z. Kornfeder expressed it: "UNESCO corresponds to the agitation and propaganda department in the Communist party. This department handles the strategy and method of getting at the public mind, young and old." [7]

The Senate Internal Security Subcommittee disclosed that Alger Hiss and Harry Dexter White were the principal architects of UNESCO along with Communists from other countries. For instance, Elen Wilkenson who had been an open Communist in England, was even elected to a city council position on the Communist party ticket, and who later called herself a socialist, was made president of UNESCO's preparatory commission. Clement Attlee had made her British minister of education. [8] And, as the Senate Committee on the Judiciary stated:

[7] "The Communist Pattern in the UN," speech by Joseph Z. Kornfeder before the Congress of Freedom, Veterans War Memorial Auditorium (San Francisco, April 1955).

[8] *Who Was Who 1941-1950* (London, A. & C. Black, Ltd.), p. 1277. Also, *The Annual Register* 1947 (London, Longmans, Green & Co., Ltd., 1948), p. 568. Also, John H. Snow and Paul W. Shafer, *The Turning of the Tides* (New Canaan, Conn., The Long House, Inc., 1953), p. 102.

What appears . . . to be by far the worst danger spot, from the standpoint of disloyalty and subversive activity among Americans employed by international organizations, is UNESCO. . . . Mr. Pierce Gerety, former chairman of the international organizations employees loyalty board . . . expressed the opinion that there existed in UNESCO a clique of people who placed the interests of the Communists and Communist ideology above any service to UNESCO, and above their own country.[9]

On August 2, 1953, Dr. Luther Evans, who was then the new director of UNESCO, inadvertently confirmed the above Senate report when he declared "that the U.S. drive against Communist infiltration in UN groups was a factor *threatening to destroy UNESCO.*" [10] [Italics added.]

The following item appeared in newspapers on September 25, 1954. The article is speaking about the Institute of Pacific Relations, which, as previously mentioned, has been officially described as Soviet dominated. The news dispatch said: "Two problems confront the organization. One is that the work it set out to do is now being duplicated by wealthier and better equipped world organizations such as the United Nations Educational, Scientific and Cultural Organization (UNESCO)." [11]

In its own literature and periodicals, UNESCO makes its position clear. The Communist *Guardian* of Melbourne, England, in its May 28, 1959, issue, recommended the UNESCO *Courier* to its readers as "a monthly magazine deserving of wide distribution." [12] The *Courier* is so blatant in its Communist propaganda that even the most unobserving reader can scarcely miss it.

As we have pointed out several times, not all of the people who are advancing the cause of the United Nations and its specialized agencies are doing so with malice aforethought. As a matter of fact there are relatively few who are. It has always been the pattern of successful Communist operation to have unsuspecting idealists do most of the work while the Communists stay in the background pulling the strings and issuing the direc-

[9] SISS annual report (1956).
[10] Congressman Fred E. Busbey, *Congressional Record* (August 3, 1953).
[11] Reuter's dispatch datelined September 25, 1954. As quoted in a speech by Florence Fowler Lyons before the Congress of Freedom, Veterans War Memorial Auditorium (San Francisco, April 1955).
[12] Ewell, p. 79.

tives. Consequently, many good people are victimized into lending their time, their reputations and their money. Unfortunately, once a person has done this he gradually acquires a vested interest in his own error and even though he finds more and more aspects of the United Nations which run counter to his sensibilities, he tends to brush them aside rather than swallow his pride and admit that he made an original mistake in judgment. Most humans are like that, but occasionally there is an exception.

Mr. John M. Larson, as an active, respected and well-known citizen in his community, had been invited by the State Department to become a member of the United States National Commission for UNESCO. Like most Americans, he considered this to be an honor and felt that it was his duty to accept, which he did. He soon discovered, however, that he had been invited solely for the prestige that his name would add to the commission. He was expected to be satisfied with the role of a yes-man for all the decisions of the full-time staff and senior members of the commission. He expressed a desire to participate in UNESCO planning sessions as he was theoretically allowed to do—volunteering to travel at his own expense. But he was not advised of the meetings. He tried to make his voice felt through correspondence and personal visits with the commission secretariat. He was ignored as were his recommendations. Finally, he resigned in protest. Here is what Mr. Larson revealed:

> With respect to UNESCO's literature, it has very little substance, and what little it does have, appears overtly or covertly to be slanted away from the spiritual and political beliefs and traditions of the United States of America toward the sterile conceptions of a nebulous one-world government or federation which is to be built upon atheistic foundations. . . . I found grave errors of omission and distortions of perspective with respect to historical trends and events and to the growth and development of certain ideas. For these reasons, it is important to analyze what UNESCO does *not* present and proclaim as well as what it *does* present and proclaim, in order to gain an understanding of what its aims are. . . . Peoples today are interested in achieving some sort of peaceful solution to the conflicts present in the world. The question is: on what foundation will the edifice of peace be built? UNESCO claims to supply this foundation, but when its claims are investigated, they are found to be empty as well as a con-

venient cover for its real activities. The foundations of UNESCO are atheistic and materialistic. For it, man is the highest product of nature rather than one created in the image and likeness of God. This view of God and man dictates UNESCO's methods and can be seen in them. Rather than being genuinely concerned with the intellectual and moral development of men through education, UNESCO makes cynical use of those whom it professes to be serving and helping; rather than assisting people to grow and accept responsibilities, UNESCO preys upon those with whom it comes in contact and is more than glad to assume covertly or overtly all responsibility.[13]

Look at a few examples. The book *How the United Nations Works* by Tom Galt is one of the children's books recommended by UNESCO.[14] It also comes highly praised by the New York *Times*, the *Saturday Review of Literature* and the New York *Herald Tribune* as well as the United Nations Information Service. In the opening paragraphs the reader is informed that the United Nations is "the most important organization that has ever been created on this earth." As for accuracy of information in this book, the following is typical. The author describes the UN organizational meeting in San Francisco in 1945. On page 20 he says that while the delegates were meeting in the opera house, *Japanese bombs drifted overhead on balloons and exploded in the hills near the city!* On page 9, the author skillfully plants a typical UNESCO attitude in the minds of his young readers by saying that when he was a boy his teachers and school books told him:

> The U.S. is always good and noble. We never fought a war except in self-defense. We have always been kind and generous to other countries. But the people of other countries are dishonest and mean. They will always cheat you. They never take baths.

You and the United Nations is another children's book highly recommended and praised by UNESCO.[15] Written and illustrated by Lois Fisher, it is designed for the very young. It is crammed with clever drawings and appropriate captions to catch the imag-

---

[13] "UNESCO Renounced," *Congressional Record* (September 16, 1961).
[14] Tom Galt, *How the United Nations Works* (New York, Thomas Y. Crowell Company, 1955).
[15] Lois Fisher, *You and the United Nations* (Chicago, Children's Press, Inc., 1958).

ination of children too young to understand the more complicated and sophisticated United Nations arguments. For instance, all pro-UN figures are characterized as wholesome and intelligent. Those who are against the UN are presented as ridiculous and evil. One classic illustration depicts our Founding Fathers as three extremely ugly and grotesque cross-eyed creatures snarling at each other while a rat watches from the floor.

This is the kind of conditioning of children's attitudes that Luther Evans had in mind when he addressed a UNESCO meeting and said:

> UNESCO's is a radical program. The rewards may be visible ten years from now; again they may not be visible for a hundred years. . . . They are instilled into the daily habits of mind of rising generations—perhaps not the first, not the second, but ultimately, it must be so. . . . To make the system of the UN and its specialized agencies work, we must sweep past traditional barriers in our thinking toward new frames of reference.[16]

Writing as one of UNESCO's special consultants in a symposium on human rights, Borris Tchechko provides us with an example of just what these new frames of reference might be. He explained that the Soviet constitution "not only constitutes one of the most decisive stages in the advance of the ideas of the democratic emancipation of man, but also—and this is of vital importance—sets man as a worker in ideal political, social and economic conditions and gives him facilities for work and intellectual life." [17]

On February 14, 1963, American newspapers carried a UPI report from Paris revealing that UNESCO had just published a booklet entitled *Equality of Rights Between Races and Nationalities in the USSR*. The book is pure Soviet propaganda denouncing race discrimination in the United States while praising Soviet race relations as one of the major social triumphs of the twentieth century:

> Only the revolution of October 1917 which . . . instituted the Soviet system, enabled the peoples of Russia to achieve genu-

[16] *UNESCO Leaders Speak,* Department of State publication #841574 (1949), p. 2.
[17] *Human Rights: Comments and Interpretations; a Symposium Edited by UNESCO* (London and New York, Allan Wingate, 1949).

ine equality of rights and freedom of development. . . . It was the Communist party which showed the peoples of Russia the true way to free themselves from social and national oppression. . . . The Soviet Union is a brotherhood of free and equal peoples comprising 15 sovereign Soviet republics in voluntary association on a footing of complete equality. Under the constitution of the USSR, each of these republics retains the right to secede from the union. Each of them embodies the collective will of its people and can decide its own future in entire freedom.[18]

Through our membership in the United Nations, the American people were required to pay for over a third of the total cost of publishing this booklet and giving it worldwide distribution —a great deal more than the Soviet Union paid.

As previously noted, William Z. Foster, who was at the time the head of the Communist party in the United States, predicted that in the future Communist world "there will be no place for the present narrow patriotism, the bigoted nationalist chauvinism that serves so well the capitalist warmakers." And in the constitution of the United States Communist party, we find the same sentiment: "The Communist party . . . fights uncompromisingly against . . . all forms of chauvinism." With this in mind, it is doubly interesting to note the following passages taken from a UNESCO publication entitled *Toward World Understanding:*

We shall come to nationalism later on. For the moment, it is sufficient to note that it is most frequently in the family that children are infected with nationalism by hearing what is national extolled and what is foreign disparaged. As chauvinism, this may be more ridiculous than dangerous; but it must, nonetheless, be regarded as the complete negation of world mindedness. . . . As long as the child breathes the poisoned air of nationalism, education in world mindedness can produce only rather precarious results. As we have pointed out, it is frequently the family that infects the child with extreme nationalism. The school should therefore use the means described earlier to combat family attitudes that favor jingoism. . . . If the feeling of belonging to the human community develops normally by extension of the feeling of belonging to the national community, it cannot possibly de-

[18] Congressman John M. Ashbrook, *Congressional Record* (March 21, 1963), p. A-1604.

velop from that caricature of patriotism which is extreme nationalism.[19]

Touching on the subject of teaching geography in our
schools, the same UNESCO publication states:

> One method much in use now is to teach geography in a
> series of widening circles, beginning with local geography (i.e.
> the classroom, the school building and its surroundings, the vil-
> lage, the county) and proceeding to a study of the nation and the
> continent. Only when that routine has been accomplished is the
> child introduced to the rest of the world. This progress from the
> particular and the immediate to the general and the remote may
> be logical, but does it serve the purpose? . . . In some atlases,
> the child's country is shown on every page on the same scale as
> the map to which it is to be compared. This is an admirable de-
> vice, but would it not be better still if the first map constantly
> before the eyes of the child were a map of the world? . . . This
> seemed to us so important that we were led to hope that UNESCO
> might persuade a publisher to prepare a world map that would
> really touch the child's imagination. . . . It should summarize
> the splendors of the earth; and when, later on, the child began
> the study of national geography, he would be already partly im-
> munized against an exaggerated sense of the importance and
> beauty of his own country; that is to say, against the error of per-
> spective which is at the root of jingoism and nationalism. . . . In
> addition, the geography teacher should never allow to go unchal-
> lenged statements from his pupils which reveal a supercilious feel-
> ing of national superiority. . . . The teacher who has, himself,
> a broad world outlook, will find many opportunities for influenc-
> ing the minds of his pupils both in normal school sessions and
> in his personal contacts with them.[20]

In Volume 10 of UNESCO's *Toward World Understanding*,
George Washington is given as an example of the "hero-type"
which has to be expunged from history. This volume condemns
all "presentation to the young of 'hero-types' in whom virtues are,
so to speak, incarnated." UNESCO bemoans the fact that such
figures are

> . . . spoken of with admiration, and there is an implicit ex-

[19] *Toward World Understanding* (19 Avenue Kleber, Paris, UNESCO).
[20] *Ibid.*

pectation that some children, at least, will look at these heroes as examples and model their own character and attitudes upon them. . . . Children do not content themselves with studying the heroes of national history simply as significant human beings [but] identify themselves with them, at least to some degree, and may attempt to mold their conduct upon theirs.

Volume 6 is rich in variations on the theme that the government must replace the family. It stresses the importance of "freeing the child more and more from the family."

Getting back to the question of ways and means, UNESCO's Volume 5 of *Toward World Understanding* said:

The kindergarten or infant school has a significant part to play in the child's education. Not only can it correct many of the errors of home training, but it can also prepare the child for . . . membership in the world society.

For older children, Volume 1 has this to say:

The idealism of youth should be appealed to, but it is essential to remember that the adolescent's enthusiasm can quickly turn to disappointment and disillusionment. . . . It will be found that children grasp more quickly and more firmly the principles of the UN and its agencies if the teaching is related to practical activities, such as the international children's emergency fund [UNICEF], or UNESCO's work of education reconstruction in the war-devastated countries.

Over the past twenty years the concept of education in America has gradually changed until today it is shockingly UNESCO-oriented. And this includes more than attitudes toward patriotism and religion. Increasing emphasis has been placed on UNESCO's program of replacing scholastic achievement with such vagaries as "human adjustment," "group consciousness," and "social cooperation." Our educational system has been shifting away from one which trains children to think and to understand, toward one which is preoccupied with turning out intellectual paralytics who do not question the authorities but readily conform with the group.

Our primary concern here, however, is not with UNESCO's program of mental paralysis, but with its assault on patriotism, religion and moral standards among our youth. One clear example of how far this poison has seeped into the air of American academic circles is a series of psychological tests called *Reading for Understanding* which was prepared by an organization known as Science Research Associates (SRA). These tests have been widely used in approximately seven thousand public school districts across the United States and are highly praised by teachers' associations and school administrators. As the following sample questions will reveal, however, the tests not only require the student to assume the veracity of a preliminary statement which is loaded with editorial opinion, but they use half-truths and untruths to undermine traditional concepts of religion, morality, and constitutional government.

Question 34-S-2: More Americans are going to church today than ever before. Some say that these new churchgoers are motivated by . . .
[Correct answer: "fear of death."]

Question 42-S-7: As religion in Medieval times permeated man's every thought and action, so science today is rapidly becoming a . . .
[Correct answer: "way of life."]

Question 64-C-3: Analyzing the failure of the League, the writer came to one basic conclusion; it had been betrayed by pride, self-interest and jealousy—in short, by unbridled nationalism. When sovereignty becomes a fetish, it produces more evil than good. The poison that killed peace, he decided, was . . .
[Correct answer: "nationalism."]

Question 72-S-8: Truth is sometimes thought of as leading an existence separate from the affairs of the world; but this author believes that truth depends on the achievement of human goals. That which leads to the goals we set up is true. Hence, truth is . . .
[Correct answer: "man-made."]

Question 78-C-5: The ultra-conservative elements of our population usually fail to impede change because they cannot spot the crucial aspects either of the new or of the old. They fight to preserve things that have existed only in their imaginations, but they yawn noisily while the cornerstones of their system are shattered to bits. They rush to bolt the stable doors long after the horses have run away, and when they do attempt to look toward the future, they display an uncanny knack of locking only the doors behind which . . .

[Correct answer: "no horses ever lived."]

Question 84-S-4: The value of historical knowledge is primarily practical. We are betraying our forebears by revering them. For their achievements were possible only because they rebelled against their own tradition. Our awe of them is an expression of a sentiment that they themselves . . .

[Correct answer: "hated."]

Question 96-C-10: Nature has placed man under the empire of pleasure and pain. We owe to them all our ideas; we refer to them all of our judgments and all the determinations of our life. . . . Evil is pain, or the cause of pain. Good is pleasure, or the cause of pleasure. . . . Good and evil are nothing else than . . .

[Correct answer: "happiness and unhappiness."]

If we would but open our eyes and look, we would be shocked at the extent to which this UNESCO virus has spread. On Flag Day in a school in White Plains, New York, American children were presented with a flag at an impressive ceremony in which even the city government participated. It was not Old Glory; it was the flag of the United Nations.[21]

A University of Chicago instructor by the name of Milton Mayer was quoted by the Syracuse *Post-Standard* as saying in a public speech: "We must haul down the American flag; and if I wanted to be vulgar and shocking, I would go even further and say, haul it down, stamp on it and spit on it!" The newspaper reported that "most of the audience of nearly 200 persons greeted Mayer's statement with prolonged applause."[22]

How did this come about? How have our youngsters been brought to accept this insidious mental conditioning? If you would really like to know the answer, write to the United States Department of Health, Education and Welfare, Office of Education, and ask for information on how to better teach about the United

---

[21] Florence Fowler Lyons, *Reports on UNESCO,* syndicated column (June 24, 1962).

[22] The Syracuse *Post-Standard* (February 16, 1947), p. 15.

Nations in our schools. One such booklet, entitled *Teaching About the United Nations in United States Educational Institutions,* goes into minute detail explaining how the following school programs can be made most effective: panel discussions, notebooks and reports, audio-visuals, reading assignments, UN clubs, UNICEF drives, essay contests, speech contests, field trips to UN headquarters, and model UN meetings. It is a total saturation program that no child can escape.

On March 4, 1962, the National Broadcasting Company put on an NBC Special entitled *Regards to George M. Cohan.* You will remember that Cohan wrote many patriotic songs including "It's a Grand Old Flag." In this NBC Special, one of the actors came forward holding an American flag and said: "I guess everybody knows that George M. Cohan wrote a lot of songs about this. The Cohan brand of patriotism is a little old fashioned and naive for these confused times." [23]

Things have even gone so far that in 1963 the community of Catonsville, Maryland, selected "Salute to the UN" as the theme for its *Independence Day* parade!

In 1958 the McDonnell Aircraft Company made UN Day its seventh paid holiday. Company officials stated that they hoped the idea would "spread throughout the world." Consequently, on June 21, the Philadelphia *Bulletin* ran a story headlined "Firm Makes UN Day a Paid Holiday." And on the very next day, the same paper had another news story with the heading: "Some Philadelphia Banks Drop Flag Day as a Holiday."

What effect has this anti-American conditioning had so far on the minds of our youth who have been subjected to it? How do we go about measuring the results? Unfortunately, there are so many unhealthy indications all around us that it is hard to begin. They range all the way from the rising juvenile crime rate, which is the inevitable result of a philosophy that says "truth is man-made" and "good is happiness," to student riots against congressional committees investigating Communist subversion. But perhaps the most tangible or measurable results were those observed among our fighting men who were captured in Korea.

These boys represented a fairly accurate cross section of the

[23] Congressman James B. Utt, *Congressional Record* (April 11, 1962).

American youth that had been processed by our educational system since this thinking came into favor. They came from the same kind of homes and backgrounds as our soldiers in all previous wars. Yet, their behavior as prisoners was startlingly different. For the first time in American military history, very few captured American soldiers escaped. Many of them signed "confessions" and in other ways collaborated with the enemy, not as a result of torture, but because they got better treatment that way and because they did not think it mattered anyway. And some even chose to defect to Communism rather than return to America after the war. The underlying reason for this unexpected behavior was explained rather dramatically by the Communists themselves. During the course of the fighting several secret Communist intelligence reports were intercepted by American forces. Some of these dealt with the handling of American prisoners of war. The following message was written by the chief of intelligence of the Chinese Peoples Volunteer Army in North Korea to the chief of intelligence of the Chinese Peoples Republic in Peiping:

> Based upon our observations of American soldiers and their officers captured in this war for the liberation of Korea from capitalist-imperialist aggression, the following facts are evident:
> The American soldier has weak loyalty to his family, his community, his country, his religion and to his fellow soldier. His concepts of right and wrong are hazy and ill-formed. Opportunism is easy for him. By himself, he feels frightened and insecure. He underestimates his own worth, his own strength, and his ability to survive. He is ignorant of social values, social tensions and conflicts. There is little knowledge or understanding even among U.S. university graduates of American political history and philosophy; the federal, state and community organizations, states and civil rights, freedoms, safeguards, checks and balances, and how these things allegedly operate within his own system. . . .
> He fails to appreciate the meaning of and the necessity for military or any form of organization or discipline. Most often he clearly feels that his military service is a kind of hateful and unavoidable servitude to be tolerated as briefly as possible and then escaped from as rapidly as possible with as little investment as possible. . . .
> Based upon these facts about the imperialist United States

aggressors, the reeducation and reindoctrination program for American prisoners proceeds as planned.[24]

In 1962 the Senate Armed Services Subcommittee conducted an investigation of *Military Cold War Education and Speech Review Policies*. During the course of the hearings, Admiral George W. Anderson, chief of naval operations, testified as follows:

> There were maybe 65% or 70% of youngsters who came in with really a lack of appreciation of discipline, either imposed or self-discipline. You might say at times they were in a state of delayed adolescence, and this is the group that it was so important that we work on and devote our greatest talents to, whether they ultimately are to stay in the Navy or return to civilian life. These are the people on which we have to depend in the service and on which America is going to have to depend. . . .

General David M. Shoup, commandant of the Marine Corps, said:

> They are the same kind of human beings [as recruited in the past] but they have not been exposed to what this country means and what it took to make this country what it is today. They have not been given a realization of the worthwhileness of our way of life and that it is worth giving your life for if necessary.[25]

All of which is right to the point. Who on earth would be willing to risk his life to defend America if he had been taught from kindergarten that love of one's own country is the major evil of our modern world? And if no one is willing to take such a stand, how long can we hold out against the fiercely aggressive force of world Communism? While the Soviet Communists are busy inculcating in their youth a strong loyalty to the Russian fatherland and to a precise dogma, UNESCO encourages Americans to deny their own children comparable convictions. When there no longer appears to be anything worth defending, America will be lost.

[24] "Communist Indoctrination: Its Significance to Americans," speech by William H. Mayer before the Freedom Forum (Searcy, Ark., April 15, 1957).

[25] *Military Cold War Education and Speech Review Policies*, hearings before the Special Preparedness Subcommittee, Senate Committee on Armed Services (1962), pt. 1, pp. 216, 266.

It should come as no surprise, therefore, to find that UNESCO has chosen to locate a western hemisphere headquarters in Communist Cuba since Cuba is, at present, the most solid Soviet satellite in this hemisphere. From there, it can carry on its subversion and propaganda activities throughout all of North and South America.

An interesting sidelight on this development occurred during a UNESCO conference held in Paris in 1960. Castro's Cuba submitted a report to the other delegates at the conference which read in part:

> Law 680 was promulgated to lay the foundations of a new, more rational and effective general system of education. UNESCO experts have cooperated in this great task. . . . As will be seen in the following account of the implementation of UNESCO's major projects, Cuba, precisely by virtue of the revolutionary movement that is the driving force of our country, is one of the foremost nations in the world in the implementation of these projects. . . . One token of the high regard in which the revolutionary government holds UNESCO and the aims it pursues, is the fact that the Cuban National Commission at present has the largest budget since it was established.[26]

And now UNESCO is hoping that the United States Senate will ratify a proposed treaty known as the convention against discrimination in education. What would this treaty accomplish? As summarized in a joint statement by Congressmen John Ashbrook, William Ayres, Donald C. Bruce, Edgar Hiestand and David Martin:

> UNESCO's proposed new treaty . . . would deliver the entire American educational system into UNESCO international control. It could close every private and parochial school in the United States. It would automatically remove education from under "domestic" law and control. It encompasses every phase and facet of American education.[27]

[26] *Reports of Member States,* presented to the UNESCO general conference at its eleventh session in Paris (November, December 1960), pp. 43-46.
[27] Minority report of the House Committee on Education and Labor (July 11, 1961).

Unless Americans wake up soon and do something to clear away this UN poison in the air, the treaty *will* be ratified and we will then learn the full meaning of Earl Browder's words when he declared:

Who wins the youth, wins the future of America.

CHAPTER

THIRTEEN | THE FRIGHT PEDDLERS

On January 21, 1962, the Communist *Worker* ran an article entitled "Birchers Take Warpath Against UN Peace Hopes." The following excerpts are taken from this article:

> The John Birch Society has instructed its members to prepare a hate campaign against the United Nations. In his secret "bulletin" for members, Robert Welch, fuehrer of the Birchites, orders his followers to place this anti-United Nations drive at the top of their 1962 political agenda. Steps on how to do his bidding are detailed by Welch and are, in fact, already being taken by ultra-rightists. . . . "The UN is a tool of the Reds," says the Birch Bulletin. "The only real function of the United Nations is to serve as an instrumentality of Communist global conquest," is how Robert Welch puts it. And this theme of the ultras runs through much of the Birch Society and similar extremist propaganda of late. Its obvious aim is to undermine the faith of the American people in the United Nations. . . . It was in the spring of last year that the ultra hate campaign to destroy the United Nations actually began. The origins of this insidious business can be traced to . . . a so-called "United States Day Committee," the purpose of which was to replace United Nations Day with "United States Day." . . .[1]

Throughout the following year, more and more people began to wake up to the terrible menace that our continued participa-

[1] Mike Newberry, "Birchers Take Warpath Against UN Peace Hopes," the *Worker* (January 21, 1962), p. 6.

tion in the United Nations represented. As the volume of mail to Washington demanding withdrawal from the United Nations began to reach sizable proportions, those politicians who have long had no opposition to their internationalist policies became irate and alarmed. Perhaps the most outspoken among these was Senator Thomas Kuchel of California. In a much publicized speech before the Senate, Kuchel lashed out at what he called a hate campaign against the United Nations conducted by ultra-rightists, lunatics and extremists. Since many of his constituents had cited cases of United Nations atrocities in the Congo, Senator Kuchel called them fright peddlers.

Gus Hall, present head of the U.S. Communist party, was delighted with Senator Kuchel's speech. Writing in the Communist *Worker* of June 23, 1963, he said that the Republican party was in danger of being taken over by what he called "fanatical ultra-right-wingers." But he made a special point to single out Kuchel's speech as hopeful evidence that "moderates" within the Republican ranks have not lost out altogether.

A few months later, CBS produced an hour-long TV documentary entitled *Case History of a Rumor*. The hero of the program was none other than Senator Thomas Kuchel who was presented as the all-American champion of restraint and common sense against all the irresponsible fright peddlers who think that the United Nations poses any kind of a threat to this country. The villain in the documentary was Congressman James Utt, also of California. Congressman Utt has been outspoken in his criticism of the United Nations and was the man who introduced legislation to get us out of the organization altogether. CBS, as has been the case in many of its other TV documentaries, did a masterful job of appearing to be objective while creating a lasting impression that definitely favors the anti-anti-Communist point of view.

Unfortunately, millions of Americans have allowed their attitudes to be affected by such professional presentations, never investigating the facts for themselves. Even more tragic is the fact that they seldom suspect their opinions have been manipulated. They have had very little cause to challenge those opinions since, as mentioned in the Foreword of this book, the other side has not yet had a chance to speak up. Pro-UN forces have easy access to our television networks, our large metropolitan newspapers, and our mass circulation magazines. Forces critical of the United Nations are shouted down, labeled extremist, and relegated to the futile circulation of mimeographed pamphlets and newsletters. As the forty-six civilian doctors of Elisabethville explained: "What could we do against an organization having the most powerful means of broadcasting false news, lies, denials? We had the weak voice of Radio-Katanga, the official telegraph service, one or two teleprinters, and the small amateur radio stations." [2]

Thoughtful Americans should ask themselves why it is that one seldom runs into strong opposition to the United Nations that is not made to appear ridiculous by most of our mass communications media. Is it because all such opposition *is* ridiculous? Is there not *one* person or organization worth listening to? Why is it that we all know that Presidents Truman, Eisenhower, Kennedy and Johnson have lavishly praised the United Nations but we have not been told that former President Hoover, as long ago as 1950, said that "unless the United Nations is completely reorganized without the Communists in it, we should get out of it"? Why is it that we are familiar with Senator Kuchel's views but no one mentions Senator Taft's position: "The United Nations has become a trap. Let's go it alone"; or Senator Langer's position: "I feel from the bottom of my heart that the adoption of the Charter . . . will mean perpetuating war"; or Senator Mc-Carran's position: "Until my dying day, I will regret signing the United Nations Charter"? We have all heard Adlai Stevenson refer to the United Nations as the "moral conscience of the world," but how many of us have heard that J. B. Matthews, former chief investigator for the House Committee on Un-American Activities said: "I challenge the illusion that the UN is an instrument of peace. . . . It could not be less of a cruel hoax if it had been organized in Hell for the sole purpose of aiding and abetting the destruction of the United States"?

In a speech before the United Nations Correspondents Association in 1961, UN Ambassador Adlai Stevenson reviewed the rules which most of our newsmen have apparently been following for twenty years. Referring to UN delegates and personnel, Stevenson said:

[2] *46 Angry Men*, p. 84.

Help us to create the sense of our overriding human concern. Interpret us to each other, not as plotters or as war mongers or as demons or demagogues, but as puzzled, yet aspiring men and women struggling on the possible brink of Armageddon to achieve a common understanding and a common approach. We are not at all like that, I have no doubt, but I believe that a majority of our delegates would accept such a description of their own attitudes. The whole press corps working at the UN has a unique part to play in projecting this picture. . . .[3]

On October 23, 1963, the Committee for United States Day held a meeting in the Dallas Memorial Auditorium at which Major General Edwin A. Walker spoke critically of the United Nations before an audience of approximately 1,200. In spite of efforts on the part of the committee, none of the news reporting media gave the meeting advance publicity nor did any of the local stations broadcast the speech. The next evening, however, Adlai Stevenson made a UN Day speech in the same auditorium to an audience of about 1,700 people. This program was sponsored by the Dallas United Nations Association and the Dallas League of Women Voters. Whereas the United States Day committee paid all of its own bills, we can be sure that Mr. Stevenson traveled from New York and stayed in Dallas at taxpayers' expense. His visit was given an enormous amount of advance publicity by local news media, and the CBS station in Dallas even donated a full hour of prime time (preempting the Perry Mason show) to broadcast Stevenson's speech.

The bias of our mass news communication media and the resultant devastating effect that this bias has had on American public opinion is, of course, a vast subject too large to be adequately dealt with here. But one need only reflect for a moment on the following episode to grasp the full significance of how far this process has gone. Mr. George Todt, a well-known West Coast columnist and news commentator, tells this story:

> On Sunday, September 5, 1954, I made some remarks about the United Nations on my extemporaneous television program telecast from the studios of the National Broadcasting Company in Hollywood, California. They were not the usual mouthings

one hears from the men in the communications field nowadays. Instead of bowing and scraping before the UN, I outlined some hard cold facts about this threat to the sovereignty of the United States and suggested an alternative plan to the UN for those Americans of honest intent who felt obliged to work for international understanding in the future. My suggestion revolved about the Constitution of the United States, however, *not* the UN Charter. Although the public responded overwhelmingly in favor of the suggestion I made in preference to the present UN plan, not so NBC. The reaction of the latter was hasty and bitter. As soon as the officials returned to their offices the following Tuesday morning, after the Labor Day holiday, it was to notify me immediately that I was off the air. Although never on the NBC payroll, they denied time to my sponsor of 57 weeks standing unless he broke my contract forthwith, and refused to allow me to go on the air for two more weeks prior to cancellation as my contract stipulated. This was done without a word of warning or prior consultation. Everything had been fine up until the time I spoke against the UN. Then I was suddenly *persona non grata* with the National Broadcasting Company.[4]

The process of squelching opposition to the United Nations is far from limited to just the mass communications media. In 1955, for instance, Ron Ramsey, a sixteen-year-old high school student in Compton, California, began writing letters to the editors of local newspapers and magazines. His letters were well written, factual, and strongly critical of the United Nations. As a result, he soon became the target of a vicious smear campaign conducted by a Communist-front group calling itself an "anti-Nazi league." This group sent out thousands of postcards calling Ramsey a "Hitlerite" and urging his neighbors and fellow students to mobilize against him "before he acquires any more power." Joseph L. Causey, a member of the board of trustees of the Compton Union High School district, charged Ramsey with the unforgivable crime. In a letter to the editor of the Los Angeles *Times*, Causey exclaimed: "This lad is opposed to the United Nations and preaches anti-UNESCO propaganda." Ramsey was subsequently committed to a county institution as a "mental case" with no formal charges ever brought against him. He was finally

[4] Speech by George Todt before the Congress of Freedom, Veterans War Memorial Auditorium (San Francisco, April 1955).

released on probation after thirty-four days of confinement, but only on the condition that he stop writing letters to the papers.[5]

The extent of radio and TV coverage favorable to the United Nations is a matter of daily record. From the very beginning, it has been an avalanche. For instance, on the occasion of the United Nations' tenth anniversary, in 1955, the Communist *Daily Worker* reported:

> Radio and TV coverage of the UN's tenth anniversary was the best in that world organization's history. The UN concert with Soviet pianist Emil Gilels, the New York Philharmonic and the Schola Cantorum was televised by WOR and heard on radio stations WQXR and WNYC. One report said that a movie of the concert was being sent to Latin America and that a tape recording of same would be aired by Voice of America. In addition, station WINS in New York and 55 other U.S. stations carried Norman Corwin's play *The Charter and the Saucer*, a British Broadcasting drama on the UN with Sir Lawrence Olivier. A quarter-hour film titled *Your Seat at the Table* with Clifton Fadiman was heard on WABC and many other stations across the country. *The Family Tree* was broadcast by ABC. Throughout the weekend of the anniversary, NBC's *Monitor* featured spot salutes to the UN from delegates and celebrities. The popular children's TV show *Let's Take a Trip* visited UN headquarters last Sunday. *Ding Dong School* also had its enormous following watching a movie on the UN. The *Carousel's* weekend show was devoted to the UN. CBS's *Morning Show* did a series of live pick-ups from the UN, and Dave Garroway's NBC show featured UN posters.[6]

As a result of this kind of pro-UN programming, it is no wonder that we have come to accept unchallenged the premise that the United Nations is the epitome of good. We have been brought to the point where the mere mention of the name strikes within us a conditioned response of devout reverence.

As important as radio and TV are in reaching and molding public opinion, however, the United Nations and those who promote it do not stop there. The American Association for the United Nations (AAUN) spends millions of tax exempt dollars

[5] "Anti-UNESCO," Los Angeles *Times* (March 2, 1955). Also, "Boy Supported," Los Angeles *Times* (March 7, 1955). Also, "Speech Freedom," Los Angeles *Times* (March 11, 1955).

[6] *Daily Worker* (October 28, 1953), p. 6.

to distribute free literature, provide speakers and promote tours of United Nations headquarters. In 1962 a U.S. Air Force recruiting poster appeared which depicted a young man and woman in Air Force uniforms walking down a street in a foreign country. It was the usual appeal to youth's desire for travel and adventure. But there was something significantly different about this poster. Aside from the happy faces of the figures, the only other conspicuous item in the picture was a huge UN flag. U.S. recruiting posters used to display the American flag.[7]

Speaking of the UN flag, this, too, has played a part in creating the desired attitude in the minds of Americans. Designing the flag was actually made the subject of a school project for children in California. As early as May 1944 the California State Department of Education issued a bulletin entitled *A Study in World Friendship—Designing a Symbol for the United Nations.* Needless to say, no one ever intended that these children would design the United Nations flag; the whole object, even then, was to begin to have all the kiddies thinking favorably toward the coming world government. What better way than to create the impression that they had a part in designing its flag? The UN flag was actually created in the presentation branch of the United States Office of Strategic Services in April of 1945. The man who headed this department at the time and who supervised the flag design was Carl Aldo Marzani. It was later revealed that Marzani was a member of the Communist party and operated under the party name of Tony Whales.[8] Considering this, it is possible that the striking similarity between the symbols of the United Nations and the Union of Soviet Socialist Republics is more than a mere coincidence.

Using children to promote UN projects has, by now, become standard operational procedure. It has the double advantage of appealing to the parental and protective instincts of adults while, at the same time, it has a profound influence on the attitudes of

[7] Congressman James Utt, "Power Shift in the United Nations," *Congressional Record* (April 11, 1962).
[8] *United Nations General Assembly Yearbook, 1946-1947,* annex 12, general records, 6th commission, p. 226. Also, Eleanor Roosevelt and William DeWitt, *The United Nations Today and Tomorrow* (New York, Harper and Brothers, 1953), p. 153. Also, *The Strange Origin of the UN Flag* (Box 2037, Fullerton, Calif., Education Information, Inc.), p. 2.

the children themselves who participate. For instance, in 1960 the United Nations Children's Fund (UNICEF) distributed a promotional folder designed for children entitled *How Children Help Children Through UNICEF*. The back page, illustrated with crude drawings of a cow, a truck and a child, reads:

> Many children in Italy call a cow "UNICEF" because they never tasted milk before UNICEF came. Many children in Brazil think the American word for truck is "UNICEF." And in the hills near Galilee, one little boy said: "My father says in Heaven there is God; here there is UNICEF—Please help my people."

This is the kind of calculated tug on the heart strings that loosens the purse strings. Tattered and starving children peer at us from billboards, baseball stars and movie celebrities urge us over radio and TV to give generously, and professional organizers appear in each community to excite an *uncritical* emotion of compassion. Community leaders are maneuvered into endorsing a project they do not understand and an organization whose budget they are never permitted to see. And then ordinary housewives, enthusiastic because *they* are sincere, march from home to home ringing doorbells. But if the person who is being solicited questions the noble cause in any way, those volunteers are apt to be miffed and feel insulted. After all, they know that their *own* motives are beyond reproach and, since they have already identified themselves emotionally with the cause, they cannot help but react with horror when they find someone so cruel and selfish as to ask questions when tiny children are starving.

In 1962 UNICEF sent out another folder entitled *How Halloween Fun Can Help Needy Children All Over the World Through Trick-or-Treat for UNICEF*. The back page reads:

> What a UNICEF Halloween can mean. One cent—five glasses of milk. Five cents—vaccine to protect five children from TB. Ten cents—penicillin to cure two children of Yaws. Twenty-five cents—125 vitamin tablets.

The amount of concern that UNICEF *really* has about the money it spends was best illustrated by Miss Florence Fowler Lyons who revealed that in one case when UNICEF received one dollar for two teacher's manuals advertised in one of its trick-or-treat promotional pamphlets, it sent not only the manuals, but a large box containing hundreds of expensively printed brochures glorifying the purposes and accomplishments of UNICEF. This unrequested and unwanted material was shipped first class *airmail* at a total postage cost of $10.40.[9] According to UN statistics this could have purchased 5200 glasses of milk. That's an awful lot of milk!

Each year, over two million dollars are raised for UNICEF by American children on Halloween night. But much of this money is consumed in administrative costs before it ever reaches the point where it is available for needy children. Even though two million dollars is a considerable amount, it is a drop in the bucket compared with UNICEF's total budget. As a matter of fact, less than two percent of UNICEF's total funds come from this trick-or-treat drive. The rest comes from tax money that has been given directly to UNICEF by the government. The *real* importance to UNICEF of this Halloween drive was inadvertently disclosed by the U.S. Committee for UNICEF in a defense bulletin which had been prepared to expose what it called unfounded charges against UNICEF. The committee said:

> The truth in connection with this is that Trick-or-Treat for UNICEF is primarily an education program. More than 2,000,000 American children [it is now 3,000,000] annually participate in the project in some 10,000 communities.[10]

On October 31, 1963, Arthur Godfrey said on his CBS network program:

> As a matter of fact, you will see a lot of them [children] around trick-or-treating for UNICEF again, the United Nations Children's Fund. When your doorbell rings on Halloween, it may be a child collecting for UNICEF. And again this year American children are helping thousands of needy children and mothers in 116 foreign countries. And that starts the avalanche of mail saying it's Communist-inspired and all this business; but our government thinks it's okay and so does the advertising council and so do other responsible parties, so I guess we'll stick with it.

[9] Florence Fowler Lyons, *Reports on UNESCO,* syndicated column (October 28, 1962).
[10] U.S. Committee for UNICEF bulletin (November 5, 1959).

An article in the May 1959 issue of the *National Education Association Journal* stated that the children were drawn into a lot of *preliminary* activity in many schools "from drawing maps and posters to writing and performing an original television play." Some schools administered "study units on the interdependency of nations." At least one school followed up the Halloween stunt "with a program lasting all year and culminated in a miniature UN assembly with each student representing the country of his choice."

The examples are endless. In 1951 the U.S. National Citizens Committee of UN Day distributed over 30,000 copies of *A Useful Teacher's Guide: Planning for United Nations Day,* and over 1,300,000 other pieces of literature were mailed out. Over 50,000 kits containing materials and instructions to make hand-sewn UN flags were distributed, and over half a million women and girls across the nation participated in the project.

United Nations propaganda is even in the comic books. For instance, the inside cover of a recent issue of *Superman* contains an illustrated tale of how the United Nations World Health Organization came to the rescue and saved a small Burmese village from the bubonic plague. At the end of the story, we find: "This is your United Nations at work! When you celebrate UN Day on October 24th, be proud your country is a member nation. Through the UN, our nation is working with other nations for better health and happiness for people the world over."

What this all adds up to was clearly stated by Mr. George D. Stoddard, president of the University of Illinois and a member of UNESCO's executive board. Speaking before a UNESCO gathering in 1949, he said:

> A Gallup Poll showing that only 1% of the people had ever heard of UNESCO is not depressing. It means that hardly anybody has been turned against it! How many people can name the five most important committees in the U.S. Senate? How many can name all the countries in Central and South America? How many persons know the official name of the Marshall plan? The important question is, how many persons will be affected by UNESCO, whether they know it or not, and in what ways? . . . UNESCO is a part of the fundamental law of 40 nations;

as such, it need not be on the defensive. Clearly, the 40 member states are themselves on the defensive.[11]

In spite of this continuous bombardment on the subconscious thinking of Americans for almost two decades, the number of people who are beginning to question the UN continues to grow. So much so, in fact, that by June of 1963 the master planners were beginning to worry. The National Advertising Council publicly announced on June 24 that it had been called in to help resell the UN to the American people because, as it put it, "The United Nations is considered by close observers . . . to have lost some of its grip on public opinion." [12] With the help of a Madison Avenue advertising firm, the National Advertising Council launched a gigantic campaign in the press, radio and TV valued at over five million dollars! As you may recall, the gimmick that was used as the main theme for this campaign was a picture of a huge and frightening mushroom cloud of an H-bomb explosion. And after thus sending a calculated chill down our spines at the thought of nuclear holocaust, the advertising experts then flashed the words: "This Is One Alternative To The United Nations!"

Now really, *who* are the "fright peddlers"?

[11] *UNESCO Leaders Speak,* Department of State publication #841574 (1949), p. 4.
[12] "Campaign Will Sell UN by Advertising," Chicago *Tribune* (June 25, 1963).

PART IV

THE FEARFUL MASTER
The Present Reality—
An Imminent Danger

*If we must again send our sons abroad to fight
for freedom, I hope they go unshackled; that no
appeasers' chains bind their arms behind their
backs.*

General James A. Van Fleet

*In carrying out the instructions of my Government,
I gained the unenviable distinction of being the
first U.S. Army commander in history to sign an
armistice without victory.*

General Mark Clark

CHAPTER

FOURTEEN

A SUBSTITUTE FOR VICTORY

One of the most famous quotations of the Korean War is General MacArthur's "There is no substitute for victory." But MacArthur was removed from command for wanting to translate this philosophy into action; and a less well-known quotation became the prevailing American policy. It was Eleanor Roosevelt who set the new pace when she said: "One of the most painful lessons we have to learn is to adapt ourselves to the kind of war which ends without total victory. . . ." [1]

Until the United States became a member of the United Nations, of course, we had never fought a war that ended in anything except victory. And we could easily have achieved victory in Korea if it had not been for our unnatural subservience to foreign interests. Since the Korean War is often cited as one of the outstanding achievements of the UN, it is worth our while to take a brief look at a few of the less obvious aspects of this tragic affair.

In 1947 General Albert C. Wedemeyer was sent to the Far

[1] Eleanor Roosevelt, "The U.S. and the UN," *ADA Guide to Politics—1954*, p. 61.

East to make an official military appraisal of conditions there. In his report to President Truman, General Wedemeyer stated:

> Whereas American and Soviet forces engaged in occupation duties in South and North Korea respectively are approximately equal, each comprising less than 50,000 troops, the Soviet equipped and trained North Korean Peoples Army of approximately 125,000 is vastly superior to the U.S. organized constabulary of 16,000 Koreans equipped with Japanese small arms. The North Korean Peoples Army constitutes a potential military threat to South Korea, since there is a strong possibility that the Soviets will withdraw their occupation forces, and thus induce our own withdrawal. This probably will take place just as soon as they can be sure that the North Korean puppet government and its armed forces which they have created are strong enough and sufficiently well indoctrinated to be relied upon to carry out Soviet objectives without the actual presence of Soviet troops.[2]

This, of course, is exactly what happened, but General Wedemeyer's report was, at Secretary of State George Marshall's insistence, suppressed and denied to both Congress and the public.

After we had withdrawn most of our troops in accordance with a United Nations resolution, our Army general headquarters in South Korea began sending repeated and urgent reports to Washington warning that there was an unmistakable military buildup just above the 38th Parallel. One such report even contained the date of the expected North Korean attack.[3] In spite of these reports, however, and despite the fact that money had been appropriated by Congress for the purpose of building up South Korea's defenses, officialdom somehow managed to stall and delay for over three months so that no military equipment—not even ammunition—was delivered to reinforce South Korea.[4] Yet, when

[2] Albert C. Wedemeyer, *Wedemeyer Reports* (New York, Henry Holt & Company, Inc., 1958), p. 475.

[3] *Military Situation in the Far East*, hearings before the Senate committees on Armed Services and Foreign Relations (1951), pt. 1, pp. 436, 545; and pt. 3, p. 1991. Also, "Accept Chiang's Troop Offer, Knowland Urges," Los Angeles *Examiner* (July 11, 1950), sec. 1, p. 4. At this time Senator Knowland was a member of the Senate Committee on Armed Services.

[4] *Military Situation in the Far East*, hearings before the Senate committees on Armed Services and Foreign Relations, final report (August 17, 1951), pt. 5, p. 3581.

the attack finally came Washington officials pretended to be surprised and taken off guard.

One thing is certain: if *we* knew that the Communists were preparing for over a year to attack South Korea, the *Communists* knew it too! That may seem too obvious to mention, yet nine out of ten Americans have never considered the possibility that the Communists *wanted* the United Nations to commit the U.S. to fight in Korea. If the Communists had not wanted the Korean War, they would not have started it. And if they had not wanted the UN to go through the motions of trying to oppose them, they would have vetoed the action in the Security Council. As part of the show, however, the Soviet delegation had stage-managed an impressive walkout supposedly in protest over the defeat of a motion to seat Red China. Consequently, when the attack came, the Soviets supposedly outsmarted themselves by not being on hand to administer the veto. But, as we have just stated, the assumption that the Communists did not know well in advance that the whole thing was coming is absurd. *They planned it!* The fact that they were conveniently absent when the issue came before the UN only shows that they needed a surface excuse to refrain from the veto.

The actual course of the war is well known by all. Our tiny occupational force had been deliberately kept unprepared for the sudden massive assault. It was overwhelmed, backed into the Pusan pocket, and hovered on the brink of being pushed into the sea. There is no doubt that the Communists fully expected to sweep us off the peninsula with hardly any opposition, which would have been quite a prestige-builder for them around the world. They would have done it, too, if it had not been for the independent Americanism of General MacArthur and the bravery of his troops. As MacArthur, himself, recalled: "The only predictions from Washington at that time warned of impending military disaster. Then, too, our ammunition was critically short. . . . General [Walton] Walker, at one stage, was down to five rounds per gun. His heroically successful efforts under unparalleled shortages of all sorts constituted an amazing military exploit." [5]

[5] Speech by Anthony T. Bouscaren before the Congress of Freedom, Veterans War Memorial Auditorium (San Francisco, April 1955).

Hopelessly outnumbered by the enemy, General MacArthur conceived one of the most brilliant maneuvers in military history: the Inchon landing. It was a daring surprise flank attack aimed at cutting off the North Korean supply lines. It worked beautifully and, as a result, the enemy forces disintegrated and were nearly destroyed. As General MacArthur stated:

> By the latter part of October, the capitol of Pyongyang was captured. These events completely transformed the situation from pessimism to optimism. This was the golden moment to translate military victory to a politically advantageous peace. Success in war involves military as well as political considerations. For the sacrifice leading to a military victory would be pointless if not translated properly to the political advantage of peace. But what happened was just the contrary.[6]

There was early evidence that the North Korean forces were being trained and equipped by the Soviets and, after the Inchon landing, that the Chinese Communists were providing actual combat troops by the thousands.[7] Lt. General Samuel E. Anderson, commander of the Fifth Air Force, revealed that entire Soviet Air Force units fought in the Korean War for over two and a half years "to gain combat experience for the pilots." All in all, some 425 Migs were being flown by Russian pilots.[8] The Soviets never even tried to conceal their part in the war. When United States Ambassador Lodge complained to the General Assembly's political committee that "Soviet planning instigated the original aggression, which was subsequently maintained by Soviet training and equipment," Vyshinsky, the Soviet delegate, calmly admitted the substance of the charge and replied, "Mr. Lodge is pushing at an open door." [9]

In spite of all this, the United States Government refused to allow General MacArthur to pursue the enemy across the Yalu River or even to bomb the bridges over which the Chinese Communists transported their troops and supplies. The *official* reason given was to prevent a war between the United States and Red China! The *real* reason, since we were already in a war with Red

[6] *Ibid.*
[7] *Department of State Bulletin* (December 11, 1956), p. 926.
[8] "Soviet Jet Units Defeated in Korea by U.S. Flyers Air Chief Discloses," New York *Times* (September 19, 1953), sec. 1, p. 1.
[9] As quoted by Manly, pp. 82-83.

China, was simply that the United Nations did not want us to obtain a victory in Korea, and we had, by this time, agreed to go along with whatever the UN wanted.

The typical view of so many of our UN allies was expressed in *The Fabian Essays*, published in London in 1952, with a preface by Prime Minister Clement Attlee. On page 31 the author, R. H. Crossman, says: "A victory for either side [in the cold war] would be defeat for socialism. We are members of the Atlantic Alliance (NATO); but this does not mean that we are enemies of every Communist revolution. We are opposed to Russian expansion, but also to an American victory." [10]

In 1950, when Congress appropriated rather substantial sums of money to carry on the Korean War, and it looked as though we just might start thinking in terms of pressing for a victory, Prime Minister Attlee rushed to the United States to confer with President Truman. His mission was aptly described by the *U.S. News and World Report* which stated:

> The British Government continues to maintain direct diplomatic relations with the Chinese Communists . . . even though Chinese armies were killing British youths. . . . To Mr. Attlee, China's Mao Tse-tung still is an official friend. . . . He does big business with the British through Hong Kong. British businessmen are accepted in China. . . . The British want to get rid of Chiang and turn Formosa over to the Communists. They oppose any move inside China that might embarrass the Communist regime. . . . Mr. Attlee still hopes for a deal covering Asia, while keeping up the appearance of a fight in Korea. [11]

Mr. Attlee was needlessly alarmed, for on November 16, 1950, President Truman announced: "Speaking for the U.S. Government and people, I can give assurances that we support and are acting within the limits of the UN policy in Korea and that we have never at any time entertained any intention to carry hostilities into China." [12]

When the Chinese crossed the Yalu, General MacArthur in-

[10] As quoted by Alice Widener, *Congressional Digest* (Washington, D.C., August-September 1960), p. 217.

[11] *U.S. News and World Report* (December 15, 1950), pp. 11-12.

[12] Speech by Anthony T. Bouscaren before the Congress of Freedom, Veterans War Memorial Auditorium (San Francisco, April 1955).

stantly ordered the bridges—six of them—destroyed by our Air Force. Within hours his orders were countermanded from Washington. These bridges still stand. In his bitterness, the general exclaimed, "I realized for the first time that I had actually been denied the use of my full military power to safeguard the lives of my soldiers and the safety of my army. To me, it clearly foreshadowed a future tragic situation in Korea and left me with a sense of inexpressible shock." [13]

Not only did we forbid our army commanders to fight for victory in Korea, we denied them access to military assistance that was readily available. The free Nationalist Chinese on Formosa had offered to send between fifty and sixty thousand fighting men to push back the Chinese Reds. They were confident that with very little difficulty a crushing military defeat in North Korea could set off widespread rebellion in Red China itself. The Nationalist Chinese would have been a valuable help to our forces in any event, since they had a reason to fight and wanted desperately to get into it. They offered troops, but General George Marshall turned them down because it was not felt that Chiang's troops would be effective, and "for other reasons." On June 27, 1950, President Truman announced: ". . . I am calling upon the Chinese government on Formosa to cease all air and sea operations against the mainland. The Seventh Fleet will see that this is done." [14]

We not only denied our own troops in Korea much-needed reinforcements which would have spared us thousands of casualties, but we even sent the U.S. Seventh Fleet to patrol the Formosa Straits to protect the Chinese Reds from attack!

In spite of these unprecedented self-imposed handicaps, General MacArthur continued to spoil the Communist plans. At another crucial point in the fighting, the enemy once again began to fall apart. In the last half of May they had been driven back twenty miles with casualties estimated at one hundred thousand. In order to save them from complete defeat and to give them a breathing spell, UN Soviet delegate Jacob Malik proposed negotiations for a cease-fire at the 38th Parallel. And so, with our forces once again poised on the brink of victory, MacArthur was dis-

[13] Charles A. Willoughby and John Chamberlain, *MacArthur, 1941-1951* (New York, McGraw-Hill Book Company, Inc., 1954), pp. 401-402.
[14] *American Historical Documents*, p. 406.

missed and our forward movement was halted. As negotiations began, our representatives carried a white flag into a formal assemblage of armed Communists in a spot held by the Communists. Pictures were taken and used for propaganda purposes all over Asia. The "paper tiger" was meekly suing for peace on Communist terms!

And make no mistake about it, they *were* Communist terms. One of the key issues of the early negotiations was that of a cease-fire line. We had insisted that the cease-fire line be that point where the fighting was going on when all other major agreements had been reached. The Communists wanted us to work it the other way around. The compromise: we gave into their demands. Then there was the matter of ports of entry into North Korea. We insisted that *twelve* major ports of entry be patrolled by our observers to insure that the Communists were not receiving military reinforcements. The Communists said that *four* ports of entry would be sufficient. The compromise: *four* ports of entry. Another issue was whether or not Chinese Communists would be permitted to remain in North Korea. We said no; they said yes. The compromise: they stayed. Another major issue was who would supervise the truce. We said the UN; the Communists said neutral nations. The compromise: neutral nations. These "neutral" nations, incidentally, included Communist Czechoslovakia and Communist Poland. As General Parks later revealed in testimony before a Senate subcommittee, this so-called neutral nations commission vetoed inspection trips to North Korea when they could, stalled the inspections that they could not prevent, and practiced outright collusion with the Chinese and North Korean Communists to conceal evidence of treaty violations.[15]

A UN group, of course, would have been little different. Consider, for example, the performance of the UN cease-fire negotiating committee which consisted of Iran, India and Canada. This group finally submitted a proposal to the General Assembly political action committee that the best solution to the Korean problem was to *give Formosa to Red China and admit Red China to the UN.*[16] Incredible as this proposal may seem, the vote was fifty in favor, seven opposed, and one abstention. Even the

---

[15] *Soviet Political Agreements and Results*, SISS publication (1959), p. XI.

[16] Lie, p. 359.

United States voted for it. The only delegate present with the courage and the conviction to speak out against the proposal as "abject surrender to Communism and aggression" was Carlos Romulo of the Philippines. John Foster Dulles was, at the time, a member of the United States delegation that supported this resolution. The official reason given for this incredible vote was that we endorsed it in hopes of winning support for *another* resolution condemning Red China as an aggressor! [17]

One final tragic glimpse at this new American no-win policy, which was put into practice in Korea, was provided in a Department of Defense press release dated May 15, 1954. It described in detail how high-ranking Russian military officers were actually on the scene in North Korea directing military operations. This, of course, was not news. But then the release stated:

> They wore civilian clothing and it was forbidden to address them by rank. They were introduced as "newspaper reporters," but they had supreme authority. . . . A North Korean Major identified two of these Russian "advisors" as General Vasilev and Colonel Dolgin. Vasilev, he said, was in charge of all movements across the 38th Parallel. Another prisoner . . . said he actually heard General Vasilev give the order to attack on June 25th.[18]

General Vasilev had been the chairman of the United Nations Military Staff Committee which, along with the office of the undersecretary-general for political and security council affairs, is responsible for United Nations military action under the Security Council. As we have already pointed out, the office of the undersecretary-general for political and security council affairs has always been filled by a Communist from a Communist country.

Just as the Russian delegates had stage-managed a phoney walkout in order to provide a surface excuse for not vetoing United Nations action in Korea, the Russian members of the Military Staff Committee had done exactly the same thing. On January 19, 1950, General Vasilev stormed out of the Military Staff Committee, supposedly because he suddenly objected to having

[17] Manly, pp. 67-68.
[18] *The Truth about Soviet Involvement in the Korean War*, Department of Defense press release #465-54 (May 15, 1954). Also, "U.S. Reveals Russ Ordered Attack on Korea," Los Angeles *Examiner* (May 16, 1954), sec. 1, pt. A, p. 2.

a representative from Nationalist China on the same committee. As the previous Defense Department statement revealed, he next showed up in North Korea as one of the top military planners directing the war against the United Nations—the very organization he had just a few months earlier served supposedly in the interest of international peace and brotherhood.

Once the war had gotten under way, the Russians returned to their seats as members of the United Nations Military Staff Committee. General Vasilev was not among them, however. He had turned over his position to another Communist, General Ivan A. Skliaro. In effect the Communists were directing *both* sides of the war!

This shocking piece of information was mentioned on the floor of the United States House of Representatives by Congressman James B. Utt of California, and was thus brought to the attention of the American people.[19] For the most part, however, the nation's press played down this news.

Secretly directing the *anti-Communist* side in this world-wide struggle is probably the most important single facet of Com-

[19] Congressman James B. Utt, *Congressional Record* (January 15, 1962). On March 21, 1960, the State Department issued a formal statement which said: "The United Nations Military Staff Committee had nothing whatsoever to do with the Korean War and it did not receive any classified military information on this subject. Nor was the Military Staff Committee involved in any way with the direction of the forces in Korea. . . . The United States did submit periodic reports to the United Nations on the conduct of the fighting in Korea, but these reports contained no classified information and were limited to a factual chronicle of events."
Incredible as it may seem, the State Department was asking the American people to believe that the UN had absolutely nothing to do with either planning, directing or influencing its own war in Korea! However, General George Marshall admitted that the "hot pursuit" policy of the United States of allowing our pilots to pursue attacking enemy aircraft back into their own territory had been abandoned because this policy failed to receive support in the UN. Secretary of State Dean Acheson further revealed: "There have been resolutions of the General Assembly which make clear the course that the General Assembly thinks wise; and the United States is endeavoring to follow the course which has tremendous international support and is not contemplating taking unilateral steps of its own."
It is clear that while the United States was theoretically responsible for the military direction of the "unified command" in Korea, in reality we were going along with whatever the United Nations decided. See *Military Situation in the Far East*, hearings before the Senate committees on Armed Services and Foreign Relations (1951), pt. 3, pp. 1937, 1940; also, pt. 5, p. 3583.

munist strategy. As long as they have a comfortable degree of control over their own opposition, they are perfectly willing to allow some realistic-looking anti-Communism to occur. Otherwise, the anti-Communist followers would soon become impatient with their leadership and take measures to replace it. But by allowing the anti-Communists to go through the motions of fighting the Communists and, if necessary, even allow them a few minor victories here and there, the Communist agents within our ranks can be assured that ultimate victory will be theirs. No better illustration of this strategy can be found then by merely observing the pattern of United States history since the 1930's. It was this pattern in Korea that prompted General Mark Clark to state that he feared Communists had wormed their way so deeply into our government that they were able to exercise an inordinate degree of power in shaping the course of America. "I could not help wondering and worrying whether we were faced with open enemies across the conference table and hidden ones who sat with us in our most secret councils." [20]

Here, then, are the significant results of the Korean War:

1. The war helped Red China solidify control over its people, who were becoming ripe for revolt because of famine and harsh conditions. (Tyrants have often used war or the threat of war to preoccupy the minds of their restive subjects.)
2. The war climate in the United States had a similar distracting influence on our people as well. Many disastrous measures were introduced with little or no opposition because "we must stand behind our government in this great moment of crisis."
3. The United States lost considerable prestige, particularly in Asia and Latin America. We became the paper tiger that could not even defeat tiny North Korea.
4. We needlessly sacrificed tens of thousands of American lives and billions of dollars because other nations in the United Nations did not want us to fight back in earnest.
5. We became further conditioned to the idea of having future control of our military forces under the United Nations.
6. For the first time in American military history the United States was not victorious.

[20] Mark Clark, *From the Danube to the Yalu* (New York, Harper and Brothers, 1954), p. 11.

This is what advocates of the United Nations hold up as the UN's greatest single achievement! The whole situation should have appeared absurd, even to the casual observer. The Communists attacked a peaceful country; the United Nations went through the motions of pushing the aggressor back to his border but did everything it could to make sure that there was no punishment for the crime. At the conference table, it treated both the attacked and the attacker as respectable equals. It is like having someone enter your home, attack your wife and shoot your children; and when you call for help, the police merely place the intruder outside your house and tell him not to come back. When he breaks in a second time, stabs you in the shoulder and sets fire to your house, the police react by setting up a neutral committee to negotiate your differences.

Do we really want this kind of UN justice? Apparently we do, for when South Korean President Syngman Rhee wanted to drive the Communists across the 38th Parallel and liberate all of North Korea, President Eisenhower wrote to him and said: "It was indeed a crime that those who attacked from the North invoked violence to unite Korea under their rule. Not only as your official friend, but as your personal friend, I urge that your country not embark upon a similar course." [21]

While we have been following Eleanor Roosevelt's advice and learning "to adapt ourselves to the kind of war which ends without victory," the Communists have done just the opposite. While Presidents Truman, Eisenhower, Kennedy and Johnson declare that the United Nations is the cornerstone of United States foreign policy, Nikita Khrushchev boasts:

> Even if all the countries of the world adopted a decision that did not accord with the interests of the Soviet Union and threatened its security, the Soviet Union would not recognize such a decision but would uphold its rights, relying on force.[22]

What an uneven contest it is when one compares that with the utterances of our own United Nations Ambassador Adlai Stevenson:

[21] As quoted by Manly, pp. 75-76.
[22] "Will UN Keep Freedom?" Rockford, Illinois, *Register-Republic* (October 29, 1961).

Every time, as a result of a confrontation of opinion, one of us says, even to himself, "I hadn't quite seen it in that light before," or "I had no idea you felt so strongly about this," or "That's a point I hadn't fully appreciated"—every time we say something like that, even to ourselves, somewhere in this vast celestial electronic board which charts our movements toward or away from atomic annihilation, a little green light flashes and the traffic of man moves an inch away from the point of collision.[23]

One can almost hear the following exchange:

Khrushchev: "Americans are criminals for having used germ warfare in Korea!"

Stevenson: "I hadn't seen it in that light before."

Khrushchev: "We will bury you!"

Stevenson: "I had no idea you felt so strongly about this."

Khrushchev: "Americans are filthy capitalist war mongers."

Stevenson: "That's a point I hadn't fully appreciated."

What Mr. Stevenson apparently has failed to understand is that when dealing with the Communists, every time we move the traffic of man an inch away from the point of collision the Communists then move the point of collision back an inch closer to the traffic of man. In other words, every time we appease them in hopes that they will now stop acting like Communists, they merely consolidate the gain we have granted them and then press forward for more. In any contest, if one of the parties is willing to fight if necessary to win, and the other states in advance that, not only is fighting unthinkable, but also that *he has no intention of trying to win,* can there be any doubt as to which will triumph?

On November 12, 1951, General Matthew Ridgway submitted to the United Nations a report stating that about eight thousand UN military personnel had been killed by North Korean forces— many of them defenseless prisoners of war.[24] It was revealed that most of these had been American soldiers who were shot in the back of the head and dumped into mass graves. Many were tortured until they died a merciful death. In some instances, gasoline

[23] *United Nations Guardian of Peace,* Department of State publication #7225 (September 1961), p. 35.

[24] UN Security Council official records (supplement for October through December 1951), p. 41-42.

This guided tour through the United Nations building is part of an extensive public relations program designed to produce attitudes favorable to the UN. In ten years, from 1952 to 1962, eight and a half million visitors participated in these tours.

The naked figure of the mythological Greek god Zeus, known in legend for his ferocity and cruelty, stands in the main lobby of UN headquarters in New York.

Completely devoid of religious symbols, the UN "meditation" room resembles a nightmarish cross between an ancient pagan temple and a Picasso modern art exhibit.

UN Photo

Most UN World Court justices come from strongly leftist countries; two are from open Communist countries. The U.S. is represented by Philip Jessup.

Arkady A. Sobolev
USSR

Konstantin E. Zinchenko
USSR

Ilya S. Tchernyshev
USSR

Dragoslav Protich
Yugoslavia

Anatoly F. Dobrynin
USSR

Georgi P. Arkadev
USSR

Eugeny D. Kiselev
USSR

Vladimir P. Suslov
USSR

UN Photos

Since its inception, the UN office of undersecretary-general for political and security council affairs—which coordinates all military, disarmament and atomic energy matters for the Security Council—has been held by an open Communist

United Nations Security Council delegates watch while pro-Lumumba demonstrators battle UN guards in the spectators' gallery.

Benjamin Davis, national secretary of the Communist Party, U.S.A., is interviewed at UN headquarters amidst demonstrators protesting the slaying of Patrice Lumumba.

Guards eject a violent demonstrator from the Security Council visitors' gallery where a riot broke out in protest over the death of Patrice Lumumba.

President Kennedy strongly supported the UN.

UPI Photo

The USSR has three votes in the General Assembly.

UN Photo   Wide World Photo

UN Photo

As Adlai Stevenson observed: "When one stops to consider the philosophical foundation of the UN, it is easier to understand why
Premier Khrushchev pounds the desk in frustration."

UPI Photo

President Eisenhower endorsed the UN Congo operation.

Nautical anti-bomb pickets sail around Manhattan. They demonstrated later in the day at the United Nations building (left).

A group of pacifists walk along the road headed for Boston on their 340-mile "peace march" to the UN building in New York City. The trek began March 11, 1961, in Portsmouth, New Hampshire, with the commissioning of the atomic submarine *Abraham Lincoln*.

This is one alternative to the United Nations

The U.N. is not perfect but it is our one best hope. Below are facts about its
work that you should know. Read what the U.N. does to help prevent global war.

"MANKIND must put an end to war, or war will put an end to mankind," said President Kennedy. "Never have the nations of the world had so much to lose or so much to gain."

Dwight Eisenhower said that the U.N. "has accomplished what no nation—or any limited group of nations—could have accomplished alone."

1. *In the Cuban crisis*, the U.N. provided the means and the place to confront the Russians before the world. World opinion turned against them.

2. *In the Congo*, the U.N. helped restore order, to prevent Russia and other powers from taking over. A "brush fire" was contained before it could ignite the world. Dag Hammarskjold died for peace.

3. *In the Suez crisis*, war between Egypt and Israel drew in other countries. Russia brandished rockets. But the U.N. helped police a cease-fire with troops from ten small nations.

4. *In Korea*, U.S. forces bore the lion's share of the burden. But 15 other U.N. nations had forces in action, and the communist tide was stemmed.

5. *Throughout·the world*, U.N. programs like UNICEF and UNESCO spread education and technical knowledge, help stamp out disease and hunger. The U.N. gets at the roots of war.

What about the Russians? No one should underestimate this problem, but history proves that the Soviet Union cannot dominate the United Nations.

Important U.N. actions have gone into effect over bitter communist opposition. These include the Congo, Korea, the defeat of the Troika proposal (a three-headed Secretariat), and the strengthening of the General Assembly. All were important victories for the West, and for world peace.

A forum for releasing pressures

The U.N. provides a forum for governments to "blow off steam." Far better to pound a shoe than to unleash a rocket. World leaders are "onstage" before the conscience of world opinion.

But there are failures, too. The U.N. was helpless in the Hungarian uprising. The U.N. protests, but has not changed, apartheid in South Africa. North Korea has not been freed. And the disarmament debates go on and on as nations arm.

The United Nations has far to go but when we mock its weaknesses, we mock ourselves.

What you can do to help

The U.N. needs the moral support of every American, not out of fear alone, but out of *understanding*. You can help. Express your views about the U.N. to your neighbors, friends, and government representatives. Get the facts. Write to the U.S. Committee for the United Nations, New York 11, for a free copy of the important pamphlet, "The U.N. in Action."

Contributed by this magazine as a public service in cooperation with The Advertising Council.

*The Advertising Council for the United States Committee
for the United Nations*

Playing on the fears of the American people, the Advertising Council
in 1963 launched a campaign to promote the United Nations. The
nationwide drive was valued at five million dollars.

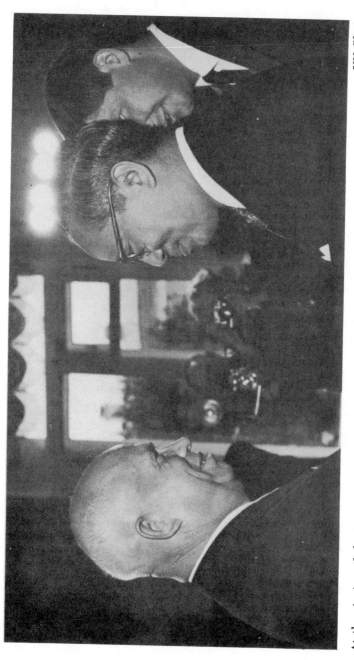

At the signing of the Moscow Test Ban Treaty in 1963, both Nikita Khrushchev and U Thant expressed satisfaction over the agreement which committed the U.S. to further disarmament moves through the UN.

UN Photo

If mere survival has become more important to Americans than freedom, then the men who sacrificed their lives for us in battles of the
past have been asked to fight, to bleed, and to die in vain.

was poured upon the wounded men and then ignited by hand grenades. When the United Nations General Assembly finally got
around to passing a rather weak resolution condemning such
practices, it even avoided coming right out and saying that the
Communists had been guilty of any of them. Yet, in spite of the
watered-down tone of the resolution, sixteen countries either refused to support it or actually voted against it.[25]

General Mark Clark reported there was solid evidence that
after the fighting had stopped in Korea and after the prisoner
exchange had been completed, the Communists still held 944
American soldiers believed to be alive.[26] United States officials
who sent these boys into battle in the first place made no formal
protest and took no action to obtain their release; nor was anything said about the matter by the advocates of justice and human
rights at the United Nations. Finally, the Chinese Communists
themselves brought the issue to public attention by announcing
that eleven American airmen captured in January of 1953 had
been sentenced as spies. The Eisenhower Administration acted
in its usual manner and courageously submitted the fate of these
American boys to the United Nations. On December 10, 1954, the
General Assembly passed a resolution against the detention of the
eleven Americans and called on the Secretary-General to inter-
cede on our behalf to see if he could persuade the Chinese Reds to
live up to their treaty agreements. Dag Hammarskjold traveled to
Red China to plead for the release of American military men being held illegally by a government that Hammarskjold was doing
everything possible to have admitted to the United Nations. It
was a perfunctory visit at best. He did not even ask to see the
captives or to survey the conditions under which they were imprisoned. Needless to say, his mission was unsuccessful.

The following year the Red Chinese "magnanimously" released the flyers as a propaganda wedge to be used at the opening
sessions of a series of discussions with the United States in Geneva. Instead of pointing out that these flyers never should have
been detained in the first place or demanding the immediate release of the hundreds of other Americans known to be still rotting

[25] Manly, pp. 91-92.
[26] Clark, p. 298.

in Red prison camps, United States officials hailed the move as a gesture of good will and spoke glowingly of the future prospects of easing world tensions.

What has happened to Americans? While Khrushchev boasts "We spit in their faces, and they call it dew," Adlai Stevenson says "We must get used to it—we who suffer from having had things our way for so long." [27] While Communists around the world shout at the top of their lungs that they are the wave of the future, Walt Rostow, the special assistant to former President Kennedy for national security affairs, proclaims: "The role of the United States in determining the outcome of the world's history over coming decades will, of course, be marginal, and success cannot be assured." [28]

What kind of insane urge for self-destruction prompted an American UNICEF official to say: "By working through UNICEF, the U.S. removes the possibility of criticism for any self-seeking ends. UNICEF itself is permitted to take the credit for the accomplishment." [29] Likewise, at the second general conference of UNESCO, an American delegate took the floor and said:

> I may say for the delegates of the United States and for the National Commission in the United States, of which Mr. [Milton] Eisenhower is Chairman, that the constant effort of each individual is to discover and to determine what is best for UNESCO. The question we ask ourselves is never "What is best for the United States?" but "What is best for UNESCO?" [30]

* * *

In 1904 a naturalized American citizen by the name of Ion Perdicaris was taken as hostage in Morocco by a lawless Arab brigand named Raisuli, and held for ransom. The sultan, Abdal-Aziz IV, was apparently not too concerned over the incident. President Theodore Roosevelt immediately sent a U.S. warship to Morocco and delivered a message to the sultan that was both

---

[27] *United Nations Guardian of Peace*, Department of State publication #7225 (September 1961), p. 9.

[28] Speech before the National Strategy Seminar held at Asilomar in Monterey, California (April 28, 1960).

[29] Testimony of Virginia Gray, Citizens' Committee for UNICEF, before the Congressional Appropriations Subcommittee (1955).

[30] *Records of the General Conference, Second Session Proceedings*, UNESCO document #2/C (Mexico City, 1947).

short and to the point. It read: "Perdicaris alive or Raisuli dead!" Within a very short time Perdicaris was safely aboard the U.S. warship.

Fifty-four years later a similar situation arose. In Cuba a bearded bandit by the name of Fidel Castro kidnapped not one but forty-five American citizens, including sailors and marines from the nearby United States naval base at Guantanamo. In this case, however, President Eisenhower sent no telegrams nor did he dispatch any warships to pick up our captured citizens. The United States Government, in fact, did nothing, for under our commitment to the United Nations Charter, such an act would have been illegal.

In 1904 we had not invented the nuclear bomb and we had not sent over 100 billion dollars of foreign aid around the world. Nevertheless, at that time the American flag and the citizens who gave it allegiance commanded and received respect and admiration everywhere. Today, it is not unusual for Americans to receive instead the jeers and taunts of the rest of the world. Our embassies have been burned, our officials have been spat upon, and in the capitals of the world "Yankee, go home" is chanted in the streets. What better proof could there be of the wisdom of General MacArthur's words: "There is no substitute for victory."

> *Shall we acquire the means of effectual resistance by lying supinely on our backs and hugging the illusive phantom of hope, until our enemies shall have bound us hand and foot?*
>
> Patrick Henry, March 1775

> *We have only to awake and snap the Lilliputian cords with which they have been entangling us during the first sleep which succeeded our labors.*
>
> Thomas Jefferson, 1796

CHAPTER

FIFTEEN | # THE SILKEN THREAD

In the story *Gulliver's Travels*, we all recall the way in which the tiny Lilliputians succeeded in rendering Gulliver powerless until they were sure he could be trusted. When they found him unconscious after being washed up on the beach, they immediately set out to bind him down with what to them was heavy rope, but was to Gulliver only the finest of silken thread. The Lilliputians worked frantically through the night knowing that they had to finish their job before the morning sun rose to awaken the giant from his slumber. When Gulliver finally came to, he found himself entirely helpless and unable to move even a finger. The thread, which he could have easily broken at any *one* place, had been carefully wrapped around his body thousands of times and was more than his match.

For the past two decades the United States, the giant among all the world powers, has been lying semi-conscious while lesser forces bind him hand and foot with thousands of strands of silken thread. Throughout these years he has, bit by bit, allowed himself to become entangled in every conceivable kind of agreement, commitment and treaty—any *one* of which would not be disastrous by itself, but the sum of which is rapidly adding up to total capture.

At the present time, there are 113 member states in the United Nations. Over fifty percent of these have a *combined* population of less than the United States! Many, like Iceland with a population of 200,000, would be hard pressed to rate even as one of our congressional districts. There are 56 members whose population is less than that of metropolitan Detroit. It is possible to get a majority in the General Assembly from nations that between themselves contribute less than seven percent of the annual budget.[1] And most of even that seven percent was first given to them as foreign aid by the United States.

When the Charter was submitted to the Senate for ratification in 1945, there were only two portions which received much publicity: the opening sentence of the Preamble, which proclaimed "To save succeeding generations from the scourge of war . . . ," and the seventh paragraph of Article 2 which states "Nothing contained in the present Charter shall authorize the United Nations to intervene in matters which are essentially within the domestic jurisdiction of any state or shall require the members to submit to such settlement under the present Charter." It is extremely doubtful that the Charter would have been ratified had it not been for this latter guarantee that other nations could not use the United Nations to meddle in our private affairs. But, as Americans were later to find out, there is *nothing* that the UN considers to be "essentially within the domestic jurisdiction" of America.

This became obvious around 1949. Mr. Levi Carneiro, writing that year in the *UNESCO Symposium on Human Rights,* stated: "Relations between states are based on the assumption that the internal policies of each nation are the concern of all nations." [2] Mr. Moses Moskowitz, a noted internationalist, made the following statement in the *American Bar Association Journal* in April of the same year: "Once a matter has become, in one way or another, the subject of regulation by the UN, be it by resolution of the General Assembly or by convention between member states at the instance of the UN, that subject ceases to

[1] Congressman James B. Utt, *Congressional Record* (April 11, 1962).
[2] *Human Rights: Comments and Interpretations,* p. 178.

be a matter of being 'essentially within the domestic jurisdiction of the member states.'" By the following year, 1950, our State Department under Dean Acheson was saying the same thing. In September it issued a formal policy statement with a foreword by President Truman which read: "There is now no longer any real difference between domestic and foreign affairs." [3] And on May 22, 1959, while speaking before the students at St. John's College in Annapolis, Maryland, President Eisenhower said: "For us indeed there are no longer 'foreign affairs' and 'foreign policy.' Since such affairs belong to and affect the entire world, they are essentially local affairs for every nation, including our own." [4]

A clear example of what far-reaching implications are carried with this philosophy was provided on August 7, 1963, when the Security Council voted nine to nothing in favor of a resolution taking action against South Africa for its policy of racial segregation. Regardless of how we may feel about racial segregation in South Africa, it is definitely the internal or domestic affair of that country. Nevertheless, the United Nations took it upon itself to impose an arms embargo and other sanctions under the justification that racial segregation in South Africa was somehow "seriously disturbing international peace and security"! The attitude of the UN was expressed during the debates by Carlos Alfredo Bernardes of Brazil who said that the question now was whether to continue to rely on persuasion or to advocate "more energetic and coercive methods of action." Nikolai Fedrinko of the Soviet Union piously described the situation in South Africa as "a reign of terror and violence" maintained by "fascist" methods.[5]

Aside from the fact that South Africa is one of the few remaining prosperous and strongly anti-Communist countries in Africa, there are several interesting points about this UN resolution. One is the clear and unmistakable violation of the Charter, as we have already mentioned. Another is the slavish way in which the U.S. almost always follows the Soviet lead in such

[3] *Foreign Affairs Policy, Series 26,* Department of State publication #3972.

[4] Clarence Manion, "This Is Where I Came In," *American Opinion* (April 1960), p. 21. Dean Manion is a former dean of the Notre Dame Law School, former director of the U.S. Department of Inter-Governmental Relations (appointed by President Eisenhower), and now is heard weekly from coast to coast over radio and TV on the *Manion Forum.*

[5] *United Nations Review* (August-September 1963), pp. 20-24.

matters. When this question came before the UN on a previous occasion, U.S. Ambassador Henry Cabot Lodge rose and said: "An item of this character invites questions about the competence of the General Assembly under Article 2, paragraph 7 of the Charter. The U.S. has observed with increasing concern the tendency of the General Assembly to place on its agenda subjects, the international character of which is doubtful." After *saying* this, Lodge then turned around and voted in favor of the resolution! That was on September 16, 1953. Ten years later, on August 7, 1963, U.S. Ambassador Stevenson was carrying on the Lodge tradition by voting with the Soviets against South Africa.

Since it has been clearly established that America's domestic affairs are all now international in character and, as such, are subject to United Nations jurisdiction, consider what might happen in the not-too-distant future if the Soviet Union should charge the U.S. with political discrimination because of its laws to limit the activities of the Communist party in this country. What would the United Nations World Court decide?

Under the terms of the Charter, we have pledged ourselves to promote full employment and social and economic progress for all peoples. If we decided to stop our foreign aid to India or Communist Poland, and these countries charged that we were not living up to our Charter obligations, what would the World Court decide?

If Fidel Castro charged the United States with threatening international peace and security by keeping its naval base at Guantanamo, what would the World Court decide?

There are fifteen justices on the World Court. Article 25 of the *Statute of the International Court of Justice* says that nine judges constitute a quorum for the Court to do business, and a majority of the nine can render judgments. This means that five judges can determine decisions. The statute also states: "The Court may, from time to time, form one or more chambers composed of three or more judges, as the Court may determine, for dealing with particular categories of cases; for example, labor cases and cases relating to transit and communications." In other words, in some matters, decisions can be rendered by as few as *two* justices!

Of the fifteen justices on the United Nations World Court,

most come from strongly leftist or Communist countries. The United States is represented on this Court by Philip Jessup, whose background with Alger Hiss and the Institute of Pacific Relations has already been discussed.

What *would* the World Court decide?

When the United States joined the United Nations, it automatically became a member of the World Court. But it was not bound by the Court's jurisdiction unless and until it filed a formal declaration in the form of a Senate ratified treaty. Senator Wayne Morse introduced in the Senate a resolution "recognizing as compulsory . . . the jurisdiction of the International Court of Justice in all legal disputes hereafter arising . . . provided, that such declaration shall not apply to . . . disputes with regard to matters which are *essentially within the domestic jurisdiction of the United States.*" [Italics added.] [6] Suspecting that there might be a little difficulty in the future definition of matters "essentially within the domestic jurisdiction of the United States," some of the senators began to look more cautiously at the whole resolution. Senator Thomas Connally was eager for the U.S. to at least go on record as accepting *some* jurisdiction of the World Court. Rather than see the whole issue defeated he proposed a simple amendment to the Morse resolution. It consisted of six words: *"as determined by the United States."* With this amendment, the resolution passed by a vote of 62 to 2 on August 2, 1946.

As of today, these six words are all that stand between us and complete legal subjection to the whims of fifteen or nine or five or even two men whose legal backgrounds and personal ideologies may be strongly antipathetic to the free world in general and to the United States in particular.

In spite of this, there has been a concerted drive in this country to generate support for the repeal of the Connally Amendment. The basic stratagem behind this drive has been to trick Americans into believing that unless we repeal the amendment we are self-judging our own case. This is then supposed to shame us into being big enough and courageous enough to openly submit our cases to impartial judgment. This, of course, is an invalid argument since all we are doing is challenging the jurisdiction of

---

[6] *Review of the UN Charter—A Collection of Documents,* Senate Committee on Foreign Relations document #87 (January 7, 1954), pp. 108-109.

the Court to try these cases in the first place. This is a common and ancient practice in American law. Just as we would refuse to submit a murder case to a traffic court, we have a right to refuse to submit a case involving domestic affairs to an international court. In view of the prevailing accepted definition of domestic affairs this reservation is more important than ever before. Nevertheless, the drive to repeal the Connally Amendment has been carried forward relentlessly by United Nations devotees under the appealing and attractive banner of "World Peace Through World Law." Not only has the Communist party pushed hard for repeal, but, unfortunately, so have Eisenhower, Nixon, Kennedy, Stevenson, Rusk and Johnson.

Accepting compulsory jurisdiction of the United Nations World Court is just one of the threads that is rapidly binding Uncle Sam into complete helplessness. It is, however, one of the most important because many of the others *could* be untied, in time, without it. Should this one be secured, though, poor Gulliver will not have a chance.

The silken thread to which we have been referring actually takes the form of international treaties. As John Foster Dulles, secretary of state, said in 1952:

> *The treaty-making power is an extraordinary power liable to abuse. Treaties make international law and also they make domestic law. Under our Constitution, treaties become the supreme law of the land. They are indeed more supreme than ordinary laws, for congressional laws are invalid if they do not conform to the Constitution, whereas treaty laws can override the Constitution. Treaties, for example, can take powers away from the Congress and give them to the Federal Government or to some international body and they can cut across the rights given the people by the Constitutional Bill of Rights.*[7]

This may come as a shock to those who have harbored the idea that they are protected as American citizens by the Bill of Rights. But, as a result of a series of Supreme Court decisions, it is now entirely possible for us to enter into a treaty with a foreign government or the United Nations which would, as Mr.

[7] Senator William Jenner, *Congressional Record* (February 23, 1954). Also, Congressman James B. Utt, *Congressional Record* (January 15, 1962).

Dulles said, "cut across the rights given the people by the Constitutional Bill of Rights." If the UN Covenant on Human Rights, for instance, should ever receive the support of two thirds of our senators—whether they realized what they were doing or not—our whole Bill of Rights would be automatically and immediately repealed. It is that simple.

Of course, our Founding Fathers, who drafted our Constitutional system, never intended for it to be this way. In 1801 Thomas Jefferson wrote:

> By the general power to make treaties, the Constitution must have intended to comprehend only those objects which are usually regulated by treaties, and cannot be otherwise regulated. It must have meant to except out all those rights reserved to the states; for surely the President and the Senate cannot do by treaty what the whole government is interdicted from doing in any way.[8]

This is the view that prevailed for many years in America. In 1836, in its decision in the case of *New Orleans v. U.S.*, the Supreme Court pointed out:

> The government of the United States . . . is one of limited powers. It can exercise authority over no subjects except those that have been delegated to it. Congress cannot, by legislation, enlarge the federal jurisdiction, nor can it be enlarged under the treaty-making power.[9]

This concept of limited government is the whole basis of the American system. By taking the chains off the people and placing them on the government, we established the formula for freedom and enterprise which has made us the envy of the world. While other nations were still laboring under a system where government officials are free to do anything they claim is in the best interests of all, American leaders had first to consult a meaningful constitution to make sure that their proposals in addition to being "good" were also constitutional. And if not, what then? George Washington answered that when he said:

[8] Thomas Jefferson, *Manual of Parliamentary Practice* (1801).
[9] Frank E. Holman "To Save the Constitution," the *Freeman* (March 1955), p. 361.

If, in the opinion of the people, the distribution or modifi-
cation of the Constitutional powers be in any particular wrong,
let it be corrected by an amendment in the way in which the
Constitution designates. But let there be no change by usurpa-
tion; for, though this in one instance may be the instrument of
good, it is the customary weapon by which free governments are
destroyed.[10]

But all that was a long time ago. Today our politicians tell
us that those concepts are out of date and antiquated; that these
modern times demand fresh approaches and greater flexibility in
order to cope with the challenge of the atomic age. Only those
who have never studied the demagoguery of past ages could accept these as fresh approaches. They may sound new, but they
are the same worn arguments used to sell dictatorship to the
people from ancient Rome to Nazi Germany.

Arthur Schlesinger, Jr., special assistant to President Kennedy
said in a speech delivered on February 15, 1962: "Jefferson is
today remote and irrelevant . . . a figure, not of present concern,
but of historical curiosity." [11]

On August 28, 1961, President Kennedy spoke to a gathering
of students at the White House and said:

After all, the Constitution was written under entirely different conditions. It was written during a period of isolation. It was
written at a time when there were thirteen different units which
had to be joined together and which, of course, were extremely
desirous of limiting the central power of the government. That
Constitution has served us extremely well, but . . . it has to be
made to work today in an entirely different world from the day
in which it was written.[12]

That same year Senator J. William Fulbright, one of the
country's most outspoken internationalists, made a speech at Stanford University. Fulbright was less guarded in his choice of words
than President Kennedy but expressed the same views when he
said:

[10] *American Historical Documents*, p. 144.
[11] As quoted by *Human Events* (Washington, D.C., July 21, 1962), p.
549.
[12] "President's Talk to the Student Interns," New York *Times* (August
29, 1962), p. 14.

The President is hobbled in his task of leading the American people to consensus and concerted action by the restrictions of power imposed upon him by a Constitutional system designed for an 18th century agrarian society far removed from the centers of world power. It is imperative that we break out of the intellectual confines of cherished and traditional beliefs and open our minds to the possibility that basic changes in our system may be essential to meet the requirements of the 20th century. . . . He [the President] alone among elected officials can rise above parochialism and private pressures. He alone in his role as teacher and moral leader can hope to overcome the excesses and inadequacies of public opinion. . . .[13]

Still at it in 1963, Senator Fulbright stated:

Government by the people is possible but highly improbable. . . . The case of governments by elites is irrefutable insofar as it rests on the need for expert and specialized knowledge.[14]

Since the Ten Commandments also date back to an agrarian society, and since they were established not 200 but *3000* years ago, it would be interesting to have the senator's views on the extent to which we must "break out of the intellectual confines" of these "cherished and traditional beliefs to meet the requirements of the twentieth century." But Fulbright did not give us the benefit of his wisdom on this subject, nor did he say just when this nation under God became dependent upon its leading politicians for moral guidance, or when it was transformed from a government of the people to a government of the elite.

It was the year 1920 that marked the beginning of a long chain of events leading up to this present repudiation of our traditional American concept of limited government. It was in that year that the Supreme Court (in *Missouri v. Holland*) reversed its previous position and declared that a federal law, which was otherwise unconstitutional, must be considered valid if it is in accordance with a treaty. In one fell swoop, nine men completely undermined our Bill of Rights and all other constitutional safeguards that had been so painstakingly erected by our Founding Fathers. While many years were to pass before the full impact

[13] San Diego *Tribune* (August 14, 1961), p. B-1.
[14] *The Elite and the Electorate* (Santa Barbara, Calif., The Fund for the Republic, 1963).

of this sweeping decision was to be felt in our everyday lives, still, the brakes had been released, and the massive machinery of totalitarianism began to inch forward.

By 1942 it had gained considerable momentum. So much so, in fact, that the concept of supremacy was extended to include not only treaties which must be ratified by two thirds of the Senate, but also executive orders, personal agreements and interternational compacts entered into by the President which do not have to be ratified nor *even seen* by the Senate or anybody else! In *U.S. v. Pink,* the Supreme Court ruled: "A treaty is the 'law of the land.' . . . Such international compacts and agreements as the Litvinov assignment have similar dignity. . . . State law must yield when it is inconsistent with, or impairs the policy or provisions of a treaty, or of an international compact or agreement." [15]

What this means is that America has now reached the point where it is legally possible for the President to issue orders to enforce some agreement which he himself has made with another government or with the United Nations, and these orders are absolute and final with no recourse to constitutional safeguards.

Recent presidents have not yet dared to exercise more than a small fraction of that power, knowing that, legal or not, they would have trouble enforcing such edicts. Nevertheless, the lever of raw dictatorship is fully operable any time the Chief Executive wishes to throw it.

President Truman tugged at it gently when he committed us to war in Korea. Remember when only Congress could declare war and send American boys to battle? Truman simply changed the name from "war" to "police action" and issued a decree. He was acting on the authority placed in him, not by the United States Government, but by the *United Nations Charter.*[16]

He pushed at the lever again when he decided to seize some

[15] Manly, p. 195.

[16] A Department of State memorandum dated July 3, 1950, explained it this way: "The preservation of the United Nations for the maintenance of peace is a cardinal interest of the United States. Both traditional international law and Article 39 of the UN Charter and the resolution pursuant thereto authorizes the United States to repel the armed aggression against the Republic of Korea." *Military Situation in the Far East,* hearings before the Senate committees on Armed Services and Foreign Relations (1951), pt. 3, p. 1936.

steel mills with uniformed soldiers. How many Americans stopped to wonder where the President got the power to do a thing like that? And how many felt any cause for alarm when he said that he was acting to uphold our commitment to the United Nations and NATO?

On February 23, 1954, the late Senator William Jenner revealed that the machinery had gained even greater forward motion when he declared:

> The doctrine that the President could make personal agreements was extended to the doctrine that agreements made by any authorized member of the government bureaucracy, in the name of the President, had the same effect as those made by the President. . . . Mr. Dulles tells us that 10,000 executive agreements have been made pursuant to NATO alone. . . . The United Nations is preparing a series of treaties which operate as domestic legislation, affecting our citizens in matters on which our Constitution does not permit even the Federal Government to legislate. They would abolish our Bill of Rights and replace it with a body of state-granted privileges and duties modeled exactly upon the Soviet constitution.[17]

At the conclusion of his speech, Senator Jenner urged his colleagues to support the Bricker amendment, which was then under discussion in both houses of Congress. The Bricker amendment was a proposed amendment to the Constitution which simply stated that the Bill of Rights and other constitutional provisions were under no circumstances to be overridden by any treaty. It was so simple, so logical and so desirable that there seemed no good reason why the proposal should not receive the enthusiastic support of everyone. The 1952 Republican platform contained a promise to support the Bricker amendment, and surprisingly enough, even Eisenhower went along with no objections. Then, of course, he was a *candidate*. After the elections Eisenhower made a complete about face and used the full prestige of his office to *oppose* the Bricker amendment. He, more than any other man, was responsible for its ultimate defeat. As Marquis Childs reported in the Washington *Post*:

[17] Senator William Jenner, "Amendment to the Constitution Relating to Treaties and Executive Agreements," *Congressional Record* (February 23, 1954).

Once the President decided to come down firmly and unequivocally against the Bricker amendment, the outcome of the contest was never in doubt. For two thirds of the Senate to vote against the President on such a crucial issue would have been, for all practical purposes, the end of the Eisenhower Administration.[18]

Secretary of State John Foster Dulles, the man who had so brilliantly explained how treaties can cut across our Bill of Rights, was now speaking against the Bricker amendment on behalf of the Eisenhower Administration. He spoke before the Senate Judiciary Committee on April 6, 1953, and assured those present that the new Administration had no intention of doing any of the dangerous things he had previously said *could* be done through treaty law.[19] In other words, under a government of such good men as Eisenhower and Dulles, who needs laws?

When the test finally came in the Senate, the Bricker amendment failed to pass by just one vote.

It is now doubly interesting to return to the pages of the April 1945 issue of the Communist periodical *Political Affairs* and read the ominous prediction:

> After the Charter is passed at San Francisco, it will have to be approved by two-thirds of the Senate, and this action will establish a weighty precedent for other treaties and agreements still to come.[20]

[18] As quoted by Clarence Manion, "This Is Where I Came In," *American Opinion* (April 1960), p. 18.
[19] Clarence Manion, "This Is Where I Came In," *American Opinion* (April 1960), pp. 20-21.
[20] "The World Assembly at San Francisco," *Political Affairs* (April 1945), pp. 289-300.

> *Government is not reason; it is not eloquence; it is force! Like fire, it is a dangerous servant and a fearful master.*
>
> George Washington

THE DANGEROUS SERVANT

In 1816 Thomas Jefferson wrote:

> The way to have good and safe government is not to trust it all to one, but to divide it among the many, distributing to everyone exactly the functions he is competent to handle. Let the national government be entrusted with the defense of the nation and its foreign and federal relations; the state governments with the civil rights, laws, police and administration of what concerns the state generally; the counties with the local concerns of the counties; and each ward direct the interests within itself. It is by dividing and subdividing these republics, from the great national one down through all its subordinations . . . that all will be done for the best. What has destroyed liberty and the rights of man in every government which has ever existed under the sun? The generalizing and concentrating all cares and powers into one body, no matter whether the autocrats of Russia or France or of the aristocrats of a Venetian senate.[1]
>
> Sometimes it is said that man cannot be trusted with government of himself. Can he, then, be trusted with the government of others? Or have we found angels in the forms of kings to govern him? Let history answer the question.[2]

Indeed, history *has* answered the question; not only the distant history to which Jefferson is here referring, but more recent

[1] From a letter to Joseph C. Cabell, February 2, 1816, *The Writings of Thomas Jefferson* (Washington, D.C., Thomas Jefferson Memorial Association, 1905), vol. 14, p. 421.

[2] *American Historical Documents*, p. 152.

events as well. In the two decades that followed the birth of this nation, men and women by the hundreds of thousands migrated here from all over the world, because they knew that here was the land of freedom and opportunity, where a man could make his own deal with life without being bowed by the oppressive yoke of government directing his daily life. Carl Schurz was one such immigrant, and his words written in 1853 serve as monumental tribute to the wisdom of such men as Washington and Jefferson:

> Here in America, you can see daily how little a people needs to be governed. There are governments, but no masters; there are governors, but they are only commissioners, agents. What there is here of great institutions of learning, of churches, of great commercial institutions, lines of communication, etc., almost always owes its existence, not to official authority, but to the spontaneous cooperation of private citizens. Here, you witness the productiveness of freedom. . . . We learn here how superfluous is the action of governments concerning a multitude of things in which in Europe it is deemed absolutely indispensable; and how the freedom to do something awakens the desire to do it.[3]

All of this, of course, was no mere accident. As we have seen, the men who drafted our Constitution and set the infant nation on its way knew full well what they were doing. They were brilliant scholars of history who had closely studied the factors that led previous nations into misery and slavery. They were determined to spare us the same fate. So when they drafted the Constitution, they inserted, among other things, Article 4, Section 4, which states: "The United States shall guarantee to every State in this Union a *Republican* form of government. . . ." [Italics added.] This means a *limited* form of government. They knew that the Union would not last if the individual states of the Federal Government itself were allowed to become despotic and unrestrained. The Constitution further stipulated: "The enumeration in the Constitution of certain rights shall not be construed to deny or disparage others retained by the people."

Compare this with the ideological foundation upon which the United Nations is built. Instead of insuring that all member states have limited forms of government, the UN assumes that

[3] "The Bricker Amendment," speech by Robert H. Montgomery (Boston, June 13, 1955).

they have unlimited power over their subjects. The UN is not concerned about the fact that a majority of its members are governments which rule with police-state methods. Instead of assuming that any power not specifically mentioned in the Constitution is reserved to the individual citizens or their smaller governmental units, the United Nations assumes that the Charter is vague and broad enough so as to authorize it to do absolutely everything! This concept of *unlimited* power was made unmistakably clear when the UN World Court declared:

> Under international law, the organization [UN] must be deemed to have those powers which, though not expressly provided in the Charter are conferred upon it by necessary implication as being essential to the performance of its duties.[4]

As a result, the United Nations has become a professional politician's paradise. It is a world forum, world court, world department of education, world welfare agency, world planning center for industry and commerce, world financial agency, world police force, and anything else anyone might want—or might *not* want.

The bedrock for world socialism upon which the United Nations is built can be found in Articles 55 and 56 of the Charter. Article 56 states: "All members pledge themselves to take joint and separate action in cooperation with the Organization for the achievement of the purposes set forth in Article 55." And the purposes set forth in Article 55 are as follows: ". . . the United Nations shall promote: (a) higher standards of living, full employment, and conditions of economic and social progress and development; (b) solutions of international, economic, social, health, and related problems; and international cultural and educational cooperation."

Since the United States is pledged to promote, among other things, the health of the world's populations, it would be well to take a look at the UN definition of "health." The constitution of the United Nations World Health Organization states:

[4] *Reparations for Injuries Suffered in the Service of the United Nations,* International Court of Justice opinion. As quoted by Abraham Feller, general legal counsel for the United Nations, in his book *United Nations and World Community* (Boston, Little, Brown & Company, 1952), p. 41.

> Health is a state of complete physical, mental and social well-being and not merely the absence of disease or infirmity. . . . Governments have a responsibility for the health of their peoples which can be fulfilled only by the provisions of adequate health and social measures.

Alger Hiss, one of the original guiding lights of the UN World Health Organization, expanded the concept even further when he said:

> . . . it includes not only the more conventional fields of activity but also mental health, housing, nutrition, economic or working conditions, and administrative and social techniques affecting public health.[5]

This simply means that the United States is bound by treaty to uphold its pledge to promote unlimited government meddling around the world; to promote the very thing against which it fought a revolution two hundred years earlier.

Advocates of this Old World concept of unlimited government quite naturally do not call it Old World; they like to think that they have discovered something new. Nor do they call it meddling; they prefer to think of it as "providing assistance." Certainly, they would not want it called socialism; "national programming" is the term. Call it what you will, the end result is still the same.

But, of course, this is a study of the UN, not a treatise on the relative merits of collectivism versus individualism. Except as this subject is unavoidably implicated in what we have dealt with so far, let us simply summarize the whole issue by saying that socialism and all other manifestations of collectivism (such as fascism, communism, etc.) would be just fine except for two considerations: first, they have never worked (as the saying goes, socialism will work in only two places: Heaven, where they don't need it; and Hell, where they already have it); and secondly, they are immoral. History has proved the first point beyond all doubt, and logic substantiates the second.

Using the police-backed power of government to force people to perform acts that would be charitable if *voluntarily*

[5] As quoted by J. B. Matthews, *American Opinion* (May 1958), pp. 8-9.

performed, is like the Good Samaritan using a club to intimidate others into helping the poor traveler who had been beaten and robbed. At the point where he threatens to use force to accomplish what is, in his mind, a noble cause, he then becomes no better than the original attacker who, for the sake of argument, might have committed the robbery to secure money for what he considered to be a noble cause. This is just a refined version of saying that the ends justify the means. If we accept that thesis, there is no end to the legalized plunder that will be our lot.

Not all of the collectivists at the UN are promoting their schemes out of ignorance or innocence. Being indifferent to the moral implications, they also know full well that their proposals are not leading to the kind of workers' utopia that they keep predicting. They know that free enterprise is far more workable and productive than socialism but they work tirelessly to promote socialism just the same. Knowing that all collectivist systems must have planners and rulers—the elite to run the lives of the rest of us—they hope to be in line for the top jobs.

Consider the following remarks made by Edward H. Carr, writing in the *UNESCO Symposium on Human Rights:*

> If the new Declaration of the Rights of Man is to include provisions for social services, for maintenance in childhood, in old age, in inadequacy or in unemployment, it becomes clear that no society can guarantee the enjoyment of such rights unless it, in turn, has the right to call upon and direct the productive capacities of the individuals enjoying them.[6]

Someone always has to pay for these schemes, of course, and in the United Nations, Uncle Sap . . . er, Sam is elected. In 1953 the General Assembly voted to create a special UN fund for world economic development. A few years later, when it was learned that this fund would need *five billion dollars,* and that Americans would be paying approximately seventy percent of the total, Mr. Hans Singer, an Englishman, casually remarked: "It will be a heavy burden on American taxpayers, but you will just have to manage that. You'll get accustomed to paying the taxes."[7]

Brock Chisholm, director-general of the United Nations

---

[6] As quoted by Ewell, p. 28.
[7] Chicago *Tribune* (October 29, 1956), pp. 1, 20.

World Health Organization, during a speech in 1957 further revealed the prevailing attitude among UN socialists when he said that it was "manifestly absurd" for a "very small proportion of the human race" (he is referring to the U.S., of course) to enjoy a "tremendous proportion of the world's natural resources." He said that this is "not a sensible arrangement" and must not last.[8]

Apparently the socialists in our own government agree with this thought, for on February 17, 1961, the State Department delivered the following official memorandum to the West German government:

> We must design formulae which . . . make allowances, as we do in our domestic taxation systems, for the principle that the richer among us shall bear a higher relative burden than the poor. In addition, we must come to recognize a principle on which the U.S. has acted in the years after the Second World War. That principle is that a sustained accumulation of gold and other international reserves by any one country is disruptive to any international community. Especially now when trade is expanding faster than gold production, we must learn to use our reserves on a *communal* basis. . . .[9] [Italics added.]

On September 20, 1963, international socialists listened with delight as President Kennedy addressed the opening session of the United Nations:

> More than four-fifths of the entire UN system can be found today mobilizing the weapons of science and technology for the United Nations decade of development. But more, much more, can be done. For example: a world center for health communications under the World Health Organization could warn of epidemics and of the adverse effects of certain drugs as well as transmit the results of new experiments and new discoveries. Regional research centers could advance our common medical knowledge and train new scientists and doctors for new nations. . . . A worldwide program of conservation could protect the forest and world game preserves now in danger of extinction—improve the marine harvest of food from our oceans—and prevent the contamination of our air and our water by industrial as well as

[8] J. B. Matthews, "The World Health Organization," *American Opinion* (May 1958), p. 31.
[9] *Department of State Bulletin* (March 13, 1961), pp. 370-371.

nuclear pollution. And, finally, a worldwide program of farm distribution—similar to our own nation's "Food for Peace" program—could give every hungry child the food he needs.[10]

At the conclusion of a previous speech by President Kennedy expressing similar views in relation to NATO, Mr. Paul Henri Spaak, leader of the Belgian Socialist party, exclaimed, "This is perfect; I have found a successor!" [11]

It should be obvious to any careful observer that there is no longer even the slightest challenge to socialist doctrine within the United Nations from *any* member nations, including our own. Any wishful thinking we might have entertained to the contrary was certainly eradicated by Secretary-General U Thant. Speaking on April 5, 1963, at Columbia University, he said:

> Not so long ago, there were quite divergent views in the membership of the UN about the desirability and wisdom for governments to set targets and adopt national plans or programs. Today . . . there is a broad measure of agreement about the usefulness of projections, planning and programing as practical tools for economic and social development, while the controversy about the relative merits of private enterprise and public undertakings is transcended by the realization that the most important aim of development is to bring about expansion and change for the benefit of all.[12]

Translated into simple, understandable English, Thant said that everyone in the UN agrees that socialism is more practical and desirable than free enterprise.

The socialistic bias of the UN is clearly revealed on nearly every page of the monthly *United Nations Review*. One can

[10] "Kennedy—A Quest for Peace Meeting," Los Angeles *Herald-Examiner* (September 20, 1963), p. A-7. Shortly after the death of President Kennedy, President Johnson addressed the United Nations General Assembly and expounded almost the identical philosophy. In fact, Johnson proposed extending the welfare programs of the New Deal period to the whole world under United Nations direction and United States financing. See "Text of Johnson's Speech to UN," Los Angeles *Times* (December 18, 1963), sec. 4, p. 2.

[11] Article by Michael Padev, the Indianapolis *Star* (February 22, 1961). Mr. Spaak, who was the outgoing secretary of NATO, was speaking about the leadership role that President Kennedy would now assume in his place within NATO economic policies.

[12] *United Nations Review* (April 1963), p. 13.

find reports on UN proceedings dealing with setting prices, production quotas, inventories, stockpiles of raw materials, labor standards, wages and monetary policies. Every conceivable sphere of human economic activity is being analyzed and then planned for so that it will come under the ultimate control of the United Nations.

As the months slip by and as we enter into thousands of additional treaties, executive orders, and international agreements, the silken thread continues to be spun around the sleeping giant. The job is so near completion that already there are a multitude of United Nations regulations that reach right down to the daily lives of American citizens. An example is the International Wheat Conference which actually decrees how much wheat our farmers may sell in foreign countries and sets the price to be paid for it. The Federal Government enforces these decrees by the authority derived from an international treaty.[13]

The International Materials Conference is another example. Set up in 1951, its purpose was to clamp down import and export quotas for certain strategic materials such as sulphur, copper, zinc and tungsten. During the Korean War, we found that these quotas severely hampered the production of critical war materials and resulted in costly layoffs in some industries. When a subcommittee of the United States Senate looked into the matter, it reported:

> . . . in effect, the International Materials Conference, an unauthorized group of persons in other countries, dictated to the Untied States how much of such critical materials could be allocated to the United States stockpile.
>
> The so-called "entitlements of consumption" established by the International Materials Conference created a shortage of critical materials in this country for the benefit of foreign powers. . . .

When the Senate received this report, it immediately withdrew authorization for the use of funds to be used in support of the IMC. The executive department under President Eisenhower, however, completely ignored the action and merely diverted the funds from other sources for this purpose. The justification used

[13] Watts, UN: *Planned Tyranny*, p. 79.

was that the IMC derived its authority from an executive agreement, a *higher* source than Congress, and, as such, must be supported.[14]

Some Americans, as they see their country gradually becoming more and more helplessly ensnared in this web of foreign entanglements, seek comfort in the thought that the real power of the United Nations supposedly resides in the Security Council where we have the right to veto anything that we dislike. As long as this is so, they reason, we have nothing to fear. But these people are in for a rude awakening. For one thing, as we have already pointed out, the Secretariat or full-time staff of the UN wields a dominant influence amounting to virtual *effective* control from behind the scenes. Aside from that, however, thinking strictly in terms of the theoretical power structure, it is true that the original setup was supposed to place the authority to wage war and other important matters in the hands of the Big Five in the Security Council, each with the protection of a veto. The General Assembly was supposed to be merely a world forum where nations could express their views and pass harmless resolutions. In fact, it is doubtful that the American people would have accepted the United Nations on any other basis. But the UN Charter is a remarkable document and, as we shall see, things are not quite the same today as they were in 1945. As Secretary of State John Foster Dulles put it:

> If a situation is arrived at where you can't accomplish a reasonable fair result through technical Charter amendments, it may very well be possible to agree on procedures which would get a very large part of the desired result. Now it would be much neater and cleaner to do it by Charter amendment, but if that process is frustrated by the fact that the five permanent members have the veto power on amendments, then *other ways* could be found. [Italics added.]

He said that the United Nations Charter was sufficiently unspecific and flexible to allow evolution in this direction, and concluded that, for this reason "future generations would be thankful to the men at San Francisco who had drafted it." [15] Trygve Lie expressed the same sentiment when he said:

---

[14] *Ibid.*, pp. 79-81.
[15] *Review of the UN Charter—A Collection of Documents*, Senate Committee on Foreign Relations document #87 (January 7, 1954), pp. 286-288.

. . . there has been a healthy shift in power from the council to the veto-free General Assembly. Thus, progress by no means alone depends upon textual revisions of the Charter. A continued liberal construction of the Charter we now have holds out great promise, and perhaps is the more practical way to strengthen the bonds of the world community.[16]

This philosophy, of course, is not original with Mr. Dulles or Mr. Lie. Centuries earlier Napoleon wrote: "A constitution should be short and obscure." While the United Nations Charter is anything but short, it certainly is obscure. A smart politician with a flair for legal language could justify almost anything on the basis of its provisions. As Dulles admitted: "I have never seen any proposal made for collective security with 'teeth' in it, or for 'world government' or for 'world federation,' which could not be carried out either by the United Nations or under the United Nations Charter." [17]

What has all this got to do with our veto in the UN? Simply this: We do not have it any more! When the United Nations called for military action to repell the Communist invasion of South Korea, technically speaking it was violating the terms of its own Charter. This has never slowed the UN down in the past, but this time the issue was important enough to demand the pretense of legality. The difficulty arose due to the Soviet's absence from the Security Council. When the United Nations was formed, it was understood that a Big Five failure to vote was automatically considered a veto. But, due to the "flexibility" of the Charter and "dynamic usage," the practice now is that failure to vote does *not* constitute a veto. At the time of the Korean invasion, this concept was right in the middle of being "evolved" and it was no time to put it to the test. Consequently, at the primary insistence of the U.S. a "unified command" was established under theoretical American control and a "uniting for peace" resolution was introduced before the General Assembly, where it passed with little difficulty. The resolution established the following profound changes in UN procedure:

1. If, due to a veto, the Security Council fails to act in a case of military crisis, the General Assembly can hold an emergency session to take up the matter.

[16] Lie, p. 424.
[17] As quoted by Manly, p. 212, from Mr. Dulles' book *War or Peace.*

2. In such a case, the General Assembly can call on member nations to make available their armed forces for whatever military action the General Assembly may recommend.[18]

Here, then, is one more thread. Loss of the veto is no small matter—as even Trygve Lie was forced to admit: "The Assembly . . . by adopting the Acheson [Uniting for Peace] Plan, engineered a profound shift of emergency power from the veto-ridden Security Council to the veto-less General Assembly—a shift the full potentialities of which have still to be realized." [19] It means that at some future date Uncle Sam will awaken from his long slumber only to find that he is completely at the mercy of a majority vote within a mob of angry Lilliputians screaming for his head; and that the harmless world forum that he thought he created has transformed itself into an all-powerful world government fully capable of performing the execution.

In an apparently calm acceptance of this grim fate for our country, President Lyndon Johnson, nonchalantly stated it this way: "In a world of 113 nations, 50 of which have had new governments in the past three years, the United States must be prepared for change." [20]

[18] *Everyman's United Nations* (New York, UN Office of Public Information, 1959), p. 75.
[19] Lie, p. 347.
[20] "Foreign Policy Critics Assailed by Johnson," Los Angeles *Times* (February 12, 1964), pp. 1, 7.

The saddest epitaph which can be carved in memory of a vanished liberty is that it was lost because its possessors failed to stretch forth a saving hand while yet there was time.

Supreme Court Justice George Sutherland, 1937

CHAPTER

SEVENTEEN | POINT OF NO RETURN

In the northern reaches of the globe live tiny rodent-like creatures called lemmings. They lead a rather solitary life and seem to be well adjusted to their environment. They look and behave in quite a normal fashion—except for one curious idiosyncrasy. Every once in a while, after several years of unusual prosperity for the lemming clan, they suddenly get an uncontrollable urge to go for a swim. Almost as though on cue, they come from all the remote parts of the terrain and, joining together into one huge army, march relentlessly to the sea. When they get there, they fling themselves into the surf and swim straight out from shore. Days later the beaches are piled deep with the tiny bodies where the tide has washed them up to decay in the sun.

Nothing resembles these lemmings quite so much as the way we Americans have been stampeding to our own destruction. We have already abandoned the secure ground of national strength and independence to leap into the boiling waters of internationalism. We are swimming straight out to sea as though there were a brighter, more secure paradise just ahead. But the water gets deeper by the minute, and our strength is beginning to ebb. Soon, even if we change our minds and decide to turn back to shore, it will be too late. We are rapidly approaching the point of no return—disarmament.

Almost everyone, of course, is opposed to war—particularly nuclear war—and we would all like to see the nations of the world throw their weapons on the scrap-heap and live peacefully together. In fact, this has been an ancient desire of noble-minded men since the dawn of history. But does getting rid of one's best weapons prevent war? Unfortunately not. It merely means that men then fight with their second-best weapons. Or it may mean that one side fights with its second-best weapons while the other uses superior weapons that everyone thought had been destroyed but which had been kept and perfected in secret.

It is true that in the past arming has always led to war; but so has disarming! Remember Pearl Harbor and Korea? As a matter of fact, most wars would never have been started but for the aggressor thinking he was sufficiently superior in military forces to overcome the opposition. A disarmed nation, therefore, is far more likely to be attacked and plunged into war than one that is armed. This is particularly true in the world of today where international Communism is carrying out its avowed program of global conquest. High ranking Soviet military officers who have defected to the West have told us that the Communists are just waiting for us to lower our guard. Nikolai F. Artamanov, for instance, a former Soviet naval captain, testified on September 14, 1960, before the House Committee on Un-American Activities and said that Soviet strategy is based upon a surprise nuclear attack on the U.S. *if* the Soviet leaders could be assured that victory would come at once.[1]

Note, however, that the Communists do not *want* to inflict nuclear devastation on America. They want to capture our great nation intact with all of our skilled labor and productive capacity to feed and support their world slave empire. Nuclear war is a last resort for them, and then only if they are positive of immediate victory.

Some people find comfort in this thought; but it is doubtful that they have any idea of what living under Communism is like. They feel that any life—even life inside a Communist slave labor camp—is better than risking death under the A-bomb. They are willing to send our young men into battle to the four corners of the world to die for their safety and freedom here at home, but they are not willing to risk their own hides for the same cause.

[1] "Ex-Russ Navy Man Plan—Sneak Attack Devised by K.," Los Angeles *Examiner* (September 15, 1960), sec. 1, p. 1.

Patrick Henry's choice of "liberty or death" has now given way to the "better Red than dead" motto of San Francisco's beatniks —and Washington's, too. As Adlai Stevenson paraphrased it: "Compared with the stake of survival, every other interest is minor and every other preoccupation petty." [2]

If mere survival has now become more important to Americans than freedom and all "other interests" or "preoccupations," then the men who sacrificed their lives at Lexington and Concord, at Valley Forge, at Saipan and Normandy must loath us from the grave, for we have asked them to die in vain.

The truly ironic part about all of this, however, is that we do not have to choose between being Red or dead at all. If we wake up and move into action, we can be both alive *and* free. All we have to do is be realistic about our situation and come to grips with the fact that so long as the Kremlin is dedicated to world domination, we have no choice but to keep ourselves well armed with the very latest weapons. Strength is the only language the Communists understand and it is the only thing that has kept their commissars out of our country so far.

That Senator Barry Goldwater is one of the realists who understands these facts of life, is clear from his voting record against disarmament proposals as well as from his following remarks:

> If an enemy power is bent on conquering you, and proposes to turn all of his resources to that end, he is at war with you; and you—unless you contemplate surrender—are at war with him. Moreover—unless you contemplate treason—your objective, like his, will be victory. Not peace, but victory. . . .
>
> Peace, to be sure, is a proper goal for American policy—as long as it is understood that peace is not all we seek. For we do not want the peace of surrender. We want a peace in which freedom and justice will prevail, and that—given the nature of Communism—is a peace in which Soviet power will no longer be in position to threaten us and the rest of the world. A tolerable peace, in other words, must follow victory over Communism. We have been . . . years trying to bury that unpleasant fact. It cannot be buried, and any foreign policy that ignores it will lead to our extinction as a nation.
>
> We do not, of course, want to achieve victory by force of

arms. If possible, overt hostilities should always be avoided; especially is this so when a shooting war may cause the death of many millions of people, including our own. But we cannot, for that reason, make the avoidance of a shooting war our chief objective. If we do that—if we tell ourselves that it is more important to avoid shooting than to keep our freedom—we are committed to a course that has only one terminal point: Surrender! [3]

Everyone knows that the Soviets have always been among the most outspoken advocates of disarmament. Unfortunately, too many Americans have taken this at face value and assumed that the motive behind this was an honest desire to spare mankind from the horrors of war. But what *are* the horrors of war? Why, death and destruction, of course. Yet, the Communists have perpetrated more death and destruction behind the iron and bamboo curtains than most of the wars of history combined. The only difference was that there was no organized opposition. The millions who have been executed did not die in combat, but in concentration camps. This, of course, is what the Communists mean when they advocate peace—the elimination of all opposition to Communism.

How sincere are they, then, when they promote disarmament? To answer that question, it is necessary to look back to the year 1928. One of the principles expounded at the Sixth World Congress of the Communist International in that year was: "The disarmament policy of the Soviet Government must be utilized for purposes of agitation . . . for recruiting sympathizers for the Soviet Union." [4]

Thirty-three years later, Khrushchev revealed that the Communist strategy in this regard had not changed one iota. Speaking in Moscow on January 6, 1961, he declared that the propaganda effectiveness of promoting a Soviet-inspired peace program was an effective means of wooing the sympathy of the masses behind the banner of Communism. He even admitted that the Kremlin's

[3] Senator Barry Goldwater, "Would a Strengthened UN Enhance U.S. Security and World Peace?—No!" *Congressional Digest* (August-September 1960), pp. 201-203.
[4] *Thesis Resolutions of the Sixth World Congress of the Communist International* (International Press Correspondents, November 28, 1928), vol. 8, no. 84, pp. 1590, 1596-1597.

plan was to make the slogan for peace fit hand-in-hand with the slogan for Communism. Speaking very candidly, he said:

> In the eyes of the masses, Communism will appear as a force capable of saving mankind from the horrors of modern destructive missile-nuclear war, while imperialism [meaning capitalism] is ever more associated in the minds of the masses as a system engendering wars. That is why the slogan of the struggle for peace is, as it were, a sputnik [meaning fellow traveler] of the slogan of the struggle for Communism.

What a beautiful strategy this has been. Appealing to the natural desire in all of us for peace, the Communists have been able to enlist literally thousands of well-meaning Americans into campaigning for disarmament and other Communist objectives. Housewives, students, professors and ministers have been enticed into supporting organizations and groups whose platforms read like a page out of the Communist *People's World*. The Turn Toward Peace movement, for instance, is one of the largest and best known of these groups. The following is just a partial list of the initiatives recommended in their official program of action:

1. Urge the opening of editorial columns of U.S. newspapers and magazines to Soviet and Red Chinese writers.
2. Double our financial support to all UN agencies such as UNICEF, UNESCO, etc.
3. Stop all travel curbs on Soviet citizens in the U.S.
4. Invite one thousand Soviet teachers and journalists to undertake at our expense a three month lecture tour of the U.S.
5. Invite five thousand Soviet "tourists" to vacation at our expense in the U.S.
6. Repeal the Connally Amendment.
7. Admit Red China to the UN.
8. Put the Peace Corps under UN administration.
9. Stop all U.S. nuclear testing even if the Soviets continue testing.
10. Invite the Soviets to plug into our missile early warning radar system.[5]

These platforms did not just happen, of course. They were carefully written by people who knew what they were doing.

[5] *American Initiatives in a Turn Toward Peace* (Cooper Station, Box 401, New York 3, N.Y., Turn Toward Peace).

Both the House Committee on Un-American Activities and various state investigating committees have reported that known Communists have penetrated into key positions within such groups as Women's Strike for Peace, The Committee for a Sane Nuclear Policy, and the American Friends Service Committee.[6] The investigators made it very clear that the majority of the members of these groups had no idea that they were being used to promote Communist objectives, and probably would not believe it if they were told. Unfortunately, most of them have never even questioned the sincerity of the leaders within the so-called peace movement and fewer still have ever bothered to inform themselves of basic Communist strategy. Consequently, Gus Hall, head of the Communist party in the United States, is able to boast that the peace movements continue to gather force and momentum. He stated quite frankly that the most active of these have been the Women's Strike for Peace and the Turn Toward Peace groups. He noted that "there are literally tons of literature for peace distributed in this country; tons and tons of it!" [7]

As pointed out earlier, however, the Communists are agitating in this country for disarmament for a far more important reason than merely fooling a lot of innocent Americans. Going back once again to the statement of principles issued by the Communist Sixth World Congress in 1928, we find: "The aim of the Soviet proposals is . . . to propagate the fundamental Marxian postulates that disarmament and the abolition of war are possible *only with the fall of Capitalism.*" [8] [Italics added.] Bringing it more up to date, Khrushchev has said: "The slogan for the struggle for peace must not contradict the slogan for the struggle for Communism. The struggle for disarmament . . . is an effective struggle against imperialism . . . for restricting its military potentialities." [9] And in December 1960 at a Moscow meeting of representatives from all over the world, Communist leaders declared: "An active, determined Communist struggle" must be

[6] Los Angeles *Times* (June 13, 1963), sec. 1, p. 2.
[7] Gus Hall, *End the Cold War* (New York, New Century Publications, 1962), p. 34.
[8] Stefan T. Possony, "The Test Ban—An American Strategy for Self-Mutilation," *Congressional Record* (March 21, 1963), pp. 4358-4370.
[9] *Ibid.*

waged to "force the imperialists into an agreement on general disarmament." [10]

As we shall see, Washington officialdom was thinking along exactly parallel lines and was putting the whole plan into operation just as fast as American public opinion would permit. Speaking in Geneva on July 21, 1955, President Eisenhower said:

> I have been searching my heart and mind for something that I could say here that could convince everyone of the great sincerity of the U.S. in approaching this problem of disarmament. I should address myself for a moment principally to the delegates from the Soviet Union. . . . I propose, therefore, that we take a practical step; that we begin an arrangement very quickly, as between ourselves, immediately. These steps would include: to give to each other a complete blueprint of our military establishments, from beginning to end, from one end of our countries to the other; lay out the establishments and provide blueprints to each other. Next, to provide within our countries facilities for aerial photography to the other country. . . . Likewise, we will make more easily attainable a comprehensive and effective system of inspection and disarmament, because what I propose, I assure you, would be but a beginning.[11]

If that was but a beginning, we got an idea of what may ultimately be in store for us when it was announced a few years later that the Defense Department had authorized several non-profit scientific agencies to prepare a comprehensive study of the conditions under which it would be advisable for the U.S. *not* to retaliate against a surprise nuclear attack. In other words, if it looked as though the Soviets had struck a killing first blow, the plan would be to surrender without fighting. They call this "strategic" surrender.[12]

Seemingly in keeping with this long range plan, President Eisenhower proposed a United Nations Atomic Energy Agency which came into existence on October 23, 1956. Three days later, before the Senate even had a chance to legally ratify our participation, Eisenhower pledged the United States to give

[10] *Ibid.*

[11] *American Historical Documents*, p. 412.

[12] "Question of When U.S. Should Surrender in All-Out Nuclear Attack Studied for Pentagon," St. Louis *Post-Dispatch* (August 5, 1958).

the new agency eleven thousand pounds of uranium 235 and, after that, to match the combined contributions of all other nations put together. Senator Joseph McCarthy fought hard against Senate ratification of our participation in this agency on the basis that Communists in the United Nations could easily take it over and use it against us. President Eisenhower assured the Senate that "the ingenuity of our scientists will provide special safe conditions under which such a bank of fissionable material can be made essentially immune to a surprise seizure."[13] Since our scientists were unable to prevent the Communists from stealing A-bomb secrets and vital parts from right under our noses, one wonders how Eisenhower thought we were going to prevent them from doing the same thing in an international organization in which they are members and over which we have no control. At any rate, the Senate ratified our commitment on June 18, 1957, and by the end of October, Communist bloc nations had gained full control of the UN Atomic Energy Agency. Not only did open Communists quickly capture over one fourth of the positions on the agency's board of directors, but the very top post, that of chairman of the board, was given to Dr. Pavel Winckler, a prominent Communist from Czechoslovakia. Eisenhower and the State Department professed to be surprised, indignant and perturbed.[14]

When President Kennedy came into office, he picked up right where Eisenhower left off. The Soviet deputy foreign minister, Vasily Kuznetsov, had complained that no progress toward easing tensions between East and West could be made as long as the U.S. maintained what he called "provocative" weapons. He specifically mentioned the manned bombers of our Strategic Air Command and our missiles deployed on foreign bases. He suggested that we scrap these weapons and build up, instead, a system of strictly secondary missiles and "conventional" non-nuclear weapons. President Kennedy's defense message to Congress in 1961 was exactly along these lines. Among the weapons deleted from the budget that year, and each year thereafter, were the B-70

---

[13] *Report of the Symposium on Military Implications of the UN,* Congress of Freedom convention, Veterans War Memorial Auditorium (San Francisco, April 1955).

[14] *U.S. News and World Report* (December 3, 1954). Also, Robert S. Allen, "Reds Grab Key Job in World Atom Agency," the *Tablet* (Brooklyn, November 2, 1957).

bomber and the anti-missile missile. We have stopped production of all manned bombers, are systematically putting into mothballs those that we have, and have now replaced our overseas missiles with Polaris submarines.

Commenting on President Kennedy's proposals, an article in the Chicago *Sun-Times* on March 30, 1961, reported:

> It is known that large sections of the President's defense message were written explicitly for the consumption of top Russian officials. Moreover, on the recommendation of Charles E. Bohlen, the State Department's leading expert on Russia, certain Communist phraseology was inserted in the message. . . . That much of the defense message was directed to the Soviet leaders is evident in the fact that Llewellyn E. Thompson, Jr., ambassador to Russia, was given a special briefing on it. . . . The message will now be forwarded to him in Moscow so he can reassure Soviet officials that the U.S. is taking care not to produce a "first strike capability." . . . Most of the sessions [at the White House leading up to the formulation of this policy] were directed by Mr. Kennedy's chief aid, Theodore Sorensen, who repeatedly made it clear that the President wanted to avoid provocative offensive weapons.[15]

Theodore Sorensen was a conscientious objector during the Korean War.[16]

As for the Polaris missiles that are now apparently the mainstay of our ability to deter a surprise nuclear attack: how good are they? Mr. Arthur I. Waskow is the man whom the U.S. Arms Control and Disarmament Agency has appointed as the expert to draft further disarmament proposals for the United States. He revealed that in his opinion the Polaris is not a provocative weapon because it is incapable of attacking an enemy's atomic force. This is because the megatonnage of the Polaris missile is too limited to damage hardened missile bases or to knock out a hidden base with a near miss. Waskow also pointed out that the Polaris, launched at sea with all the difficulties of precise and accurate aiming that any ship encounters, is incapable of direct hits on mobile missiles. He said that in order to avoid turning the

---

[15] "Inside Story of a Big Switch—Kennedy's Defense Strategy Tailored to Ease Red Fears," Chicago *Sun-Times* (March 30, 1961).

[16] "Do Unilateral Disarmers Influence Defense Policy?" *Human Events* (Washington, D.C., August 10, 1963), p. 9.

Polaris into a provocative weapon, the Navy should restrict the number of its Polaris submarines to no more than 45. Secretary of Defense McNamara has scheduled construction of a total of 41! [17]

As a result of the last series of Soviet underwater tests of the one hundred megaton bomb, it was revealed that underwater shock waves were so great that they could easily damage or destroy a submarine anywhere within hundreds of miles. A few such blasts in waters within striking distance of the relatively short-range Polaris missile could likely wipe out our entire fleet of submarines deployed there.

Mr. Paul H. Nitze as assistant secretary of defense delivered a speech in 1960 to a group of business and professional men at Asilomar on California's Monterey Peninsula. In his speech, which was sponsored by the 6th U.S. Army, the Western Sea Frontier U.S. Navy, and the 4th Air Force, Mr. Nitze advocated that we unilaterally reduce our armaments; that we scrap all our fixed-base bomber and missile bases; that we place our Strategic Air Command under NATO direction; and that we inform the United Nations "that NATO will turn over ultimate power of decision on the use of these systems to the General Assembly of the UN." [18]

When the press reported the substance of these proposals, alarmed citizens began to write their objections to Washington. Government officials responded by tripping all over themselves contradicting each other's assurances and denials. For instance, Dr. Lawrence G. Osborne of Santa Barbara, California, received one reply from the Defense Department stating flatly that a proposal to turn SAC over to NATO was definitely not under consideration. Another reply from then Vice-President Lyndon B. Johnson said: "The proposal that the Strategic Air Command be placed under the overall administration and command of NATO is one that is being given a great deal of thought and deliberation."

[17] James Roosevelt, ed., *The Liberal Papers* (Garden City, L.I., Doubleday & Company, Inc., 1962), pp. 131-132. Also, "Now the Whiz Kids Are Tackling the U.S. Navy," *U.S. News and World Report* (November 25, 1963), pp. 59-60.

[18] *Proceedings of the Asilomar National Strategy Seminar,* prepared by the Stanford Research Institute. As quoted by Congressman James B. Utt, *Congressional Record* (April 11, 1962).

Mr. Nitze has also recommended that Quemoy and Matsu be turned over to Red China, that we extend diplomatic recognition to Red China, and that Red China be admitted to the United Nations. Consequently, President Kennedy appointed him secretary of the navy.

In September of 1961 the State Department finally brought forth the grand product of its long labor in the form of publication 7277, entitled *Freedom From War—The U.S. Program for General and Complete Disarmament*. This attractively printed booklet contains the disarmament proposals that the United States Government submitted to the United Nations, and outlines in detail the point of no return that is now a reality right before our eyes. The following excerpts speak for themselves:

> Set forth as the objectives of a program of general and complete disarmament in a peaceful world:
>
> (a.) The disbanding of all national armed forces and the prohibition of their reestablishment in any form whatsoever other than those required to preserve internal order and for contributions to a United Nations peace force;
>
> (b.) The elimination from national arsenals of all armaments, including all weapons of mass destruction and the means for their delivery, other than those required for a United Nations peace force and for maintaining internal order;
>
> (c.) The establishment and effective operation of an international disarmament organization within the framework of the United Nations to insure compliance at all times with all disarmament obligations.
>
> . . . no state would have a military power to challenge the progressively strengthened UN peace force. . . .

Explaining in more detail just what lies behind the rather vague term "disarmament," President Kennedy said that it means:

> . . . A revolutionary change in the political structure of the world; creation of a radically new international system; abandonment of most of the old concepts of national states; development of international institutions that would encourage nations to give up much of their national sovereignty; acceptance without question or reservation of the jurisdiction of the international court; willingness to depend for national security on an international

peace force under an immensely changed and strengthened United Nations.[19]

Commenting further on these proposals, Walt Rostow, chairman of the State Department policy planning board, wrote:

> It is a legitimate American national objective to remove from all nations—including the U.S.—the right to use substantial military force to pursue their own interests. Since this residual right is the root of national sovereignty and the basis for the existence of an international arena of power, *it is, therefore an American interest to see an end to nationhood as it has been historically defined.*[20] [Italics added.]

Adlai Stevenson spelled it out for all to understand when he said: "In short, the U.S. program calls for total elimination of national capacity to make international war." And then, as though inscribing the epitaph on our national tombstone, he added: "It is presented in dead earnest." [21]

The same month that the State Department submitted the U.S. proposal for complete disarmament to the United Nations, Congress passed the necessary legislation authorizing the President to carry out all the terms of the proposal. The so-called safeguard in the act was that no disarmament steps could be taken "except pursuant to the treaty-making power of the President," which, as we have seen, poses no limitations at all. And so the U.S. Arms Control and Disarmament Agency was created and empowered to enter into whatever disarmament agreements it desired, even without congressional consent. After the newly created agency began to swing into action, several of the congressmen who had voted for it began to wake up to the insidious nature of the whole scheme. Congressman William Bray, for instance, said:

> Many of us, including myself, had great hopes for the future of the Arms Control and Disarmament Agency when we voted for the authorization and appropriations for its operation. After observing the operation of this agency for one year, I am deeply

[19] Washington *News* (April 19, 1962).

[20] *Congressional Record* (June 6, 1963), pp. A-362, A-363.

[21] Mr. Stevenson was addressing the first committee of the UN General Assembly on November 15, 1961. See, *Documents on Disarmament— 1961*, U.S. Arms Control and Disarmament Agency publication #5, p. 623.

disappointed. Instead of working on plans to represent the interests of America and the free world in disarmament plans, this agency has apparently been studying reasons for the free world to surrender to the Kremlin to avoid the strife and turmoil that is inherent in freedom.[22]

In 1963 there was a great deal of excitement about the Moscow Test Ban Treaty. Military men testified that such a treaty would seriously hamper our ability to keep abreast of recent Soviet weapon advances. The Senate Armed Services Preparedness Subcommittee issued a report stating that such a test ban treaty would "result in serious and perhaps formidable military and technical disadvantages."[23] The treaty was ratified, nevertheless, on the strength of so-called political advantages which were never clearly defined.

The truly amazing part of it was that there was so much widespread public opposition to the treaty. There should have been, of course, but it was interesting to see such universal concern and alarm over a test ban treaty that was nothing compared to the far more disastrous steps that had already been taken, and were still being taken at that very time. Here, the American people were getting all excited over the possibility of a Communist military *superiority*, while still continuing to support policies leading to a Communist military *monopoly!* What difference does it make whether our missiles are as good as theirs if they have control of them both?

This being the case, it was puzzling at first to understand why both Washington and Moscow were pushing so hard for this particular treaty. Was it to divert attention away from the more sinister disarmament measures now being taken? Was it to further reinforce the false image that our greatest danger is from outside military attack rather than from internal subversion? Or was it primarily a propaganda weapon for the Soviets to use showing that the United States is now so fearful of the military superiority of Communism that it was willing to travel to Moscow and sign a treaty which was clearly to its military disadvantage?

[22] William Bray, "Arms Control Switch," *Human Events* (Washington, D.C., December 7, 1963), p. 15.
[23] *Congressional Record* (September 13, 1963), pp. 16072-16075.

All of these purposes played a part, of course, but the most important feature of the entire treaty was one which received practically no public attention or concern. Buried deep within the terminology of the treaty was a phrase that took disarmament out of the proposal stage and put it in the commitment stage. When the Senate ratified the treaty it created a "supreme law of the land" which now binds the U.S., in the words of the treaty itself, to *the speediest possible achievement of an agreement on general and complete disarmament under strict international control in accordance with the objectives of the United Nations.*

The true significance of the Moscow Test Ban Treaty, therefore, was simply to take us one more very important step closer to the ultimate transfer of our nuclear weapons to the United Nations. The first step was our formal *proposal* to the UN in 1961. The second was the passing of the Arms Control and Disarmament Act, which made it legally possible. The third step, the Moscow Test Ban Treaty, has *committed* us to carry out the plan. All that is now left is to do it. Nothing else stands in the way. Without consulting Congress or the Senate, the President and the Arms Control and Disarmament Agency can surrender our weapons whenever they wish.

And so, on September 20, 1963, President Kennedy addressed the UN and said:

> Two years ago, I told this body that the United States had proposed and was willing to sign a limited test ban treaty. Today, that treaty has been signed. It will not put an end to war. It will not remove basic conflicts. It will not secure freedom for all. But it can be a lever. As Archimedes, in explaining the principle of the lever, was said to have declared to his friends: *"Give me a place where I can stand—and I shall move the world."* [24]

Exactly four months later, on January 21, 1964, President Lyndon Johnson spoke over nationwide radio and television and, parroting the sentiments of his predecessor, said:

> This morning in Geneva, Switzerland, the eighteen nation committee on disarmament resumed its work. There is only one

[24] "Kennedy—A Quest for Peace Meeting," Los Angeles *Herald-Examiner* (September 20, 1963), p. A-8.

item on the agenda today of that conference. It is the leading item on the agenda of all mankind, and that one item is peace. . . . We now have a limited nuclear test ban treaty. We now have an emergency communications link, a "hot-line" between Washington and Moscow. We now have an agreement in the United Nations to keep bombs out of outer space.

These are small steps, but they go in the right direction, the direction of security and sanity and peace. Now we must go further. . . . The best way to begin disarming is to begin. And we shall hear any plan, go any place, make any plea, and play any part that offers a realistic prospect for peace.[25]

For years, the master planners have been telling the innocent assembly line workers that the UN is only a debating arena, an international forum where world opinion focuses on events of the day. As such, we have been led to believe that there is no way for the UN to legislate or to impose its will on anybody. Events in Katanga, however, should enable anyone with even a modicum of intelligence to see through that subterfuge. If the UN is successful in its present drive to acquire the full control of the complete military apparatus of the United States, including our nuclear weapons, and our national armies, there will be many more Katangas to come. Some of them will be on our soil.

Special UN forces have already made practice seizures of American cities. U.S. soldiers, carrying the United Nations flag, and wearing UN armbands, staged a mock take-over of nine California cities on July 31, 1951. The same occurred in Lampasas, Texas, on April 3, 1952. The same at Watertown, New York, on August 20, 1952. In 1963 the Army announced that it was conducting similar exercises in North Carolina, South Carolina, and Georgia. What are they practicing for?

The point of no return is here *now!* If we cross it, we will find ourselves living in a world where the realities of peace are worse than the horrors of war; and where the suffering of life is worse than the agony of death. It will be a world of our own creating; and it will be one from which there is no escape.

While there is yet a little time, the choice is ours.

[25] *Department of State Bulletin* (February 10, 1964), pp. 223-224.

CHAPTER

EIGHTEEN | OUR LAST BEST HOPE

Before proceeding with a discussion of possible solutions to this gigantic United Nations dilemma, it seems appropriate to examine the principle arguments so often used by sincere Americans to justify our continued support of the United Nations. These can be the equivalents of mental short circuits in an otherwise logical thinking process—a pre-conditioned substitute for rational thought. If repeated often enough without challenge, these clichés gradually seep their way into the subconscious where they can then command the emotions to their uncritical defense. For this reason, let us be sure that we clearly understand the basic flaws and fallacies that lurk behind the most typical clichés.

It is our last best hope for peace. This is, without a doubt, the most universal cliché used to defend the United Nations. It takes many forms and subtle variations. It is safe to say that over ninety percent of all pro-UN speeches, magazine articles and books hinge around this central theme. Unless we can spot the fallacies, we are completely at their mercy.

The first fallacy is clear to anyone who has taken the trouble to follow the UN's action to bring about peace in Katanga. There are two kinds of peace. One is the kind that most of us think about when we hear the word—a peace that includes freedom. But, if we define peace as merely the absence of war, then we *could* be talking about the peace that reigns in a Communist slave labor camp. One thing is certain, the wretched souls imprisoned there are not at war! But would they call it peace?

222

Alfredo Cardinal Ottaviani expressed it well when he said:

> While Cain can still massacre Abel without anyone's no-
> ticing it; while entire nations are still held in slavery without any-
> one coming to the assistance of the oppressed; while . . . years
> after the Hungarian revolt, the bloodletting still continues with the
> condemnation to death of students, peasants and workers guilty
> of having loved a freedom that was stamped out by foreign tanks,
> without the world showing any horror at so great a crime—while
> such things persist, it is impossible to speak of a true peace, but
> only of a consent to a massacre.[1]

The second fallacy, however, is far more important. How on
earth can an organization promote peace in the world when
strategically entrenched within it is the most aggressive peace-
destroying force the world has ever seen? International Communism recognizes only the principle of brute force. When it was
suggested at Teheran that the Pope request Hitler to guarantee
the humane treatment of prisoners, Stalin remarked, "The Pope?
How many divisions does *he* have?"[2] Having the Communists
sitting in key spots within a so-called peace-keeping force is as
logical as having members of the Mafia on a police commissioner's
board to prevent crime in Chicago!

It is curious to observe how so many people apparently grasp
this fact when applied to Red China, but fail to apply the same
principle to Soviet Russia. They become excited over the possibility of admitting Red China to the United Nations, but never
advocate throwing out the other Communist countries. Former
UN Ambassador Henry Cabot Lodge, as a typical example, once
argued that Red China should not be admitted to the United
Nations because the organization "is not a place where the virtuous and the criminal sit side by side."[3] Yet, we *do* sit side by
side with the Soviets. According to this kind of logic, either the
U.S. is criminal or the Soviets are virtuous!

Obviously there can be no peace without order; there can
be no order without justice; and there can be no justice when the
criminal directs the police and judges his own trial. This is why,

[1] Rev. Richard Ginder, "Key to Your House," syndicated column *Right
or Wrong, Our Sunday Visitor* (Huntington, Ind., 1961).

[2] As quoted by Lie, p. 242.

[3] As quoted by Manly, p. 82.

since the UN was created supposedly to prevent the rise of another world-grasping tyrannical power like Nazism, the equally ruthless and blood-thirsty regime of international Communism has spread at a fantastic pace and has massacred and enslaved more people, broken more families, destroyed more homes and conquered more land than Hitler even came close to doing. If *that* is our last best hope for peace, we have lost all semblance of sanity.

The UN must be hurting the Communists, otherwise why would they rant and rave against it so much? The answer to that one is very simple. They do *not* oppose the UN at all. The only time they appear to is when it is a public performance before news cameras or at press conferences. These dramatic performances are obviously for propaganda purposes only. What the Communists really think about the United Nations can be seen quite clearly from the glowing praise it receives in the Communist press which is aimed, not at the general public, but at the party members, themselves. But, to answer the question of why they *pretend* to oppose the UN, one of the best explanations was provided, unintentionally no doubt, by Adlai Stevenson when he said:

> The Soviet Union has attacked the UN, has refused to pay its share of the Congo expenses, and has laid siege to the institution of the Secretary-General. Thus, as often before, the Soviets have pressed their attack at a moment when the [UN] Community seems most divided against itself. But, once again, that very attack makes the members realize more keenly that they are members of a Community *and causes them to draw together.*[4] [Italics added.]

At least while we're talking we're not shooting. This is really only an extension of the peace cliché. But it is so widely used that it deserves special consideration. In addition to all the observations previously made, it should be further noted that this argument presumes an either-or situation that does not exist. It assumes that we either talk with the Communists or shoot them. Nothing could be further from reality. The best way to get yourself into a barroom brawl with a bunch of thugs is to go into

[4] *United Nations Guardian of Peace,* Department of State publication #7225 (September 1961), p. 24.

the bar and start talking with them. The smart thing to do is to stay out and mind your own business!

The theory that as long as nations are talking over their problems there will not be war, sounds fine. Unfortunately, it does not work that way. Americans surely remember what happened on a December morning some years ago while Emperor Hiro Hito's envoys were in Washington—*talking*.

The UN is merely doing between nations what we did so successfully with our thirteen colonies. This, in essence, is the plea for federalism, and is based on the idea that the mere act of joining separate political units together into a larger federal entity will somehow prevent those units from waging war with each other. The success of our own federal system is most often cited as proof that this theory is valid. But such an evaluation is a shallow one. First of all, the American Civil War, one of the most bloody in all history, illustrates conclusively that the mere federation of governments, even those culturally similar, as in America, does not automatically prevent war between them. Secondly, we find that true peace quite easily exists between nations which are *not* federated. As a matter of fact, members of the British Commonwealth of Nations seemed to get along far more peacefully after the political bonds between them had been relaxed. In other words, true peace has absolutely nothing to do with whether separate political units are joined together—except, perhaps, that such a union may create a common military defense sufficiently impressive to deter an aggressive attack. But that is peace between the union and outside powers; it has little effect on peace between the units, themselves, which is the substance of the UN argument.

Peace is the natural result of relationships between groups and cultures which are mutually satisfactory to both sides. These relationships are found with equal ease within or across federal lines. As a matter of fact, they are the same relationships that promote peaceful conditions within the community, the neighborhood, the family itself. What are they? Just stop and think for a moment; if you were marooned on an island with two other people, what relationships between you would be mutually satisfactory enough to prevent you from resorting to violence in your relationships? Or, to put it the other way around, what would cause you to break the peace and raise your hand against your partners?

Obviously, if one or both of the others attempted to seize your food and shelter, you would fight. Their reaction to similar efforts on your part would be the same. If they attempted to take away your freedom, to dictate how you should conduct your affairs, or tell you what moral and ethical standards you must follow, likewise, you would fight. And if they constantly ridiculed your attire, your manners and your speech, in time you might be sparked into a brawl. The best way to keep the peace on that island is for each one to mind his own business, to respect each other's right to his own property, to respect the other fellow's right to be different (even to act in a way that seems foolish or improper, if he wishes), to have compassion for each other's troubles and hardships—but to *force* each other to do nothing! And, to make sure that the others hold to their end of the bargain, each should keep physically strong enough to make any violation of this code unprofitable.

Now, suppose these three got together and decided to form a political union, to "federate," as it were. Would this really change anything? Suppose they declared themselves to be the United Persons, and wrote a charter, and held daily meetings, and passed resolutions. What then? These superficial ceremonies might be fun for a while, but the minute two of them out-voted the other, and started "legally" to take his food and shelter, limit his freedom, or force him to accept an unwanted standard of moral conduct, they would be right back where they all began. Charter or no charter they would fight.

Is it really different between nations? Not at all. The same simple code of conduct applies in all human relationships, large or small. Regardless of the size, be it international or three men on an island, the basic unit is still the human personality. Ignore this fact, and any plan is doomed to failure.

When the thirteen colonies formed our Federal Union, they had two very important factors in their favor, neither of which are present in the United Nations. First, the colonies themselves were all of a similar cultural background. They enjoyed similar legal systems, they spoke the same language, and they shared similar religious beliefs. They had much in common. The second advantage, and the most important of the two, was that they formed their union under a constitution which was designed to prevent any of them, *or a majority of them,* from forcefully intervening in the affairs of the others. The original federal government was authorized to provide mutual defense, run a post office, and that was about all. As previously mentioned, however, even though we had these powerful forces working in our favor, full scale war did break out at one tragic point in our history.

The peace that followed, of course, was no peace at all, but was only the smoldering resentment and hatred that falls in the wake of any armed conflict. Fortunately, the common ties between North and South, the cultural similarities and the common heritage, have proved through the intervening years to overbalance the differences. And with the gradual passing away of the generation that carried the battle scars, the Union has healed.

In the United Nations, there are precious few common bonds that could help overcome the clash of cross-purposes that inevitably must arise between groups with such divergent ethnic, linguistic, legal, religious, cultural and political environments. To add fuel to the fire, the UN concept is one of unlimited governmental power to impose by force a monolithic set of values and conduct on all groups and individuals whether they like it or not. Far from insuring peace, such conditions can only enhance the chances of war.

There is nothing wrong with the basic argument for a world society or a world union of nations. But not just *any* world federation will do. Otherwise, we should have let Hitler conquer us all; that is precisely what he was working toward. In order to work, such a one-world system will have to be based on the same rules of conduct, the same principles of limited government that we have just outlined. The system will have to be one which, instead of using the police-backed force of government decree to cram every human being into a single mold, will set out systematically to reduce even the existing government restrictions on man's freedom.

When speaking about the United Nations, however, we are not talking about *a* United Nations, or *some* United Nations, or the *idea* of a United Nations; we are talking about the *existing* United Nations. And any thought that the existing United Nations will bring peace and happiness to this earth is merely the temporary triumph of hope over reason.

We don't want to turn back the clock to a period of isolationism, do we? This is two clichés wrapped into one. The first assumes that all change is progress. In other words, today is better than yesterday and tomorrow will be better than today. That is implied in the phrase "turn back the clock." In the realm of material things—inventions, gadgets, consumer products, etc.—this is often a valid observation. But when it comes to human relationships, there can be no such presumption. Change may or may not be an improvement. Each case must stand on its own merits.

The word *isolationism* is the basis of the second cliché; it has become a scare word to intimidate all critics of the United Nations. The so-called isolationism of the United States in past years is basically a myth. We have never been totally isolated from the world, either in diplomatic affairs or commerce. On the contrary, American influence and trade have been felt in every region of the globe. Private groups and individuals spread knowledge, business, prosperity, religion and good will throughout every foreign continent. It was not necessary then for America to give up her independence to have contact with other countries. It is not necessary now. Yet, in the summer of 1963 a Gallup Poll asked the following question: "Would it be better for the U.S. to keep independent in world affairs, or to work closely with other nations?"

How many people saw through the intellectual deception of the presumption that in order to work closely with other nations, we cannot stay independent? Apparently not many, for eighty percent of the answers favored "working closely with other nations." [5]

With the use of such clichés and loaded phrases, many Americans have been led to believe that this country is so strong it can defend and subsidize half the world, while at the same time believing it is so weak and "interdependent" that it cannot survive without pooling its sovereignty and independence with those it must subsidize. If wanting no part of this kind of "logic" is isolationism, then it is indeed time that it was brought back into vogue.

[5] *Los Angeles Times* (July 3. 1963), sec. 1, p. 8.

The UN provides a valuable vehicle for contact between nations. This may be true, but is it necessary? What is wrong with the traditional method of maintaining contact between nations through the use of ambassadors, envoys and a diplomatic corps? The United States has such contacts in all the major capitals of the world. Why not use them? In fact the traditional approach is far more likely to produce results than the debating arena of the United Nations. Consider what would happen if every time a small spat arose between a husband and wife they called the entire neighborhood together and took turns airing their complaints in front of the whole group. Gone would be any chance of reconciliation. Instead of working out their problems, the ugly necessity of saving face, proving points, and winning popular sympathy would likely drive them further apart. Likewise, public debates in the UN intensify international tensions. By shouting their grievances at each other, countries allow their differences to assume a magnitude they would otherwise never have reached. Quiet diplomacy is always more conducive to progress than diplomacy on the stage.

Nationalism fosters jealousy, suspicion and hatred of other countries which in turn leads to war. Here again we are dealing with a problem of semantics and false logic. If we merely substitute the word "independence" for "nationalism," this cliché begins to fall apart right away. We *should* be desirous of not having men hate each other because they live in another country, but what kind of logic assumes that loving one's own country means hating all others? Why can't we be proud of America as an independent nation, and also have a feeling of brotherhood and respect for other peoples around the world? As a matter of fact, haven't Americans done just that for the past two hundred years? What country has poured out more treasure to other lands, opened its doors to more immigrants, and sent more of its citizens as missionaries, teachers and doctors than ours? Are we now to believe that love of our own country will cause us to hate the peoples of other lands?

In order for a man to be a good neighbor within his community, he does not have to love other men's wives and children as he does his own.

We must support the UN because it is working to eliminate

the roots of war—ignorance, poverty, hunger, and disease. The fallacy in this argument is the assertion that ignorance, poverty, hunger and disease are the roots of war. Some of the bloodiest wars of history have been fought between nations that were highly educated, affluent and healthy. What country hovering on the brink of poverty and disease ever started a major war? How could it? To wage war requires armaments and large armies— hardly the products of destitute states. As for the thought that low educational standards and lack of international understanding (whatever that means) are the cause of war, consider the fact that Germany and England were enemies in two world wars. Yet both have extremely high educational standards, and it would be difficult to name two nations that had a more thorough understanding of each other.

There is no challenging the fact that the United Nations, through its specialized agencies, has done some good—perhaps much good in many areas. Food and clothing have been distributed to the needy; medical care has been provided for the sick and the lame. But for each child so fed and clothed, for each person relieved of suffering, the UN system is destined to condemn a hundred who can never be reached. When the United States stood for individual freedom rather than government subsidies, it spearheaded a century of life-saving and relief from famine and pestilence that far exceeded anything UNICEF or WHO can ever approach. What America gave was not *primarily* food, clothing and medicine (although it did give these things in large quantities), but rather it provided an example of what could be achieved through a system of economic freedom.

It is impossible to uplift the masses of the world through a redistribution of the existing wealth. If every man, woman and child in America gave everything he had but the shirt on his back, the poverty-stricken peoples of the world would hardly notice a change in their misery. There are so many of them and so few of us. But by providing the example, the encouragement and the assistance for these people to follow in our footsteps, they can build their own economies to the point where real and sustained progress is possible. The only way that the needy of the world will ever be helped, other than with sporadic and temporary measures, is for governments to abandon the futile paternalistic programs which are draining the economies of those countries to the point where they cannot flourish. Only when free enterprise is introduced will the full productive capacity of these areas be released so that their people will no longer have to worry about nutrition or health.

The cause of war is simply the use of force to require a nation or group to accept the dictates of another nation or group. Since the United Nations is committed to the use of force "if necessary, in the last resort" as the cornerstone of its approach to world problems, it can never get at the roots of war.

Instead of scrapping the whole thing, we should reorganize the UN and use it to our own advantage. The proponents of this idea never explain how we should go about revising an organization in which we have only one vote against 112 who do not want to revise it. This approach may be less controversial than the "get US out" school of thought, but it simply will not work.

With what would we replace the UN? This is, perhaps, the greatest cliché of the lot. The implication that it has to be replaced at all is very seldom challenged, even by critics of the UN who consequently begin to search for a NATO or a western alliance or organization of free states. This would be like a patient who, upon being told by his doctor that he has a cancer that must be removed, replies, "Just a minute, doctor. What would you replace it with?"

When something is evil and dangerous it is not necessary to find a replacement before getting rid of it. But, in the case of the UN, this is not an entirely superfluous idea. True, we must get out of the UN whether we replace it with anything or not. But, to be perfectly realistic, when the United States does withdraw, the UN *will* be replaced—but not by NATO.

When the UN finally topples, it will be the result of a ground swell of renewed patriotism and a rebirth of the American spirit of victory over tyranny—a return to the traditional American principles which made this country great.

Instead of looking to the rest of the world for collective security, we will rely on our own strength and vigilance.

Instead of trying to finance the expansion of socialism in every country around the world, we will encourage, by example, the spread of free enterprise capitalism.

Instead of coddling agents of our sworn enemy within the top echelons of our own government, we will replace them and their sympathizers with men who are loyal only to the United States. And unless this very important *first step* is taken we are not going to even come close to getting out of the UN. Until we disconnect this end of the Washington-Moscow "axis," our government will continue to support and promote the UN, as it has from the very beginning.

Instead of coexistence with the evil thing called Communism, we will direct our energies toward ultimate victory.

Instead of continuing to build a welfare-socialist system here at home, we will move once again in the direction of reducing government restrictions on our daily lives and, thus, in the direction of increasing personal freedom.

Instead of trying to *buy* friendship around the world, we will offer the sincere qualities of mutual respect and good will. American investment abroad by private citizens and business enterprises will create far more prosperity in foreign lands than foreign aid ever could; and the commerce that springs from such investment will do more to bring our peoples together than all the Peace Corps and other government programs put together.

In short, the United Nations will be replaced with *freedom*—freedom for all people, everywhere, to live as they please with no super-government directing them; freedom to succeed or to fail and to try again; freedom to make mistakes and even to be foolish in the eyes of others. Americans will, once again, be free to work where they please, employ whom they please, buy and sell what they please, and, in an infinite number of ways, do what they please—with only one government restriction upon them: that they not interfere with anyone else's access to the same freedom.

This is the meaning of a republic; a *limited* government. This is what we Americans once had until the socialists, Communists and other collectivists turned back the clock to the ideas that dominated the political systems of the Dark Ages. Many Americans today, thinking that collectivist ideas are new, argue that we must place more and more power into the hands of the Federal Government so that it will be strong enough to cope with the challenges of the modern world. But, as Thomas Jefferson stated in 1801:

I know, indeed, that some honest men fear that a Republican government cannot be strong, that this government is not strong enough; but would the honest patriot, in the full tide of a successful experiment, abandon a government which has so far kept us free and firm, on the theoretic and visionary fear that this government, the world's best hope, may, by possibility, want energy to preserve itself? I trust not. I believe this, on the contrary, the strongest government on earth.[6]

As for peace in the world, until all nations follow the concept of limited government, it is unlikely that universal peace will ever be attained. Unlimited, power-grasping governments will always resort to force if they think they can get away with it. But there is no doubt that there *can* be peace for America. As long as we maintain our military preparedness, the world's petty despots will leave us alone.[7]

To make sure that we do not get caught up in the middle of the endless squabbles between the countries of Europe, Asia and Africa, we must put an end to the insane practice of trying to entwine our economic and political affairs with those of the rest of the world.

Let us, then, move the clock *forward* to that point where we were when this great nation was infused with the only really new political concept the world has seen in thousands of years. Let us throw off these Old World ideas and heed the sage advice of that true "modernist," George Washington, who told his countrymen:

[6] *American Historical Documents*, p. 151.

[7] A perfect illustration of this was provided at Pearl Harbor. The United States was not militarily prepared to defend itself against foreign aggression. As a matter of fact, we had even gone so far as to deliberately bottle up our fleet within Pearl Harbor so that it was vulnerable to surprise attack. For the complete and shocking story of how high officials in Washington clearly knew well in advance of the so-called "surprise" attack at Pearl Harbor and did nothing to prevent it—even going so far as to keep this information from naval commanders of the fleet so they could not deploy their ships to less vulnerable locations, see *The Final Secret of Pearl Harbor* by Rear Admiral Robert A. Theobold with forewords by Rear Admiral Husband E. Kimmel and Fleet Admiral William H. Halsey (New York, The Devin-Adair Company, 1954). The military and political policies which led to Pearl Harbor have a shocking parallel in our times. This nation is following a deliberate program of increasing military vulnerability. Reversal of this policy is imperative. We must follow a policy of military preparedness and vigilance if we are to prevent another Pearl Harbor.

Observe good faith and justice toward all nations. Cultivate peace and harmony with all. Religion and morality enjoin this conduct. And can it be that good policy does not equally enjoin it? . . . Against the insidious wiles of foreign influence—I conjure you to believe me, fellow citizens—the jealousy of a free people ought to be constantly awake; since history and experience prove that foreign influence is one of the most baneful foes of republican government. . . . If we remain one people, under an efficient government, the period is not far off when we may defy material injury from external annoyance; when we may take such an attitude as will cause the neutrality we may at any time resolve upon to be scrupulously respected; when belligerent nations, under the impossibility of making acquisitions on us, will not likely hazard giving us provocation; when we may choose peace or war, as our interest, guided by justice, shall council. Why forego the advantages of so peculiar a situation? Why, by interweaving our destiny with that of any part of Europe, entangle our peace and prosperity in the toils of European ambition, rivalship, interest, humor or caprice?

The next time you hear someone speak lightly about sovereignty or national independence, remember that this was the one single accomplishment of the American Revolution. Our present involvement in the United Nations has put us right back where the shooting began in 1775.

The Declaration of Independence states:

When in the course of human events, it becomes necessary for one people to dissolve the political bonds which have connected them with another, and to assume among the powers of the earth the separate and equal station to which the laws of nature and nature's God entitles them, a decent respect to the opinions of mankind requires that they should declare the causes which impel them to the separation. . . .

It then lists the causes. It is stunning that this bill of grievances and complaints can be justly applied to the present encroaching tyranny of the United Nations and, to some extent, our own expanding Federal Government. It speaks of a "multitude of new offices" and "swarms of officers to harass our people and eat out their substance" (taxes); it complains about being subject to "a jurisdiction foreign to our Constitution and unacknowledged by our laws" (supremacy of the World Court); it deplores "transporting large armies of foreign mercenaries to complete the works of death, desolation and tyranny already begun with circumstances of cruelty and perfidy scarcely paralleled in the most barbarous ages and totally unworthy of the head of a civilized nation" (Katanga).

The men who put their signatures to the bottom of the Declaration of Independence were signing their own potential death warrants. Most of them were prosperous and comfortably situated with every reason to go along with the existing bureaucracy. Besides, what chance did inexperienced farmers have against the British Army, at that time the most invincible fighting force in the whole world? If the colonies had been overpowered, as it appeared more than likely they would be, these men who signed the Declaration would have all been hanged or shot as traitors. Yet, without hesitation they stood up for what they believed to be right and declared: ". . . and for the support of this declaration, with a firm reliance on the protection of Divine Providence, we mutually pledge to each other our lives, our fortunes, and our sacred honor."

In signing the Declaration of Independence, John Adams turned to his colleagues and spoke these words:

> If it be the pleasure of Heaven that my country shall require the poor offering of my life, the victim shall be ready. But while I do live, let me have a country, or at least the hope of a country —and that a free country. But whatever may be our fate, be assured . . . this declaration will stand. It may cost treasure, and it may cost blood; but it will stand, and it will richly compensate for both. . . . And live or die, survive or perish, I am for the declaration. It is my living sentiment, and, by the blessing of God, it shall be my dying sentiment: independence now, and independence forever!

Can it be that modern Americans are not equal to their ancestors? Are we not willing, if necessary, to make sacrifices in the cause of freedom? Is it more important to enjoy the temporary comforts of the "good life," the security of a non-controversial social status, than to pass on to our children the cherished liberty we ourselves inherited? As Patrick Henry would have replied, "Forbid it, Almighty God!"

As you read these final words, you must come to a decision

as to your *own* reply to these questions. Each man and woman will soon be called upon for his answer. The rapidity of world events will no longer permit us to remain aloof and unaffected by them. Disinterest will no longer purchase a ticket for escape. Tyranny demands unqualified allegiance: We are either for it or against it. There is no middle ground.

Which will it be, America?

INDEX